DISAPPEARING THE PRESIDENT

TRUMP, TRUTH SOCIAL, AND THE FIGHT FOR THE REPUBLIC

Lee Smith

New York • London

First American edition published in 2024 by Encounter Books,
an activity of Encounter for Culture and Education, Inc.,
a nonprofit, tax-exempt corporation.
Encounter Books website address: www.encounterbooks.com

Manufactured in the United States and printed on
acid-free paper. The paper used in this publication meets
the minimum requirements of ANSI/NISO Z39.48-1992
(R 1997) (*Permanence of Paper*).

FIRST AMERICAN EDITION

LIBRARY OF CONGRESS CATALOGING-IN-PUBLICATION
DATA IS AVAILABLE UPON REQUEST UNDER ISBN 978-1-64177-457-4

For Steven Biss, Joshua Cremeans, and Matthew Perna — Patriots

CONTENTS

1

THE SILENCING

" I had no voice," says Donald Trump. He's talking about the campaign to silence him and drive him out of public life after the 2020 presidential election. "I didn't know what to do," he says, "because I have so many things to say, and I have so many people that want to hear them, and I had no voice."

Silencing the 45th President of the United States was part of a larger campaign to disappear him altogether. After Trump left office, the Biden administration mounted a massive lawfare operation—four cases total, with two federal, one in Fulton County, Georgia, and another in Manhattan—to impoverish him and distract him from his 2024 re-election efforts, with the ultimate goal of imprisoning him for life. After the legal attacks fell apart, the government exposed him, through incompetence or malice, to an assassination attempt at a Pennsylvania rally.

Instead of the tragic ending scripted by the would-be murderer, however, Trump rose from the ground with blood on his face and his fist in the air. "Fight!" he shouted to the relieved crowd, which broke into chants of "USA!" as Secret Service agents rushed Trump off the stage.

"There's never been spirit like there is right now," Trump tells me. "We did great in 2016. We won, and then we did much better in 2020. We got close to 12 million more votes. The spirit for each was unbelievable. The spirit now blows it away. There's more spirit now. And I think we're doing much better this time. The spirit's never been like this."

I met with him at Mar-a-Lago, his Palm Beach, Florida mansion and headquarters for his 2024 re-election efforts. He shows me a schedule of his day—rallies, speeches, meetings, fundraising events. It seems the crowds he meets on the campaign trail replenish and ready him for his fights.

Accordingly, the crusade to stop him is larger, his opponents more driven, and their language scored with the violent rhetoric that incited a Pennsylvania man to fire on him. Media reports regularly describe Trump as a would-be dictator and characterize his possible second-term as the end of "our democracy." Precedence suggests that the breathless press accounts are early indicators that the groundwork is being laid for broad resistance to another Trump presidency that will prove even more disruptive and destructive than before.

In 2020, most of the election-interference operation was conducted behind the scenes. It only became clear later that even in Trump's own administration, special units at the FBI and Department of Homeland Security partnered with the private sector to censor the incumbent, his top aides and supporters, and to tilt the election against him. Citing the January 6, 2021 demonstrations in Washington, D.C. as a pretext, Facebook and Twitter banned Trump from their platforms.

The January 6 protests were weaponized to silence opposition supporters and keep them out of public view. As the 2020 George Floyd riots and the pro-Hamas demonstrations four years later were meant to show, the streets and other public forums belonged to the political faction still led by Barack Obama. Should other Americans manifest their displeasure with the ruling establishment's preferences and policies—vaccine mandates, open borders, inflation, climate change regulations, etc.—they'd have their lives ruined, like January 6 defendants. Naturally, January 6 was also exploited to target the leader of the opposition.

"When I was silenced, it was shocking," says Trump. "I was number one on Twitter, and a lot of people said that I built Twitter."

He'd called Twitter his "typewriter." He'd told a 2019 White House audience how he drove the news cycle with his phone and a few remarks on Twitter: "I go, 'Watch this.' Boom. I press it, and within two seconds, 'We have breaking news.'"[1]

Trump was also one of the showcase accounts on Facebook. The company's founder Mark Zuckerberg courted him regularly.

"Zuckerberg would call me all the time because I'm president," says Trump. "And you would never think that he could be against me because he just could not have been nicer. He came over probably three times, with his very beautiful wife to ask if we could have dinner or meetings, and he'd be in the White House every once in a while, and I'd see him. One time he walked into the White House and he said to me, 'Congratulations, you're number one.' I said, 'number one on what?' He said, 'number one on Facebook. You're number one far and away. Congratulations!' And it was very nice. And I did very well with all that stuff. And then one day I had nothing."

Silencing the leader of the opposition was part of the rolling coup that started at the end of Obama's term almost exactly four years previously. In a January 5, 2017 White House meeting, the outgoing president greenlighted the FBI's continued surveillance of the president-elect, based largely on a forged document funded by Hillary Clinton contractors alleging that Trump had been compromised by Russian intelligence. In supporting a propaganda campaign accusing his successor of treason, Obama interfered with the peaceful transfer of executive power and destabilized the country he was twice elected to lead. Russiagate cost Trump his most trusted aide outside his family—National

Security Advisor Michael Flynn—and hobbled his ability to govern with a special counsel investigation that lasted nearly two years.

"They try and do the coup all the time," says Trump. "Whether it's the Russia, Russia, Russia hoax or impeachment number one and impeachment hoax number two. All hoaxes and scams, and they never stop. You win one, and you wait a couple of weeks, and you got another one. You know, it's misinformation, disinformation. But that's all they're good at."

That's why, says Trump, Biden was a bad president. "He was always a dumb guy," says Trump "Ted Kennedy told me a long time ago. He lived in Palm Beach. And I got to know him very well. And we had a very good relationship, considering that we had pretty different views on things, but we had other things that we talked about. I asked him, who's the smartest guy in Congress? He said a certain name. I said, who's the dumbest? He said, probably Joe. I said who's Joe? Joe Biden. He can't understand anything. And this was his prime time, don't forget that's 20 years ago."

By the time Biden was inaugurated on January 20, 2021, the outgoing president had been all but pushed out of the public sphere. "I went from having almost 300 million people between all of the social media platforms to having no voice," Trump says. "And what they did was so wrong."

It wasn't just the former President who was silenced. Pro-Trump accounts across social media—Twitter, Facebook, YouTube, etc.—were shrunk, some losing hundreds of thousands of followers or being wiped out entirely. Thus, thanks in part to the cadres hunting him, Trump was already the Republican Party's 2024 frontrunner. As the most censored man in the history of a constitutional republic that enshrines freedom of expression, Trump became the de facto leader of America's free-speech movement. The former president was now the free world's leading dissident.

DELIVERING TRUTH

Trump explains how he was in talks to take his social media account to various platforms, including Parler. But within a few days of January 6, the Twitter alternative started by Republican donor Rebekah Mercer became another casualty of the Great Purge when Amazon, Apple, Google, and other tech firms conspired to destroy it. So President Trump looked for other options.

In May 2021, he started to post messages on a webpage under the heading, "From the Desk of Donald J. Trump." "I called it a press release," he says. "I dictated to the secretary or somebody and they'd put it out. They were well-structured. They looked beautiful. I didn't think it would do very well because it wasn't a mechanically good situation. But they went through the roof. Now nobody else's would, but mine did."

But it didn't allow users to interact with Trump. "I had millions of people trying to reach me," he says. The platform shut down in June in anticipation of a communications platform that would give Trump his voice and offer his audience a chance to reply.

In October, the newly founded Trump Media & Technology Group announced development of a social networking application to debut the next year: Truth Social. Two months later, Trump hired Devin Nunes as the new company's CEO.

When the ten-term congressman from California's Central Valley announced he was resigning from the House of Representatives to lead Truth Social, Republican voters were alarmed. Nunes was one of the few GOP legislators who fought hard for them. As chairman of the House Intelligence Committee, he led the investigation of abuses and crimes the FBI had committed during its Trump-Russia investigation. Nunes' early hunch that the Trump team had been spied on eventually proved right, but when he first spoke up he found himself alone. Other Republican legislators were either scared of challenging the intelligence services or reluctant to stick their necks out for an outsider president who expressed as much contempt for the establishment GOP as he did for Democrats. But Nunes kept at it, revealing the scope of the FBI's unlawful activities and eventually rallying Republican House members to his side.

Thanks to Nunes' efforts exposing the Russia plot, when the same people who had framed Trump as a tool of Moscow set about impeaching him for a phone call with the Ukrainian President, Congressional Republicans and the GOP electorate saw it as a variation of the same putsch, the next link in an unbroken series of information operations to topple Trump.

Now with Nunes set to leave, Republican voters were nervous. Just as the Biden White House began sweeping up Trump supporters who'd attended the January 6 protests and bringing absurd charges against Americans who'd simply exercised their rights to assembly and free speech, it appeared as though there were no one left to fight for them in Washington.

Nunes says he appreciates those concerns but, he tells me, "I would have been wasting my time on the Hill." He wasn't leaving the fight, it's just that the scope of the war had expanded.

I'm sitting with Nunes in the Truth Social offices in downtown Sarasota, a three-and-a-half-hour drive across the width of Florida to the Atlantic coast and Mar-a-Lago. He's dressed in slacks and a polo-shirt, "tech-start-up casual" as the programmers in the office call it—a very different setting from Capitol Hill. "It's a different battlefield," he says. "But it's the same fight."

He's brought half a dozen members of his congressional team with him to Truth Social, while Kash Patel, the former Nunes staffer who led his probe of the FBI, joined the company's board. Team Nunes was hardly surprised to find that in their efforts to bring Truth Social online they were facing many of the same adversaries they'd fought while exposing Russiagate, including former Hillary Clinton campaign operatives, federal government lawyers, and of course the media.

Given the correlation of forces, Nunes was the ideal choice for the Truth Social job, and when Trump asked him to take it he felt obliged. "Trump called my bluff when he offered me the position," he says. The former congressman had been warning about Big Tech's black hand of censorship dating back to the earliest days of the Russia investigation. He'd acquired hundreds of thousands of followers on Twitter but saw that his reach had been throttled—he'd been shadowbanned, hindering his ability to inform Americans about the biggest political scandal in U.S. history.

Another problem was the prestige press. Outlets like CNN, the *Washington Post*, and the *New York Times* had played a crucial role in credentialing Russiagate by disseminating leaks of classified intelligence fed to them by intelligence officials in order to prosecute a campaign against Trump. Nunes watched the same process unfold in Trump's first impeachment as the media, Democratic Party operatives, and intelligence officials joined once again to run an information operation that hamstrung the president and his ability to effect the policies he was elected to implement.

Seeing social media, the press, and technology as the left's communications infrastructure, Nunes mapped out the problem in his 2020 pamphlet, *Countdown to Socialism*. Published months before the election, his short book argued that the political operatives, Big Tech oligarchs, spy services, and the media driving the plot against the republic are socialists. And socialist regimes, wrote Nunes, "excel at propaganda. That's by necessity—socialism is a resentful ideology that exploits and widens class conflict, racial strife, and other social cleavages, pitting countrymen against one another. They have to have an intensive propaganda operation to make this ideology seem appealing. In America today, among the Democratic Party, the mainstream media, and the social media barons and tech oligarchs, this propaganda network already exists."

According to Nunes, social media is "the central component"

of the propaganda network. "It's the distribution center," he wrote. "Nearly 70 percent of Americans use Facebook, and more than half of all Americans use it as a source for news. Social media takes the radical, anti-American messages developed by socialist activists and disseminates them to the public at large. This process of developing and distributing propaganda is the key to the success of the fake news complex—I call it the 'Disinformation Funnel.'"[2]

Nunes continued, "The purpose of the Funnel is to filter, refine, direct, and amplify propaganda ultimately disseminated through laptops, tablets, and smart phones. From there it goes directly into your brain, with the goal of leaving no room for anything besides socialist propaganda."

Nunes had predicted what happened after the 2020 election. "I said what was coming," he says, shaking his head. "The Great Purge started before the election, but after January 6 they kicked everyone off."

Parler, a multi-billion-dollar company, was wiped out by the tech oligarchs. Nunes had been one of the app's earliest advocates. Moreover, he had at least a million followers there, and he explains that he received greater engagement there than on Twitter.

"Then the tech platforms stopped playing around with shadow-banning and banned people outright," says Nunes. "I said at the time, and still believe, that what happened in 2021 was the worst thing that has ever happened to our country—the destruction of millions of Americans' First Amendment rights. They targeted Trump, but the purpose was also to take total control, consolidate their power, and take away our freedom of speech. I had to do something. I couldn't just complain anymore. When Trump offered me the job at Truth Social, I had to take it."

Since social media was the core component of the information chain, as Nunes had written, he now had a social media platform of his own to run, a powerful instrument in the fight for the republic. And to succeed, says Nunes, "I had to make it indestructible."

THE MISSION

Nunes had Truth Social up and running by February 2022. "It was an immediate smash," says Trump. "All the while we'd been developing the site. They're not easy to develop. They're very complex and expensive. But we have great engineers and they're patriots too. They're conservative patriots these guys. I have the best engineers. You know, the Truth site works better than X. It's a better site. Looks better, works better mechanically."

Trump talks about the money it took to get it going—mostly lawyers' fees. "But the actual cost of running this thing is not much once you have it set, and you can't be taken down because, we have our own everything," says Trump. "So with the other ones, you could be taken down. You say one controversial thing about Crooked Joe Biden and they can take you down. I noticed at the end before they did take me out, they were red-flagging every statement I made. I could make a statement that was out of the Encyclopedia Britannica and they'd red-flag it. 'This is false in our opinion.' Practically anything I said was red-flagged. I said at the time that these people are disgusting, and they are disgusting."

Truth has given Trump a platform for short video clips to explain proposed second-term policies—like mass deportations of illegal aliens ushered across the border by the Biden administration. He also uses Truth to endorse candidates. For instance, there was the Republican primary for Ohio's U.S. Senate seat in which he endorsed Bernie Moreno. "He was wrapped up in a little bit of a problem," says Trump, "and he was down ten three days going in. I did a rally for him, but I did a series of Truth endorsements for him. He won by 21 points. I endorsed Mike Rogers in Michigan, who was essentially in a group of 5 or 6 people that are running. He went up 61 points. That race is over. It's done. And every endorsement I do it through Truth. Every single one."

He uses the platform to support allies, like Texas Attorney General

Ken Paxton. The outspoken lawman was under attack by House Speaker Dade Phelan who was pushing to impeach him in September 2023.

"Phelan's a big guy in Texas," Trump says. "But he's a RINO. And he tried to impeach the attorney general. I see on television that the vote is going to happen the next morning and there were 17 Republican senators who were going to vote against him. I didn't like it, and I like him. So I wrote a Truth—it said the Republicans always eat their young. We have a wonderful attorney general in Texas and you should be ashamed of yourself. All of you senators. Everybody immediately changed. I put that out at 12:30 in the evening. I got a call at 1:30. Sir, everybody's gone aboard. And he didn't get impeached."

Truth, says Trump, "has tremendous power. Look, it's my voice, but the power comes through Truth because every one of those things is done on Truth. It's been fun doing it. And it's also created some good value."

In March 2024, Truth Social went public by merging with a special purpose acquisition company (SPAC). The merger followed a long struggle with the U.S. Securities and Exchange Commission, possibly the hardest and most contested SPAC merger in history. "It was another vector they used to fight Trump," says Nunes.

The stock began trading on the Nasdaq exchange under the ticker symbol DJT. Quickly, the stock appeared on the Nasdaq Reg SHO Threshold list—a signifier of abnormal trading activity that could indicate a company's shares are being illegally manipulated by hedge funds or other sophisticated investors. "It's a little bit of a roller coaster," says Trump. "The shorts are in there trying to kill it, but it won't get killed because we have more than $300 million in cash and we don't have very many expenses. And even at low numbers, it's worth billions of dollars."

Trump pauses and reflects on Truth. "It's sort of a strange thing," he says. "My enemies forced me out of the mainstream stuff. And so I said, 'well, I have to get a site,' and I open up Truth, and it's worth a lot of money, but it really wasn't done for the money. It was done because I need a voice."

So did the many millions of Americans who questioned the integrity of the 2020 election, and the many thousands who went to Washington, D.C. on January 6 to support their candidate and exercise their rights to assembly and free speech. For nearly a year prior to the 2020 presidential election, they'd been told by political, corporate, and media elites that the establishment intended to rig the vote against their candidate, render their vote worthless, and there was nothing they could do to stop it.

In fact, they had no say in their own lives at all. When they challenged state and local governments' right to exploit Covid to pen them in and strip them of their rights, or questioned the lockdowns, or doubted the official story of the origins of the virus, or circulated news of Covid treatments not sanctioned by the health bureaucracy, they were censored. When Democratic operatives moved to rewrite election laws to accommodate the lockdowns, those who questioned the integrity of mass mail-in-voting or voting without an ID were banished from what was once called the marketplace of ideas.

After 2020 Election Day, when Democrats in key toss-up states conjured just enough ballots during the extended vote counting to put Biden over the top, Americans were resolved to make their voices heard. They came from all around the country on January 6 to rally for their candidate, their vote, and their country.

The protest devolved into violence at the Capitol, including fights with security officers, broken windows, and legions of false media reports that officers had been murdered. In the subsequent ferocious crackdown, authorities targeted thousands of January 6 defendants and sent a message to millions, to anyone who'd dare challenge an American government that flashed its whip hand like an Arab security regime. The regime's response to the protest marked a turning point. Shunned, silenced, and some imprisoned, Americans knew that something fundamental had changed—they were losing control of their country and losing their sovereignty.

OUT OF THE SHADOWS

Since Nunes exposed the FBI's anti-Trump machinations, the America First movement has used the phrase "Deep State" to describe the country's number-one adversary. The term derives from Turkish politics to describe a cadre of intelligence and military officers who wield extensive power over the elected government. In the U.S. context, "Deep State" gives a sharper edge to what constitutionalists often refer to as the "administrative state." It comprises the unelected officials who staff Washington, D.C.'s federal bureaucracy and believe their more or less permanent tenure and technocratic expertise justify their usurpation of executive powers, regardless of the elected president's policies.

The catch is that identifying the "Deep State" as the core issue both minimizes the problem and makes it unsolvable. In reality, the Deep State is a menacing but essentially inert piece of bureaucratic machinery. It's not a force in its own right but an instrument weaponized to advance a cause. Contesting it means committing to an endless struggle against a shapeless leviathan feeding on paper, the life source of all bureaucracies. Fighting it means using more paper to root out bad actors, and maybe even an entire institution, but every time one is knocked down, another piece of paper rises with another bureaucrat hiding behind it. Taking on the Deep State is, in the end, a misdirection of energy and resources.

The FBI's espionage against Donald Trump's 2016 campaign was much more than a skirmish with a political outsider to retain bureaucratic privileges. It was rather the origin point of the ongoing coup against the republic. The question is, who weaponized the bureaucracy and on behalf of which causes?

The answer has to begin by recognizing that it was not just the Beltway that fought Trump. It was also the media, Wall Street, academia, the culture industry, and every other citadel of establishment power. All were mobilized to wage a broad counterinsurgency campaign using the weapons at their disposal—financial, cultural, academic, technological, and bureaucratic. The arsenal they pointed at the voting public comprised propaganda, surveillance, and censorship, all deployed to advance a comprehensive, even totalitarian, project to transform America.

So who led it?

Trump revealed the answer only months into his presidency. "Just found out that Obama had my 'wires tapped' in Trump Tower just before the victory," Trump tweeted on March 4, 2017. With that and a subsequent series of tweets, he identified the power behind the surveillance and propaganda operation that unlawfully targeted his presidential campaign—the president under whose authority U.S. spy chiefs managed the anti-Trump plot. This operation rolled into the special counsel investigation, the first impeachment, widespread election irregularities in battleground states, the January 6 insurrection hoax, the second impeachment, the FBI raid on Mar-a-Lago, the indictments and efforts to get Trump thrown off the ballot, and finally the attempt on his life.

Eight years on, it's time to acknowledge Barack Obama's leading role in the counterinsurgency targeting Trump, his aides, and his supporters. Yes, it's terrifying to think that a man elected twice to lead the country had such poisonous designs against it. But starting with the aftermath of the 2016 election when he assumed control of the intelligence operation targeting Trump, to the present, as the first president in over a hundred years to stay in Washington after his term ended, it's Obama.

Few, however, want to recognize it. The end of normalcy in American politics has left normal Americans in a daze, struggling to recognize the contours of the new political anatomy. Those who can are often hesitant to call it what it is. But when Obama's own lieutenants leak to the media that Obama is calling the shots, there's no reason to look the other way. He wants the credit. It's in his nature. The same is true for the faction he leads.

A month after January 6, Obama's whole-of-society network boasted openly about its counterinsurgency efforts to disappear Trump. The February 4 edition of *Time Magazine* published, "The Secret History of the Shadow Campaign that Saved the 2020 Election," in which "dozens" of participants explained how the 2020 presidential election was rescued from Trump by, as *Time* described it, "a well-funded cabal of powerful people, ranging across industries and ideologies, working together behind the scenes to influence perceptions, change rules and laws, steer media coverage and control the flow of information."[3]

During the 2024 campaign cycle, it became impossible to ignore Obama's role when he abruptly walked out of the shadows and virtually raised his hand to claim credit. At a Hollywood fundraiser for Joe Biden in June hosted by George Clooney and other A-list celebrities, the guest of honor was incapable of exiting the stage on his own. Obama physically guided Biden to safety.

It was a public show intended to allay fears about the candidate's mental health, as if to say, "Fear not, friends, you're not really being asked to fund an aging and increasingly feeble man who walks into walls, speaks to imaginary interlocutors, and can't finish a sentence without gliding into gibberish. I'm propping him up here to show you what's really happening behind the curtain. The party and the country are in safe hands, my hands." Obama was pulling back the curtain on his shadow presidency.

The reality is that Biden 2024 was the same as Biden 2020, when Democrats turned his cognitive decline to their advantage by running the campaign out of his basement. For instance, his caution in the face of Covid, coupled with the fact that his rallies were attended by only a handful of people spaced yards apart from each other, demonstrated not that the political careerist lacked charisma and a vision for the country, but rather highlighted his mature leadership during a pandemic.

Under the aegis of Obama's shadow presidency, Biden's term was a stunning success, checking off major items on the progressive wish list. Among other accomplishments, it institutionalized and monetized the trans agenda, opened our borders, and gifted trillions to Democratic donors and China via the climate change agenda.

Nevertheless, the June 2024 Trump-Biden debate convinced the media and most Democrats that Biden had to be ejected from the Democratic ticket. But who should replace him? The final decision, of course, belonged to the shadow president. "Although you called for an open process," he told Kamala Harris, "and you know, Democrats have, have put in place an open process, it appears that people feel very strongly that you need to be our nominee."

But without a primary, without a popular referendum, without even the open convention that Obama was rumored to be favoring, who was really making their will known? Was it social media influencers? Mass rallies across the country? Media chronicling the excitement surrounding a Harris candidacy? No, it was nothing like that. Obama is the people. The people are Obama.

Jill Biden reportedly opposed Kamala both as her husband's pick for vice president and as his replacement on the Democratic ticket. She didn't fully grasp that it was never truly Biden's presidency in the first place. He was merely serving in a ceremonial role on behalf of a politburo thanks to the patronage of his former boss, who saw him as the most reliable vehicle through which to exercise power. Biden was just an imperfect placeholder for Obama, and it was only a matter of time before an improved avatar would be slotted in to serve as Obama's empty vessel to relay his message directly.

"We need to chart a new way forward to meet the challenges of today," Obama said in his speech keynoting the Party's August convention. "And Kamala understands this."[4]

To signal that she understood she is Obama's New Way Forward, the candidate repeated the slogan he devised for her in her acceptance speech, twice. She represented, she said, "a chance to chart a new way forward." And as she repeated a dozen paragraphs later, "We are charting a new way forward."[5]

In her first interview as the Democrats' nominee, a month and a half after her selection was publicly announced, she broke the phrase down, with each word spoken like a separate sentence: "The American people deserve," she said, "A. New. Way. Forward."[6]

But it's not new, it's just more of the same, what friendly media call "the female Obama."[7] She's an ideologue committed to the causes advanced by her party and patron, including censorship of her political opponents. As a senator, Harris was one of the first to call for Trump's banishment from social media, writing a letter to Twitter's management in October 2019 demanding the American President be silenced.[8]

And now there's no more mystery as to what has happened the last eight years. A political party employed third-world tactics—surveillance, censorship, election interference, political prosecution, and political violence—to put America under the thumb of a totalitarian faction invested in controlling every aspect of American life. That's Obama's faction. I call it the Shadow Network.

Most of the network's key players are names already well known to the American public—oligarchs from the tech and finance sectors, political donors, operatives who go back and forth between the private and public sector, leading journalists, and top spy chiefs. It's not a sprawling bureaucratic behemoth like the Deep State, but smaller, tightly knit, well-funded, and focused.

As Nunes discovered, the same people and institutions that he fought during the Russiagate investigation also resisted his efforts to bring Truth Social online. He estimates that the actual number of operators across the political, corporate, and cultural landscape who seek to bring America to its knees is small. But they're powerful. "It's not the 'Deep State' we're up against," he says. "It's all those same people we've been fighting from the start."

This book aims to bring the Shadow Network into the light—to reveal who it comprises and how it seeks to achieve its goal of disappearing President Trump from public life. Domestic spying and election rigging are vital parts of its modus operandi. The network, however, has increasingly identified communications as a central battlefield. Its members wage information warfare operations by dominating the public discourse with their own narratives, preferences, and arguments while suppressing the speech and even the personal freedom of their opponents. These attacks have given rise to parallel communications platforms such as Truth Social and Rumble, which fight to provide a safe harbor for free expression outside the influence of the Shadow Network.

The normalization of political violence by the Shadow Network, culminating in the attempt on Trump's life, underscores the fundamental issue—the fight is to restore our constitutional republic. It's an existential contest that will decide our future and whether we remain a free people or forfeit more than 250 years of American history and once again succumb to tyranny. And like so many of the anti-democratic policies and practices adopted by our ruling establishment in recent years, the Shadow Network first showed its hand with Russiagate.

2

THE JANUARY 5 CONSPIRACY

Barack Obama wanted a word with Mark Zuckerberg. It was a week and a half after Donald Trump's November 8, 2016 victory, and the sitting president was looking for someone to blame. Eventually, he would use his executive authority to delegitimize Trump's presidency as the fruit of a foreign plot. But in the meantime, he was mad and wanted to take off someone's head—the legacy he had built with his phone and pen was now vulnerable. When he saw the Facebook chief at a conference of world leaders in Lima, Peru, the outgoing leader of the free world read him the riot act.

Zuckerberg's company was perhaps the most problematic part of the Shadow Network. The issue is less Zuckerberg himself, who may be sincere when he professes his affinity for free speech, than the company's financial model. What makes Facebook a crucial instrument for the Shadow Network is its size—it is the largest social media platform in the world. But massive purges of users and flagrant censorship jeopardize the company's reputation and thereby its influence. So, Zuckerberg must be managed with carrots as well as sticks.

Even before the election, the media had accused him of allowing his platform to proliferate "hoax or fake news" that might enable a

Trump victory.[1] So after Trump won, the Facebook founder became public enemy number one.

One post-election assessment blamed Facebook directly for the dissemination of fake news that led to Trump's victory. "Facebook's enormous audience, and the mechanisms of distribution on which the site relies," claimed *New York Magazine*, "makes it the only site to support a genuinely lucrative market in which shady publishers arbitrage traffic by enticing people off of Facebook and onto ad-festooned websites, using stories that are alternately made up, incorrect, exaggerated beyond all relationship to truth, or all three."[2]

Zuckerberg argued it was "pretty crazy" to blame Facebook for fake news, since "more than 99% of what people see is authentic." He explained, "Only a very small amount is fake news and hoaxes."[3]

Obama wasn't having it. In a November 17 joint press conference with German chancellor Angela Merkel in Berlin, he lamented that "there's so much active misinformation and it's packaged very well and it looks the same when you see it on a Facebook page or you turn on your television." He continued, "If everything seems to be the same and no distinctions are made, then we won't know what to protect."[4]

Obama was using a word that would soon become part of the American left's political lexicon—"misinformation" (also called "disinformation")—a word employed to describe information deemed distasteful and dangerous due to its association with Trump. Neither Obama nor any of Facebook's critics ever explained how the problems they attributed to the platform differed in any real way from supermarket checkout counters, where the *World Weekly News* and other sensationalist tabloids occupy the same space as glossy magazines produced by Madison Avenue publishers. But no one ever claimed salacious scoops detailing Hillary's intimate extraterrestrial liaisons cost her the White House.

Obama's real problem with Facebook was that it drove the bulk of the $250 million the Trump campaign raised online. "Social media was Trump's primary communication channel," the online magazine *WIRED* reported a week after the election. The campaign had largely bypassed traditional media advertising to target audiences receptive to the candidate's message. Trump was an innovator. From the campaign's perspective, *WIRED* explained, Facebook "wasn't a platform for broadcasting pre-planned messages, but for interacting with supporters and starting new conversations."[5]

The Trump campaign raised millions from Facebook Live events.[6] With a little more than two weeks before Election Day, Trump campaign officials organized a nightly half-hour Facebook Live news show to run through November 8.[7] Trump understood the medium and mastered it. Facebook was happy to help. A Trump campaign official told the press that the company even sent staff to show them how to exploit the platform's advertising tools to maximize response.[8] And for Obama and his faction, that alone was enough to make Zuckerberg complicit in Trump's great crime—defeating Clinton.

So, the Shadow Network concocted an elaborate plotline charging that the social media giant was part of a Russian plot that put Trump in the White House—for Facebook, the narrative contended, had also been infiltrated by Russian intelligence agencies.

According to one report, "Facebook detected elements of the Russian information operation in June 2016 and then notified the FBI."[9] Many social media cybersecurity experts are essentially detailees from the U.S. Intelligence Community, so it is no mystery why Facebook's security team named APT28, also known as Fancy Bear, as the culprit. It was the same hacker group alleged to be tied to Russian military intelligence that former feds working for the Clinton campaign claimed had hacked and leaked her emails. The purpose was to make Moscow responsible for anything that looked like election interference and then link the Russians to Trump.

Dragging Facebook into the Russia collusion narrative filled out the information operation weaponized to rationalize censorship as well as surveillance of Trump, his circle and, eventually, half the country. But when Obama pulled Zuckerberg aside in Peru, the message he wanted to convey was simple and direct: for helping put Trump in the White House, he and his then $400 billion-dollar company were on notice.

Perhaps it struck Zuckerberg as odd that the outgoing president was so animated about an election in which he was not a candidate. Sure, the loss was bad for the party Obama had led for eight years, but wasn't he leaving the White House to pursue other interests, like every other former commander in chief? Why had Obama taken it to heart as if he were still an active participant in U.S. politics? Because the bigger message he was sending was that he wasn't going anywhere, especially now with Trump entering the White House.

FORTIFYING THE SURVEILLANCE CAMPAIGN

Zuckerberg's company was one of several tech juggernauts—along with Apple, Microsoft, Google, Skype, and others—that gave the National Security Agency (NSA) direct access to their servers to spy on Americans. In June 2013, a report sourced to documents stolen by former NSA contractor Edward Snowden revealed the details of a secret NSA collection program called PRISM that tapped into Facebook and other platforms to collect user data and conduct surveillance on live communications.[10] Zuckerberg and other Big Tech oligarchs denied that Facebook gave the government "direct access," but Obama admitted it was true—and said it was a good thing.

"You can't have 100 percent security and then have 100 percent privacy and zero inconvenience," Obama told the press a day after the report was published. He added, "There are some trade-offs involved." What did he mean by that? If you don't want the government to spy on you through a website where you post pictures of your children's birthday parties, do you then have to live with terror attacks on U.S. soil?

PRISM, Obama officials explained, was part of a collection program under the authority of Section 702 of the Foreign Intelligence

Surveillance Act (FISA). Congress enacted 702 during the George W. Bush years when the FBI and other agencies tired of having to obtain a warrant to spy on foreign targets whose emails and other electronic communications were carried by U.S. service providers. Given the logic of the post-9/11 security state, it was hardly surprising that after collecting emails, phone calls, etc., culling information from social media would be the next step.

Obama tried to allay Americans' concerns. "Nobody is listening to your telephone calls. That's not what this program's about," he insisted. "They are not looking at people's names, and they're not looking at content." But they were.

The law stipulates that the communications of U.S. citizens and anyone located within the United States is off-limits, but the intelligence services use a loophole to collect against Americans called reverse-targeting. The agencies pretend to focus on a foreigner when what they're really after is the American with whom the foreigner is communicating.

"Section 702 collects on foreigners and foreign state-sponsored actors when they are on foreign soil," says former FBI agent Stephen Friend. "It's illegal to reverse-target on Americans. But they do it anyway."

And shortly before leaving office, Obama broke down the few barriers built to protect our liberties and thereby spare U.S. intelligence officials the trouble of having to contrive cover stories in order to spy on Americans.

Executive Order 12333, issued by President Ronald Reagan in 1981, regulates how the NSA collects, retains, analyzes, and disseminates foreign signals intelligence. It also stipulates that the names of U.S. citizens are redacted, or "masked," in transcripts and other records of intercepted communications to protect their privacy rights. Obama amended 12333 to give every U.S. intelligence service and law enforcement agency access to the NSA's raw, unredacted signals intelligence.

In short, he pre-empted the debate about privacy vs. security by handing U.S. spies the keys to the kingdom.

Previously, says Friend, "12333 had established a wall between the NSA and the other agencies. If the NSA found something in their collection they couldn't just go to the FBI and say, 'hey, here's the name of this guy we picked up.' The FBI had to have a reason to have the information and go through proper channels and use proper processes like search warrants to get it."

Friend left the FBI in August 2022 after making protected whistleblower disclosures to his superiors about January 6 investigations assigned to the field office where he was based. Within a month, the FBI weaponized the security clearance process to remove him from active duty. I spoke with him and another whistleblower, former FBI analyst and Marine veteran George Hill, and they explained how the Bureau was already becoming politicized by the time they arrived.

First was the appointment of Robert Mueller to lead the post-9/11 FBI and implement George W. Bush's domestic security agenda. As Hill recalls, "Bush told Mueller, 'I know you're going to catch the guys who did it, Bob, but what are you going to do to stop the next one?' So Mueller made the FBI into a domestic intelligence agency. And it's not just me saying this, but history shows that a domestic intelligence service has only one master, not the people it's supposed to protect, but the government that pays it."

At first the FBI staffed its new intelligence cadres with veterans, but that began to change around 2005. "I did 26 years in uniform," Hill says. "And with vets like me, our loyalty is to the constitution. But the FBI started recruiting right out of college and when you're hired right out of college your loyalty is to the people writing your paycheck."

Moreover, he adds, they were hiring people who were already political. "We see what's happening on college campuses," says Hill. "These are young men and women who are ideologically bent. And they're arriving that way at the FBI and finding a ready-made mechanism to push their agenda forward."

The FBI had been primed for political warfare, and Obama armed them by giving the Bureau access to raw signals intelligence. "Before Obama amended it," says Hill, "12333 put up really high walls and delineated which intelligence agency could do what. I had to test out every year to show that I knew the procedures."

The NSA would notify agencies about electronic communications they'd collected and whether the particular agency, the FBI for instance, had any interest in the individual.

"The NSA would provide a phone number, or an IP address, or something of that nature, without giving out the name," says Hill. "And then we would have to go and look at our own database to say, 'No, we don't have any cases here related to this individual. So the answer's no, no need to unmask him.' But if we had information matching what the NSA provided and we wanted the individual unmasked, there was a formal process to get the name."

Plans were afoot to amend 12333 during Obama's last year in office, and the FBI knew it was coming.[11] "They already had the servers and everything in place to ingest the same raw signals intelligence traffic that the NSA was collecting," says Hill. In mid-December Director of National Intelligence James Clapper signed off on the new rules, and on January 3, 2017, Attorney General Loretta Lynch finalized them.[12]

The FBI now doesn't have to go through any formal procedures to get the names of Americans unmasked because, says Hill, "nobody is masked. The American citizens that are in that intelligence traffic are not masked. Now, it's a straight shot. You get to see everything."

The FBI, says Friend, "and actually all federal law enforcement can just go and have access to all the raw information that the NSA collects. And when you have that ability, you can really abuse people. Because you can just go in there and shop for whatever you want, and if you're an intelligence person who's politically motivated, you can create an intelligence product or open an investigation on anything or anyone you want."

For a time, the left was panicked about the new rules. Civil libertarians and journalists couldn't fathom how Obama had blundered so badly by leaving to Trump what he'd surely use as a political weapon. "*WIRED Magazine* did a piece about it shortly after 12333 was amended," says Friend.[13] "They were worried that the Obama administration had given the agencies unfettered access to all that material and the incoming Trump administration was going to use it to go after the left."

But that was the opposite of Obama's plan. Rather, he left to his allies a powerful arsenal to target their political enemies—access to all their communications. "He knew that the left had already captured institutions like the FBI," says Friend. It was only a few months later, says Hill, that "the left stopped complaining when they saw Russiagate and the other shenanigans and realized Obama had left it out there to target Trump."

Obama's move was masterful, says Hill. "He had created an environment that was favorable for people with political leanings to run wild and get whatever they need."

OBAMA'S COUP

Obama disciplined the owner of the world's largest and most influential social media platform and gave factional allies access to raw intelligence for the purpose of targeting political opponents. But there was more to put in order before he left the White House.

On January 5, 2017, two days after 12333 was amended, Obama met in the Oval Office to discuss the FBI's Trump-Russia collusion investigation with top aides, including Deputy Attorney General Sally Yates, FBI director James Comey, National Security Adviser Susan Rice, and Vice President Joe Biden. They all already knew there was no evidence of any ties between the president-elect and Russian officials.

It was a phony investigation that had been stood up to serve the interests of Hillary Clinton's presidential campaign. But it never would have gotten off the ground without Obama's greenlight. Espionage was a crucial component of the Obama White House's style and ethos. Thus, unsurprisingly, everyone in the Oval Office for the January 5 meeting had spied on Trump transition officials, in particular General Michael Flynn, the incoming National Security Advisor.

At least forty Obama aides had spied on Flynn by unmasking his identity from transcripts of foreign intelligence intercepts, the most significant of which documented Flynn's conversations with the Russian ambassador. In the January 5 meeting, Biden suggested Flynn could be arrested for speaking with Moscow's envoy to the U.S. and charged under the Logan Act, an obscure and never-enforced eighteenth-century law that bans private individuals from conducting official foreign policy.

Maybe the other lawyers in the room wondered how Biden even knew about the Logan Act. But that's easy to explain. He had received countless legal briefings on how to side-step every possible infraction he might have committed during his decades-long career billing foreign officials and businessmen to massage U.S. foreign policy to their advantage. Biden's coin-operated family machine was a coarser, shanty version of the racket Hillary Clinton was running with the Clinton Foundation. She used a private email server to keep journalists and opposition researchers from accessing her communications through Freedom of Information Act requests. But then she was hacked, and the FBI was forced to investigate whether she had mishandled classified information.

It was exactly six months before the January 5 meeting that Comey cleared her. On July 5, the FBI director had personally exonerated the Democratic Party candidate. Of course, there was no chance the Department of Justice was ever going to bring charges. Every senior Obama official, including the president, would have been implicated. They had all corresponded with her, knowing she was using a non-government account. Comey acknowledged she was "extremely careless," but judged "that no reasonable prosecutor would bring such a case."[14]

The Clinton campaign's main concern was never the FBI investigation but rather that there were emails from her private account floating around in cyberspace. If potential evidence of her financial arrangements with foreign officials and enterprises went public, it might ruin her candidacy. So, the FBI set up a sting operation targeting Trump aides to see if they knew anything about her emails that might be used as an October surprise to hurt Clinton.

Also in early July, FBI informant Christopher Steele had begun sending fake reports to his handler about Trump's alleged ties to Russian officials. Steele was a London-based fixer, once employed by British intelligence and later by Russian oligarchs, who was hired by the Clinton campaign to make its anti-Trump smears look authentic. Democratic Party media operatives managed the makeover, turning the midlevel MI-6 washout into a real-life James Bond who risked his life to disclose the supposed dark secret he had uncovered in less than a month: Trump had been compromised by Moscow's intelligence services in an operation overseen by Vladimir Putin himself.

In reality, the FBI tasked Steele to put his byline on fake reports about Trump's ties to foreign officials in order to secure a FISA warrant to spy on the Trump campaign.

Obama's CIA chief John Brennan says he told Obama in an August 2016 meeting at the White House that he had intelligence showing the Russians knew the Clinton camp was running a dirty tricks campaign against Trump, smearing him as a Russian agent to deflect attention away from her use of a private server.

This information—that Russia knew of Clinton's plans to frame Trump as a Russian spy—appears to have been the only genuine piece of Russian intelligence that U.S. spy services ever collected during the FBI's investigation of Trump's ties to Russia. And it's not hard to see how Moscow figured it out. By then, the public phase of the Russia collusion hoax was well under way. At the outset of the 2016 Democratic convention, Clinton campaign manager Robby Mook suggested Russia had hacked the DNC to help Trump win the election, while campaign chairman John Podesta accused Trump of having a "bromance" with Putin. It would have been obvious to Russian officials that the Clinton campaign was seeding the Trump-Russia story.

At the same time Brennan acknowledged that the Russia collusion story was a campaign hoax, he was furiously advancing that very narrative. He later testified that he gave the FBI every piece of information he had on Trump and Russia, and that his information was the basis of the FBI's investigation. But Brennan never had anything on Trump and Russia. No one did because they made it up.

Time was running out, and Brennan was keen on helping Clinton and keeping his job into the next administration. So he publicly pressured Comey to get the warrant to spy on the Trump campaign. The CIA director went to Senate minority leader Harry Reid and got him to write a letter to the FBI director telling him to act on the information supplied by the Bureau's informant, Steele.

Now Comey was feeling the heat. He asked about the status of the FISA warrant to spy on the Trump team and was frustrated by delays. The case agents were aware that the White House wanted to know everything they were doing. When the secret FISA Court finally green-lit the warrant, largely based on the fraudulent reports from Christopher Steele, it turned up nothing. The FBI had counted on finding an October Surprise of their own by scouring the Trump circle's electronic communications—something, anything to drop on the GOP candidate before the election. FBI agent Peter Strzok was so confident in the FBI's talent for targeting political enemies that he assured his FBI mistress Lisa Page that "we'll stop" Trump from winning.

But they didn't. Trump won, and with the inaugural barely two weeks away, Obama called for a meeting at the White House. He'd resolved to keep Russiagate alive.

According to Susan Rice's notes from the January 5 meeting:

President Obama began the conversation by stressing his continued commitment to ensuring that every aspect of this issue is
handled by the Intelligence and law enforcement communities
"by the book." The President stressed that he is not asking about,
initiating or instructing anything from a law enforcement perspective. He reiterated that our law enforcement team needs to
proceed as it normally would by the book.[15]

Her memo continues, "From a national security perspective, however, President Obama said he wants to be sure that, as we engage with
the incoming team, we are mindful to ascertain if there is any reason
that we cannot share information fully as it relates to Russia."

When Rice's notes were first made public midway through Trump's
term, Republican officials wanted to know why she emailed them to
herself in the Obama administration's final hours on January 20. GOP
investigators and Trump supporters speculated she was covering for
Obama—and herself, should anyone come asking questions about the
White House's role in the unlawful surveillance of the Trump circle.
It's not Obama's fault—he told them to go "by the book."

But Obama wasn't covering up anything. He knew the FBI's Trump
investigation was a fraud and that there was no evidence to support it.
No, Rice's January 5 memo documented something else: Obama wasn't
trying to hide his role. He wanted his national security advisor to get
it on the record that *he* was in charge, that *he'd* made the call to turn
Russiagate into an instrument to undermine his successor. Understanding that this phase of the investigation, spying on a President, marked
the start of something historic, a counter-revolution leaving America
under the rule of a unified regime, Obama wanted the coming generations to know it was he who had set it in motion. It's in his nature to
demand credit for what he's done.

The next day, January 6, the directors of the CIA and the Department of Homeland Security established the precedent for censoring,

surveilling, and propagandizing Americans and turning the country into a permanent one-party security state. There would be no need for tanks or planes to finish this coup because what Obama's faction institutionalized would give it control over elections and the authority to silence anyone who resisted the radical regime, even a former president and the opposition party's leading presidential candidate. Obama was moving the pieces in place to topple the American republic.

"THE FIX WAS IN"

Truth Social CEO Devin Nunes remembers when he received his first post-election intelligence briefings about the 2016 presidential campaign. "It was around Thanksgiving," says Nunes. He was then chairman of the House Intelligence Committee.

"It was just the usual stuff," he says, "Nothing abnormal. They told us what everyone already knew—'Hey, the Russians are bad actors and they're always playing games. They've been doing it since before the Cold War. Even before the Russian Revolution they had active intelligence services and operations. And here's what they did this time.'"

But a December 9, 2016 article in the *Washington Post* signaled that the spy services had changed their assessment and it was not what Nunes had been told. "The CIA," according to the article, "has concluded in a secret assessment that Russia intervened in the 2016 election to help Donald Trump win the presidency."[16] Obama's counterterrorism advisor Lisa Monaco told the press that the outgoing president wanted that finding documented in an official report—an Intelligence Community Assessment (ICA)—before Trump's inauguration.

In the meantime, Obama's spy chiefs used media leaks to delegitimize the incoming administration. "American intelligence agencies have concluded with 'high confidence' that Russia acted covertly in the latter stages of the presidential campaign to harm Hillary Clinton's chances and promote Donald J. Trump," reported the *New York Times*.[17] And according to NBC News, Moscow's pro-Trump operation was run by the head of the regime: "Russian President Vladimir Putin became personally involved in the covert Russian campaign to interfere in the U.S. presidential election, senior U.S. intelligence officials told NBC News."[18]

This was not the assessment Nunes had been given, and he asked for an explanation. "They just clammed up and said they wouldn't brief us again until the ICA was finished," says Nunes. "The fix was in—that was already obvious."

Between the time of his talk with Zuckerberg in mid-November and the first week of December, Obama had decided he was going to use Russia to frame Trump and cripple his administration. He put Brennan in charge with this goal in mind.

"Brennan cooked the process, to keep the experts out," says Derek Harvey, a U.S. Army combat veteran and former intelligence officer who was a senior investigator for Nunes' committee. "They kept senior Russia analysts at the CIA out of it. They kept out the joint staff, the Defense Intelligence Agency (DIA), the State Department's intel shop and others."

The analysts were handpicked by Brennan. "He kept it small to keep everyone else out. He didn't want anyone looking at process, methodology, and tradecraft," says Harvey. "He wanted to avoid scrutiny because he was purposefully manipulating intelligence to support this illusion that Trump had colluded with Russia."

Harvey continues, "When we got briefed on Russia's actions in 2016, it made no sense. No one disputed Russia meddled in some ways. But there were no specific actions or identifications of intelligence that showed support for their claims that Putin had interfered to help Trump. Brennan, Clapper, Comey, Rice—they had nothing."

Harvey explains that a team of former CIA and DIA analysts looked at Brennan's work on the ICA. "They meticulously researched and examined all of the source documentation used and not used but available to Brennan and his cohort," he says. "They unambiguously determined that the sourcing was manipulated and changed."

In the end, all Obama spy chiefs had was the FBI informant's reports. Brennan, says Harvey, lied to Congress. "He said the Steele dossier was not used in the ICA, but it was." A summary of the dossier was attached to the ICA in a two-page document, called Annex A. "The ICA's principal finding is that Putin and the Russian government's influence campaign aspired to help Trump," says Harvey. "The footnote to support that key judgment about Putin's intentions and strategy refers to Annex A, which is the dossier."

Nunes called the ICA "Obama's dossier." "Everything about it—how they researched it, how they wrote it, the rushed timing, the leaks, the changing assessments, the way they stonewalled us on what they were doing—it was all crooked," says Nunes. "It was a purely political project that had nothing to do with intelligence."

"It was critical for setting up the collusion narrative," Harvey says of Brennan's memo. "It gave credibility to everything. What Obama ordered gave political operatives, the press, and his intelligence chiefs a second shot at Trump."

The immediate aim was to undermine Trump and force him from office. Mike Pence was perhaps amenable. His aides were letting on in private that the vice president despised Trump. Pence later helped the FBI force Flynn, Trump's closest advisor, out of the White House amid a media frenzy over his alleged Logan Act violation.

The longer-term goal was to destabilize the country and set Americans against each other in an atmosphere of relentless anger and unremitting fear, the necessary conditions designed to facilitate the Shadow Network's permanent takeover.

DHS BOLSTERS THE COUP

"Until the CIA's Russia memo came out, Russiagate was a stupid, bad joke," says Mike Benz. He served in the Trump administration's State Department, formulating and negotiating U.S. foreign policy on international communications and information technology. He now serves as executive director of Foundation for Freedom Online, a civil society institution championing digital freedom.

"Between November and January," says Benz, "everyone was like, 'really? You're going to blame this on Russia? It's the stupidest thing. You're never going to get away with this.' And then the CIA came out and said, 'Oh, no, it's true.'"

The ICA went beyond delegitimizing Trump's presidency. According to Benz, it was also the pretext for internet censorship. "It basically said that 2016 was an illegitimate election because Russia had taken over U.S. social media. So people weren't really supporting Trump. They were manipulated into it by Russian influence online."

According to Benz, the CIA's assessment of Russian actions "never laid out a case for how Russia had interfered on social media. It was all smoke and mirrors. All they claimed is that Russian press organizations like *Russia Today* (now RT) and *Sputnik* grew massively on social media, especially comparing their growth rate to the BBC and other state-backed media. But that means nothing."

Indeed, the ICA's own charts showed that RT far surpassed the reach of CNN and BBC on YouTube, but was dwarfed by the same outlets on Twitter and Facebook.[19]

Benz says the ICA's implicit argument is "that social media can't be trusted because the Russians took it over and they elected Donald Trump. And once the CIA—America's first line of defense—made that its formal intelligence finding, well then, are you against protecting America from Russian interference online?"

Brennan's memo also asserted that Russian military intelligence was behind the hack of DNC emails. The problem is that there was no evidence for that assessment except for claims made by a private cybersecurity firm CrowdStrike, that was under contract with the Clinton campaign. CrowdStrike executive Shawn Henry later admitted in congressional testimony that there was no evidence Russia had stolen the DNC emails.[20] Nonetheless, the claim had already been used to justify Obama initiatives to consolidate control over political institutions, including elections.

The same day the unclassified version of the CIA assessment was released to the public, Obama's Department of Homeland Security secretary Jeh Johnson published a memo of his own. Because Russia had "orchestrated cyberattacks" on the U.S. "for the purpose of influencing our election," claimed Johnson, alluding to the DNC hack, DHS was adding election infrastructure to a list of critical infrastructure sectors like energy, food, and nuclear facilities, entitling them to DHS cybersecurity assistance and protections.[21]

Johnson's memo was crafted to piggyback on Brennan's. Because, according to the CIA, a foreign power had elected a president against the will of the U.S. electorate, the DHS was adding elections to its portfolio. A handful of state officials, rightly protective of the states' sovereign authority over elections, understood Johnson's move for exactly what it was: the first step toward nationalizing elections. "This action is a federal overreach into a sphere constitutionally reserved for the states," said then-Georgia Secretary of State Brian Kemp.[22]

"It seems like now it's just the D.C. media and the bureaucrats, because of the DNC getting hacked, they now think our whole system is on the verge of disaster because some Russian's going to tap into the voting system," Kemp told the media. The future Georgia Governor had reason to be concerned about Obama's larger project. "The question remains whether the federal government will subvert the Constitution," said Kemp, "to achieve the goal of federalizing elections under the guise of security."[23]

Johnson's gambit was supported by a press corps that had driven the public into a mass panic attack, worrying where the omnivorous Russian bear might strike next. A December 31 *Washington Post* story, for instance, reported that the Russians had hacked a Vermont utility.[24] The *Post* got it wrong and walked back its story, but not before it had supported the flimsy premise for designating elections as infrastructure:

with the Russians attacking energy infrastructure, it was high time to harden democracy infrastructure.

Johnson had been pushing to federally "fortify" elections since the June leak of DNC emails. "The FBI and the DNC had been in contact with each other months before about the intrusion, and the DNC did not feel it needed DHS's assistance at that time," according to Johnson. "As summer 2016 progressed, my concerns about the possibility of a cyberattack around our national election grew."[25]

In an August conference call with state election officials, he pitched the administration's big idea, but there were few takers. "Those who expressed negative views stated that running elections in this country was the sovereign and exclusive responsibility of the states, and they did not want federal intrusion, a federal takeover, or federal regulation of that process," said Johnson. So he bided his time and pushed the Russia collusion hoax.

On September 8, Johnson joined Comey and Lisa Monaco in an unusual meeting with congressional leaders intended to show "solidarity and bipartisan unity" against Russian interference. In reality, the purpose was to get GOP lawmakers to join Democrats and smear the Republican candidate as a Russian stooge. The gathering included both parties' leaders in the House and Senate, the chairmen and ranking members from the House and Senate Intelligence Committees, and the chairmen and ranking members from the House and Senate Homeland Security committees.

Johnson, Comey, and Monaco discussed Russian efforts to shape the upcoming presidential elections. But they had no details.

"Just like everything they were doing back then on Russia issues, the briefing was weird and suspicious," Nunes recalls. "They were implying that the Russians were involved in some major assault, but they had no specifics and no evidence of anything. If this was just the usual meddling the Russians try to do in every election, then why were they treating it as a DEFCON 1 event? And if it was something more than that, then why wouldn't they tell us what the Russians had actually done?"

After Trump took over the White House, his DHS Secretary John Kelly blundered terribly by keeping the Obama initiative in place. The agency was tasked with protecting election-related structure, such as polling places, voting machines, and computer systems. In the run-up to the 2020 vote, DHS operatives would expand the definition of "critical infrastructure" to include voters themselves.

"By 2019," says Benz, "whatever DHS labeled 'foreign disinformation' on social media would be framed as a 'cyber threat to election infrastructure,' justifying the censorship of millions of American voters."

In the inverted language employed by the Obama faction, defending democracy meant stripping citizens of their First Amendment rights. And protecting election "infrastructure" was simply a pretext to seize control of elections. The Shadow Network was determined that Trump, or anyone who challenged its vision, would never win another election. And with Obama securing the two central pillars of surveillance and censorship, it was all but guaranteed.

3

THE COUNTERINSURGENTS

With Devin Nunes' investigation verging on a major breakthrough in early 2018, a broad coalition rose up to prevent the House Intelligence Committee Chairman from making public the evidence he'd amassed of FBI crimes and abuses committed during its probe of Donald Trump's presidential campaign.

What came to be called the Nunes memo was a four-page document showing that the FBI's warrant application to spy on Trump associate Carter Page was based extensively on false information from FBI informant Christopher Steele and his fraudulent dossier. As Nunes went through the procedures to legally reveal this information to the public, speculation about the memo's contents spread rapidly. Conservatives rallied behind Nunes and his investigators, showing their support with a hashtag on social media, #ReleaseTheMemo.

"The spread of the hashtag was a great, grassroots campaign by conservatives who'd become skeptical of 'Russia collusion,'" says Nunes. "They didn't yet know what was in the memo, since it was still classified, but they wanted to see it for themselves and reach their own conclusions. The more they saw Adam Schiff, the Democratic Party, the media, and the Intelligence Community panic over the memo and fight its release, the more they believed there was something there that the establishment wanted to hide—and they were right."

The committee's then-spokesman Jack Langer, now at Truth Social, remembers they knew they were close to an important win and gratified they had the public with them. "Conservatives really supported our efforts to get the memo out," says Langer. "There was a sense that Devin was on to something big."

Nunes and his team were accustomed to media attacks, and federal law enforcement had stonewalled them every step of the way. But with the impending release of the memo, a larger coalition had been assembled to shut down Nunes, including private sector partners from Big Tech and civil society organizations. It was what Beltway insiders and NGO executives call a whole-of-society mobilization.

The scope of the operation showed the stakes involved. They were not just protecting the politicized FBI and DOJ officials who had run the unlawful Russia investigation. The larger problem was the movement of which Trump had taken leadership—it threatened to unseat them, then hold them accountable for their failures and corruption. They saw it as an insurgency.

To better understand the information warfare operation run against Nunes and Trump, let's take a brief look at the evolution of the U.S. government's data-gathering and surveillance techniques, and how these weapons intended for foreign foes were eventually turned on Americans.

THE INTERNET AND COUNTERINSURGENCY

It is a little known fact that the internet emerged from a surveillance tool to help America battle communism.

After the Soviet Union's 1957 Sputnik launch, President Eisenhower resolved to keep U.S. technology a step ahead of its Cold War rival and established the Advanced Research Projects Agency (ARPA). Now called DARPA, the agency joined industry, academia, and government to execute "research and development projects to expand the frontiers of technology and science far beyond immediate military requirements."[1]

In the 1960s, ARPA researchers developed the earliest precursor to the internet, ARPANET, rumored to be a communications network designed to survive a nuclear war. Rather, as ARPA director Charles Herzfeld, explained, "The ARPANET came out of our frustration that there were only a limited number of large, powerful research computers in the country, and that many research investigators, who should have access to them, were geographically separated from them."[2]

The Pentagon launched its first major deployment of ARPANET during the Vietnam War, when it was used to collect and disseminate data as part of the counterinsurgency campaign against the Vietcong communist guerillas. ARPANET's purpose was two-fold: to collect intelligence on the enemy's military activities and on Vietnamese society as a whole.

"The Pentagon designed projects to cover the Ho Chi Minh Trail, the major North Vietnamese supply route, with a vast network of surveillance sensors to give U.S. forces advance warning of an attack," says writer Jacob Siegel. "The other major aspect of the ARPA Vietnam initiative entailed large-scale social science research and survey projects to determine what was motivating the Vietcong and how to keep the rest of the population from joining the insurgency."

Siegel is the author of a forthcoming book on the rise of the information state and a former U.S. Army officer who served in Iraq and Afghanistan. He explains how the precedent for the Global War on Terror (GWOT), including the freedom agenda and counterinsurgency doctrine, or COIN, was set decades earlier in Vietnam, where the Pentagon first made mass collection of data a war-fighting priority. Eventually, these experiments in social engineering would also become the template for the Shadow Network's campaign to suppress and disenfranchise Americans.

"Surveillance technologies are dual purpose," says Siegel. "The same targeting instruments used to pinpoint the enemy for kinetic strikes on enemies can also be used by online marketers to deliver customized ads or by governments as part of a social engineering effort. And in Vietnam, the Pentagon came to believe that fighting insurgencies required extensive research into the attitudes of the local population."

From this perspective, an insurgency is evidence of an unstable society, and the goal of counterinsurgency is to stabilize it while killing the insurgents. This is where the social engineering component comes in, says Siegel. "The question that the academic researchers wanted to answer is, 'what will bring the population back into balance and separate it from the insurgents? Is it that they want more money, or more safety, or more freedom, or whatever? What does it take to keep them from joining the insurgency and to re-balance society?'"

Vietnam is where the whole-of-society counterinsurgency concept first appeared. Siegel explains that "with the social engineering aspect, social science researchers were forward deployed like a military academic branch as part of the war effort."

That model would later be replicated during the GWOT and then turned against supporters of Donald Trump, the insurgent candidate. The 9/11 attacks helped solidify the whole apparatus.

"People were anguished and also confused," says Siegel, a native New Yorker who joined the Army shortly after the 2001 attacks on his hometown. "How could this have happened? The consensus was that it was the greatest intelligence failure in the nation's history. And in some sense, that was obviously true. But what did that mean?"

"According to the 9/11 Commission report," says Siegel, "all these bureaucratic agencies, the FBI, and CIA had pieces of the puzzle, but because they didn't communicate, they didn't put those pieces of the puzzle together."

Federal agencies attempted to fix the problem by adding more bureaucracies, like Department of Homeland Security and the Office of the Director of National Intelligence.

"They also decided that the real problem was not a failure of under-standing," says Siegel, "which is something that humans are responsible for, not a failure of strategic vision, again, something that individual leaders, statesmen are responsible for. No, they decided that the problem was that we'd failed to capture enough information."

In fact, he says, "they wanted to capture all the information in the world. And that was because terrorists were distributed in different parts of the world, so the consensus was that we need to surveil everything, everywhere. Put all of that into centralized databases and do predictive analysis. Once it had enough data fed into it, the database would tell you where you needed to be looking to find the next attack."

The name of the program was Total Information Awareness (TIA), created under the auspices of the Information Awareness Office, established by DARPA a few months after 9/11. It was the largest mass surveillance program in the free world, collecting the personal information of everyone in the United States, including emails, phone calls, social networks, financial and medical records, and other information.

"It was similar to predictive policing, like something right out of *Minority Report*," says Siegel. But TIA wasn't just about predicting the future, it was also about shaping it. Mass surveillance, like censorship, is an instrument of social engineering. Knowing that they're being watched, or that some of their ideas are subject to official disapproval, people adjust their behavior to avoid public shame and other punishment.

"The TIA program only survived about six months because word of it got leaked," says Siegel. "But after it was shut down officially, it was moved to other agencies like NSA, where it was rebranded."

And the Pentagon also used components of it in Afghanistan, where Siegel saw first-hand how it affected military strategy and dictated Washington's decision to try to re-engineer Afghan society.

"With Afghanistan there was an uncertainty about the terms of victory from the very beginning," says Siegel. "And I believe that America's defeat in Afghanistan was a product of our investment in these informational systems. It came at the expense of, or instead of, clearly defined criteria for victory, such as the toppling of the adversarial government, for instance."

It wasn't enough to destroy al Qaeda in Afghanistan, bring down the Taliban, and declare victory. Instead, the U.S. adopted nation-building as a strategy to eliminate terror. The freedom agenda for the Middle East presupposed that terrorism was the inevitable result of authoritarian governments crushing the political voices of their people. Implant democracy, and there would be no more rationale for terror.

The George W. Bush administration adopted the freedom agenda not because of mission creep—where the objectives expand beyond their initial scope. Rather, the American regime reverted to form—as in Vietnam, the social engineering component became decisive.

And so during the GWOT, the whole-of-society effort to re-shape nations truly took root. "You start with the military and the intelligence agencies and the State Department," says Siegel.

Soldiers, spies, and diplomats constitute the political cadre's chief instruments in the conduct of war, but given the ambitions of U.S. leadership, more cadres were needed. "When you start to generate these large civil affairs projects," says Siegel, "you're bringing in people from the Justice Department, because they are going to train the Afghan judges. And you're also bringing in NGOs through the State Department who are going to educate Afghan women and create a new parallel school system for Afghan girls."

Victory, according to the terms dictated by U.S. policymakers, depended on fundamentally remaking Afghan society. America, however, could no more remake Afghan society than it could shape the Vietnamese. "Nor could we make the Afghans want us there," says Siegel. "The acquisition of data and the manipulation of data allowed U.S. leadership to pretend that it had things under control. And if you can create a realistic enough digital model of the war, then winning is no longer a brute force exercise with one side imposing its will on the other. Now it becomes an informational problem that can be solved by the application of the right algorithms and the acquisition of the sufficient volume of data."

So how does this data-driven approach affect the prospects of actually winning a war?

"The reality of the war was too demanding for our leadership to manage, so they find these systems that promise to manage it and rein in the chaos, to organize the information that would otherwise overwhelm them," says Siegel. "And once the war becomes a matter of adjusting metrics and of repositioning avatars on the screen, it can go on indefinitely. Because you have lost track of what victory is, you're disinclined to risk enough to put yourself in a position that would force the end of the war. So the stakes are lowered and you're not facing the prospect of the kind of defeat that might make you reevaluate what you're doing there in the first place."

The U.S. loss in the Global War on Terror, the trillions spent while Beltway contractors got rich and Washington became the emerald city on the Potomac, and—most despicable of all—the cheapening of American life, helped give rise to a protest movement inside the United States that the U.S. regime could only understand as an insurgency. And it is true that veterans of the GWOT, their families, and their communities were the core component of the American First movement.

But it wasn't veterans who brought the war home. It was U.S. political and corporate elites who collected mass data on Americans to change how they live and the character of the republic.

The U.S. government put the electorate who had chosen them under surveillance, censored them, and propagandized them. It even deployed the same counter-terrorism instruments it used against foreign threats, like the FISA warrant targeting Trump's campaign. It fiddled with institutions and interfered with elections to get the outcomes it wanted and to re-engineer American society.

As in Vietnam and Afghanistan, U.S. leadership never asked what it had done to turn the locals—in this case, Americans—against it. The difference was this: in foreign theaters they reasoned that giving the population a political voice would quell the insurgency; but when it came to Americans, they focused instead on stripping them of their rights, dehumanizing them, and ultimately destroying them.

REVENGE OF THE GATEKEEPERS

The fight over censorship, surveillance, and propaganda is about what takes place online because the internet is the underlying infrastructure for mass media, both print and broadcast, as well as private communications like emails, texts, and phone calls. The internet is not just a surveillance device, it is also a colossal historical archive. "It's our library of Alexandria," says online freedom activist Mike Benz.

"When you censor the internet, you are censoring the physical world," says Benz. "If you've got a radio show, it will play on your frequency. But you'll also stream on the internet. And oftentimes, those audiences are multiples larger than what first hears it live. Whatever cable TV show you watch, you can watch it live, but for replay you'll go to the internet." It's the same for newspapers, magazines, and even books to a certain extent. "The distinction between what is cyber and what is physical is effectively dissolved," says Benz. "And we've passed the point of no return."

By the mid-2000s, smart phones and social media moved everything to cyberspace, and the great migration was accompanied by a heady optimism that the world was entering a new phase of global freedom. "Facebook, YouTube, and Twitter were all created in the mid-2000s," says Benz, "and the iPhone comes online in 2007. The internet was supposed to democratize information because it bypassed traditional gatekeepers of information. A random shit-poster could have more influence on the internet than the *New York Times*. The promise was that the internet would be a force for democracy. And for decades the U.S. has argued that a country without a free and open internet is effectively perpetrating a human rights violation."

Freedom and democracy were useful slogans, but the inherent power of the technology is what appealed to U.S. government leaders. For the first time in history, public media and private communications were wrapped up in the same package where they could be monitored and controlled as well as amplified or stifled, depending on the mission. If an anonymous social media account could project as much power as the world's most prestigious media organization, then the internet was the nuclear bomb of propaganda. You could shape the destiny of nations if you controlled the internet, and the U.S. had the inside track because the Pentagon invented it.

What a free and open internet meant for adversarial regimes, like Russia or Iran or North Korea, was exposure to the Americans' destabilizing measures. "The intelligence agencies used social media to create insurgencies abroad," says Benz. "They mobilized revolutions digitally, creating hashtags, paying YouTube influencers, setting up Facebook groups. With the internet you have an instant regime change tool."

The 2010–2011 "Arab Spring" revolutions in the Middle East, and the "color" revolutions in Russia's backyard culminating with the 2014 Ukrainian coup, were driven by local social media activists trained by American institutions, chiefly the State Department and the National Endowment for Democracy.

In the context of coups, says Benz, "free speech is an insurgent activity to destabilize target regimes and topple them. And internet censorship is an instrument of counterinsurgency to stabilize the regime."

In 2016, the revolution came home. "Due to the outcome of democratic processes," says Benz, "namely the UK's Brexit referendum resolving to leave the European Union and the election of Donald Trump, various institutions decided that there was a little bit too much democracy happening."

Since Trump's victory owed in part to his innovative social media campaign, the Shadow Network adopted counterinsurgency measures. Obama warned Zuckerberg he should have shut Trump down.

"To save democracy," says Benz, "they needed to curtail the capacity to use the internet for democratic participation. And there was effectively a whole-of-society push to apply censorship to the internet to change the way we interact with the information ecosystem. What we're living in right now is essentially the revenge of the gatekeepers."

"AN ONGOING ATTACK BY THE RUSSIAN GOVERNMENT"

Nunes was fighting the gatekeepers, who were recasting #ReleaseTheMemo as a Russian influence operation in order to throttle the movement.

"The national security state thinks of information economies as something like a sound system," says Benz. "They want to turn the volume up on their speaker and turn down the speech of opposition voices."

First, there was federal law enforcement. To prosecute the anti-Trump campaign, they weaponized the classification system, and that too was a form of information warfare. Naturally, America has secrets it rightly conceals from adversaries. But federal officials also use the classification system as an instrument to target bureaucratic rivals and prevent the public from holding them accountable for their failures and crimes.

The FBI team investigating the Trump circle had used the classification system to hide its unlawful surveillance of a presidential campaign. They categorized their operation as a classified counter-intelligence investigation, code-named "Crossfire Hurricane," and classified the documents they had forged to obtain a warrant to spy on the campaign in a secret court whose procedures are classified.

Former DOJ prosecutor Kash Patel knew how to find what they had hidden. Nunes tasked him to lead the Russiagate investigation. "I hired him to bust down doors," says Nunes. It was Patel who gave the committee's investigation its name—"Objective Medusa."

Patel would eventually serve in several high-level positions in the Trump administration, including chief of staff to acting Defense Secretary Christopher Miller. During his time at the DOJ, Patel had worked with many of the same people he investigated as part of Nunes' team, including Comey and McCabe. "I told Devin that we will find that the people running the Russia investigation will have done inappropriate things," Patel tells me. "That was my experience having worked with them and seeing it."

Nunes saw it, too. "We kept finding things that shouldn't have been classified but were," says Nunes. "The FBI was just hiding what they'd done."

Nunes and his team were eager to get the evidence to the American public, and the memo was nearly finished by Thanksgiving. Accordingly, the volume was turned up to drown out their message.

Patel had shown a draft of the memo to Director Christopher Wray and other senior FBI officials. "We asked them," Patel says, "'based on the information you've given us, is this correct?'" They said it was, but FBI and DOJ officials simply redoubled their efforts to discredit the memo through media leaks targeting Patel—in the *New York Times*, the *Washington Post*, and the *Daily Beast* among others—as well as Nunes.

"The FBI is essentially labeling this a partisan document that uses lies to undermine law enforcement," reported the *Washington Post*.

According to *Vox*, "The question is not whether there was a plot against Trump at the FBI, as the Nunes memo reportedly alleges. There is no evidence for such a claim, and it doesn't pass the smell test. The real question is this: Will the FBI and Justice Department remain semi-independent agencies that check the president's authority—or will they be brought under President Donald Trump's direct control?"

Lawfare, a DOJ fan site published by the Brookings Institution, claimed that Nunes "is committed to releasing to the public a document that the FBI says has grave concerns, contains sufficient omissions of fact as to be effectively a lie, and that the Justice Department describes the release of as an extraordinarily reckless act."

"None of the media had read it," says Nunes aide Jack Langer. "It was still classified at the time. But they reported as fact what the intelligence agencies told them to say: 'It's going to destroy national security.' 'It's full of lies.' 'Nunes cherry-picked facts,' etc."

The Justice Department knew that the memo was bad news for them, says Nunes, "because they were trying to cover it up and they were trying to stop this from getting out publicly. They said it's going to do irreparable damage to national security. It's going to jeopardize our relations with allies. Comey and Clapper and Brennan were out selling the same message. But in reality, if people learned that DOJ and FBI leaders used the Steele dossier to justify spying on Americans, the only damage would be to these agencies' own reputations."

In January 2018, after Patel told the Justice Department that he wanted records of the Crossfire Hurricane investigation, Deputy Attorney General Rod Rosenstein threatened Patel that he would subpoena his communications. Rosenstein later denied to Congress, under oath, that he had made this threat.[3] But as Patel discovered five years later when Google alerted him that it had turned over his personal email and phone data in response to a DOJ subpoena, Wray and Rosenstein had already issued the subpoenas months before Rosenstein's threat.

"The FBI and DOJ spied on a presidential campaign," Nunes says, "and when Congress began investigating and exposing what they were doing, they spied on us to find out what we knew and how we knew it."

Nunes was under surveillance, too. His phone was hacked, and his family was dragged into the regime's dark world of surveillance and violence. "They used technology to mimic my phone number so that family members thought I was calling them," Nunes says. "And then they made it sound like I was kidnapped and that I'd better back off or something bad's going to happen to me and to them. There was a political structure built to bring tremendous pressure on me and my family to stop me from investigating. It was clearly being run by professionals. They didn't want any of what we'd found to come out. And they did everything they could to stop it."

As the grassroots support for releasing the memo intensified, the counterinsurgents moved to bar the door. On January 23, Congressman Adam Schiff and Senator Dianne Feinstein wrote to Twitter and Facebook demanding they investigate the #ReleaseTheMemo hashtag.[4]

"It's the ultimate absurdity that the House Intelligence Committee's ranking member and a former chairwoman of Senate intelligence demanded the investigation of a hashtag," says Langer.

According to the Schiff-Feinstein letter, #ReleaseTheMemo was part of a Russian bot operation to manipulate public opinion, influence congressional action, and undermine the special counsel investigation. "We are witnessing an ongoing attack by the Russian government through Kremlin-linked social media actors directly acting to intervene and influence our democratic process," they wrote. "This should be disconcerting to all Americans, but especially your companies as, once again, it appears the vast majority of their efforts are concentrated on your platforms."

Furthermore, Schiff and Feinstein claimed the hashtag had gained "the immediate attention and assistance" of Russian accounts. The Democrats' letter claimed #ReleaseTheMemo was "'the top trending hashtag among Twitter accounts believed to be operated by Kremlin-linked groups,'" and was being used "'100 times more than any other hashtag' by accounts linked to Russian influence campaigns."[5]

Nunes says none of this surprised him. "Everything and everyone, including me, who questioned the hoax back then was denounced as a Putin stooge."

Schiff and Feinstein's claims were sourced to a website called Hamilton 68 run by the German Marshall Fund, a Washington, D.C . think-tank.

"Hamilton 68 had been around for about 5 or 6 months at that point," says Nunes. "I'd seen some of their work. They'd denounce some online discussion as a Russian influence operation, and the media would unquestionably report their accusations as unassailable fact. They were useful to those who were spreading this paranoia that unseen, nefarious Russians were everywhere and were behind everything."

The information flow repeated the pattern established by the Steele dossier: it originated with a class of experts and moved through the press to the political echelon. The machine spit out the same answer every time: Russia.

WHY RUSSIA?

Russiagate was designed to smear Trump as a Russian agent but, say Siegel and Benz, it was also a lingering after-effect of the national security establishment's resentment at having suffered a loss to Russia. Military and intelligence professionals believed that Moscow had outfoxed them in an information war just a few years before and were hence inclined to see Russian hands everywhere they looked.

"By the late 2000s, information warfare had become the new end-all-be-all of military operations," says Siegel "And the concerns about Russian information warfare were very influential within the Pentagon and NATO in these years. It cemented in the minds of the defense establishment that control of the internet is the determinative factor in warfare."

NATO and the Pentagon, says Benz, "came to believe that war is about control over social media. For them tweets are as important as weapons. NATO secretary general Jen Stoltenberg actually said as much when he told an audience that 'NATO must remain prepared for both conventional and hybrid threats: From tanks to tweets.'"[6]

The Obama administration tested that thesis when it backed the 2013-14 coup in Ukraine that toppled a government friendly to Russia and installed what was effectively a puppet regime. The Russians responded by invading Crimea, which then voted to join the Russian Federation.

"When the people of Crimea voted to side with Russia," says Benz, "the U.S. and NATO saw it as a major foreign policy disaster. And they believed they'd lost because the Russians had manipulated the hearts and minds of the Ukrainians by inundating them with propaganda. The Russians had gotten around the traditional Western gatekeepers of information narratives and beat them in an information war."

Siegel says that "the annexation of Crimea convinced the U.S. and NATO defense establishment that control over the internet was now the crux of warfare. They were legitimately alarmed by Russia's success at media operations. But the crucial point is that they used the Russian success with media operations to excuse their inability to contain Russia geopolitically. They are delusionally invested in information warfare as a way to avoid responsibility."

That is, if hybrid warfare is a combination of information warfare and real shooting, the Americans had emphasized the tweets so much they'd forgotten about the tanks.

"If Putin had feared an American or NATO response for invading Crimea, he wouldn't have invaded Crimea," says Siegel. "You could have a thousand information operations leading up to the invasion of Crimea, but you're not going to invade Crimea if you fear sufficiently punitive retaliation in response to it. An information operation is not a deterrence like threatening to bomb someone's tanks off the field of battle."

The U.S. hadn't lost an information war—Russia won a real war because the Americans had simply continued along the same path it first walked in Vietnam, then the GWOT. Because U.S. leadership could not muster the resolve to win wars, it squandered American prestige even as it tried to remake other nations in its own image.

Plus, Obama added a layer of crippling self-consciousness to the American regime's collective neurosis. He wouldn't dare push back on Russia with anything but information warfare for fear of forfeiting his chief foreign policy goal—a nuclear agreement with Russia's ally, Iran. So he failed to deter Russia not only in Crimea but the Middle East too, where Russian forces were supporting Iran's ally Syria in the Syrian regime's war against its own people.

There was something else that happened with the Crimea referendum. It confirmed to the Americans that nationalist movements were driven by foreign subversion. Why else would Crimeans decide for Russia and against all that Washington had to offer?

It's true, as Siegel explains, "that some of the populist voices popping up in Eastern Europe were ideologically aligned with Russia," says Siegel. "And in response, counter-disinformation efforts targeting Russian messaging started cropping up in the Czech Republic and Poland."

Thus, when anti-globalist movements started to grow in Europe and the U.S., the national security establishment applied the same explanatory model—that the movements must also be somehow connected to Russia—and showed their lack of self-awareness. The Brexit and America First movements reflected popular demands for governments responsive to the national longings of their citizens. But because technocratic elites can find no fault in themselves, they could hardly fathom why they were rejected by a citizenry they held in contempt—unless, of course the Russians were behind it.

Many of the analysts obsessed with Russian information warfare played crucial roles in Russiagate, like Hamilton 68 founder Clint Watts. "I was talking to him at the time and quoting him in stuff I was writing because I thought what he said made sense," says Siegel. "And some of what he said didn't make sense. People lose track of reality when they talk about information warfare."

A West Point graduate, Watts joined the FBI after leaving the Army, and in 2011 he joined a think-tank based in Philadelphia, the Foreign Policy Research Institute. During the 2016 election cycle, he was a go-to talking head on Russian information warfare. "Regardless of the extent of Trump's direct knowledge about Russia's intelligence activities, active measures [by Russian intelligence] have achieved enormous success on the back of his presidential campaign," he wrote in a 2016 article that supported the collusion narrative. "Russia sees Trump as a tool to undermine its American adversaries. In that regard, they've already achieved their goal and possess the potential to exceed their expectations."[7]

The name of Watts' organization, Hamilton 68, refers to the 68th essay from *The Federalist Papers*, in which Alexander Hamilton discusses the presidency and foreign influence: "These most deadly adversaries of republican government might naturally have been expected to make their approaches from more than one quarter, but chiefly from the desire in foreign powers to gain an improper ascendant in our councils. How could they better gratify this, than by raising a creature of their own to the chief magistracy of the Union?"[8]

The reference was clear: Trump had been raised by a foreign power. Thus, the purpose of Watts' organization was not to track Russian "disinformation" and influence operations on social media, but was rather to add another branch to the counterinsurgents' propaganda campaign vilifying the chief magistracy of the Union—Trump—as a Russian agent.

Watts was supported by the Alliance for Securing Democracy (ASD), a project of the German Marshall Fund, a Washington, D.C.-based think-tank funded by private donors; government agencies like the U.S. Agency for International Development; foreign governments like Norway, Sweden, and Belgium; Big Tech oligarchies Google, Microsoft, and Amazon; and major Democratic Party donor George Soros, a Shadow Network giant.

ASD was founded in 2017 by a left-right coalition of anti-Trump activists who had supported and promoted Russiagate. Its board of advisors included:

- John Podesta, chairman of Hillary Clinton's presidential campaign
- Jake Sullivan, a longtime Clinton aide and now Biden's national security advisor
- Michael McFaul, Obama's ambassador to Russia
- David Kramer, aide to Senator John McCain. Kramer gave a copy of the Steele dossier to *BuzzFeed*, which published it in January 2017.
- Bill Kristol, anti-Trump editor of the now-defunct magazine, the *Weekly Standard*
- Michael Morrell, former acting CIA director and longtime deputy director under President Obama

Morrell explained the ASD's purpose as it was getting off the ground in July 2017. "In a perfect world, we would have a national commission that would be looking into exactly what happened, exactly what did the Russians do and what can we do as a nation to defend ourselves going forward and deter Putin from ever doing this again," Morell told a journalist. "We all know this is not going to happen, so things like the GMF [German Marshall Fund] effort are hugely important to fill the gap."[9]

In reality, ASD and Hamilton 68 were partners in the FBI's ongoing anti-Trump operation, which had been offboarded to Robert Mueller's team when the special counsel investigation began in May 2017.

When the #ReleaseTheMemo hashtag appeared, Hamilton 68 reported that it was being spread by Russian bots.[10] Schiff and Feinstein's letter on the hashtag relied exclusively on Hamilton 68's data.

Even as the corporate media dutifully reported Hamilton 68's declarations as fact, however, the Big Tech platforms were becoming increasingly wary of Watts' analyses.

The *Daily Beast* offered a glimpse of this skepticism with a January 23, 2018 story reporting that Twitter analysts had determined the

#ReleasetheMemo hashtag was spread by legitimate American accounts, not by Russian bots.[11]

Behind the scenes, Twitter officials were coming to believe that Hamilton 68 was a fraud. Twitter's trust and safety head Yoel Roth told colleagues that a secret list of around 600 Russian bot accounts that Hamilton 68 monitored was "weird and self-selecting. They're so unwilling to be transparent and defend their selection that I think we need to just call this out on the bullshit it is."[12]

Twitter identified the 600 accounts tracked by Hamilton 68 and found they were neither Russian nor bots. Rather, Roth wrote to colleagues, "they appear to strongly preference pro-Trump accounts, which [Hamilton 68] use to assert that Russia is expressing a preference for Trump." Roth wanted to confront Hamilton 68 publicly. "My recommendation at this stage is an ultimatum," he wrote, "you release the list or we do."

Some Twitter employees were worried about taking on an organization that represented a powerful consortium of political and intelligence officials. Others represented those same interests inside the company. "We have to be careful in how much we push back on ASD publicly," wrote Emily Horne, who later landed a job in the Biden White House. Another Twitter executive, Carlos Monje, wrote, "I also have been very frustrated in not calling out Hamilton 68 more publicly, but understand we have to play a longer game here." Monje later became a senior advisor to Biden's Transportation Secretary Pete Buttigieg.

Twitter lawyers drafted a careful response to Schiff and Feinstein explaining that the company's initial inquiry regarding #ReleaseTheMemo had "not identified any significant activity connected to Russia." Twitter wrote that "because the Hamilton Dashboard's account list is not available to the public, we are unable to offer any specific context on the accounts it includes. …We have offered to review the list of accounts contained in the Dashboard and this offer remains open."[13]

Facebook responded simply by noting that Hamilton 68's allegations concerned content on Twitter, not Facebook.[14]

Those responses were not good enough for the California Democrats. On January 31, Schiff and Feinstein sent another letter demanding that Twitter and Facebook try harder. "It is unclear from your responses whether you believe any of the Russian-linked accounts involved in this influence campaign violated your respective user policies," the duo warned. "We reiterate our request that you immediately take necessary steps to expose and deactivate such accounts if you determine that they violate your respective user policies." The letter continued, "Twitter inexplicably…neglected to answer the question of whether Russian sources were actively engaged in promoting the #ReleaseTheMemo hashtag, as illuminated by the Hamilton 68 dashboard of the German Marshall Fund."[15]

In other words, *You must find a way to tie pro-Trump accounts to Russian bots and then censor them—or else.*

"In the end, Schiff, Feinstein, and the Dems just beat Twitter down," says Langer, the Nunes aide. "They were threatening to take all kinds of retaliatory action if the platforms didn't produce the right results. And eventually, Twitter found a way to connect #ReleaseThe Memo to Russian bots, even though there was no evidence for it and they knew Hamilton 68's findings were fraudulent."

The following January, Twitter released a report detailing its research into a new batch of 418 accounts that "appeared to originate in Russia." The company admitted it could not determine if they actually were Russian bot accounts, but claimed they behaved *similarly* to Russian bots. Of the top three hashtags employed by these 400 accounts, number two was #ReleaseTheMemo, which was included in approximately 38,000 Tweets.[16] Thus, based on a few hundred accounts that may or may not have been Russian, Twitter insinuated that a grassroots campaign among American conservatives might really be a Russian influence operation.

"These possible Russian bot accounts comprised less than one-half of one percent of activity on the hashtag," says Langer. "That's a drop in the ocean. It's statistically irrelevant. But Twitter left that out of the report."

The release of the Nunes memo on February 2, 2018, exposed Russiagate as an instrument of information warfare, paid for by the Clinton campaign and directed by Obama's spy chiefs. It was the Shadow Network's counterinsurgency campaign targeting Trump, his allies, and supporters.

"What we're now experiencing is what countless other countries around the world have experienced since the start of the Cold War," says Benz. "When the U.S. government controls your information ecosystems, controls your political leadership, censors you, spies on you, and propagandizes you. People in Boston are now experiencing what people in Baghdad did. This is what it feels like when the U.S. government deploys its military, its intelligence, and civil society partners and media in a whole-of-society campaign to re-engineer your country."

4

COERCED AND CAJOLED: BIG TECH JOINS THE FRAY

Christopher Wray's first major initiative as FBI director was to formalize the law enforcement agency's election interference protocol that Nunes and his team had uncovered.

Former Director James Comey's coup-squad had hidden the anti-Trump plot by making its investigation of the Trump campaign, code-named Crossfire Hurricane, a classified, counterintelligence investigation, which made it easier to conceal it from congressional oversight by Nunes' committee. Meanwhile, running Crossfire Hurricane out of Washington, D.C. headquarters helped to hide the operation from the FBI rank-and-file who might have opposed weaponizing the Bureau against a Republican candidate.

After all, in summer 2016, Obama's spy chiefs couldn't be certain how the public or its elected representatives would respond to the feds' interference in a political campaign. It turned out that many people, prompted by the media, supported unconstitutional means to undermine a presidential election. So, when Christopher Wray took over the FBI, he made the Russiagate infrastructure public.

Soon after being named director in August 2017, Wray told Congress that he had set up the Foreign Interference Task Force (FITF) "to identify and counteract malign foreign influence operations" through "strategic engagement with U.S. technology companies." He was referring to Big Tech giants like Amazon, Google, and Uber, and social media platforms like Facebook and Twitter.[1]

"Technology companies have a front-line responsibility to secure their own networks, products, and platforms," said Wray. "But we're doing our part by providing actionable intelligence to better enable them to address abuse of their platforms by foreign actors."[2]

It was a two-way street. While the FBI was feeding social media platforms fraudulent information to suppress political speech and violate Americans' civil rights, companies like Facebook and Twitter were also sending the FBI tips based on their surveillance of users' private messages and other communications. As we'll see, the FBI had informants at the Big Tech companies supporting the work of former FBI agents and other national security personnel who had landed jobs at social media companies.

Thanks to Trump's successful use of social media, online discourse became the focus of the FBI's new initiative. Wray made that clear through the coded language spy agencies used to reference the 45th U.S. President. The problem was Russia, said Wray—by which he meant Trump.

"Russia attempted to interfere with the last election," said Wray, and "it continues to engage in malign influence operations to this day."[3] Because they saw Trump's 2016 breakthrough victory as the product of "Russian interference," the FITF's focus on "Russian operations" was simply an extension of the ongoing campaign to stop Trump. During the 2020 election cycle, the unit grew to at least 80 agents.[4]

In 2020, the FBI provided the same service it had four years previously, because the Democratic Party's presidential candidate had the same problem. Back in 2016, Hillary Clinton's use of a private email server had made her communications vulnerable to foreign intelligence agencies. Accordingly, one of her campaign's top concerns was that a leak of her correspondence—for instance, with foreign donors to the Clinton Foundation—would hand her opponent an October surprise and endanger her candidacy.

With the next election cycle, Joe Biden's candidacy was also exposed after his son Hunter left his damaged laptop at a computer repair store in Delaware in April 2019. The laptop contained a family album of the Bidens' corruption, with emails, texts, images, and other evidence of their arrangements with foreign officials and enterprises. The job of the FBI's new social media unit was to ensure it did not see the light of day—by blaming the Russians and tying the opposition party to Moscow.

And so, censorship was pushed to the top of the Shadow Network's bag of dirty tricks.

OBAMA AND BIG TECH MERGE

By the time Obama left the White House, he and Silicon Valley had virtually merged. Dozens of aides throughout his administration rotated back and forth between the White House and tech firms like AirBnB, Amazon, Apple, Facebook, Google, Twitter, and Uber, among others. For some Obama staffers, Silicon Valley felt like home. Here, said deputy CIA chief of staff Nick Shapiro, "I was surrounded by many of the same people I was surrounded by in the White House itself." He added, "There's a feeling of familiarity knowing you have a strong support network. Probably if I needed something at another company, one of my first calls would be to another Obama alumni."[5]

Obama wanted to absorb Big Tech, and he wanted his people to fill Big Tech companies. He had to own it or someone else would. In 2014, he relocated the U.S. chief technology officer, a position Obama created, to Silicon Valley, changed his job title, and tasked him with "recruiting more top tech talent" for the administration.[6]

The symbiosis with tech had begun during Obama's first run for president. His 2008 campaign, said one Obama adviser, resembled a startup, and that's why "there's a lot of cultural affinity between Obamaland and Silicon Valley."[7] What made Big Tech love Obama, a Silicon Valley entrepreneur and Democrat donor told the press, was Obama "betting the whole campaign on the principle that disruptive tech can take down an unbeatable giant." He added, "The campaign and the president believed you could beat the system using technology."[8]

Former Google executive Andrew McLaughlin wrote Obama's tech policy agenda and later joined the administration. Tech money also played a big role, with top executives like Facebook's one-time chief operating officer Sheryl Sandberg and Yahoo's chief executive Marissa Mayer hosting fundraisers for the Obama campaign.

Facebook co-founder Chris Hughes was the candidate's "online organizing guru" and managed the My.BarackObama.com site, which campaign staff referred to as MyBo. "One of my fundamental beliefs from my days as a community organizer is that real change comes from the bottom up," Obama told the media. "And there's no more powerful tool for grass-roots organizing than the Internet."[9]

Zuckerberg's company had been a central piece of Obama's new media strategy that helped him raise millions of donations in small donations and mobilize supporters for the primaries.[10] Credited with "revolutionizing" the use of the Web as a political tool, it's not hard to see why Obama was enraged when Facebook helped Trump's 2016 campaign: the Republican outsider had not only thwarted his political program and broken the chain of post-Obama succession, but he had also stolen his thunder. With 2016, Trump had become the innovator.

For Obama's 2012 re-election campaign, it was his relationship with Google that defined his mind-meld with Big Tech. According to a report from Campaign for Accountability, Google lobbyists made more than 427 trips to the White House, and 363 of those were by

Google employees themselves. At least 169 Google executives attended meetings with 182 different White House officials. Google executives met with Obama himself more than twenty times, but Todd Park, Obama's U.S. Chief Technology Officer, accounted for the most meetings with Google executives. Google lobbyist Johanna Shelton made 128 trips to the Obama White House, nearly double that of the next most frequent visitor.[11]

Google CEO Eric Schmidt, another Shadow Network figure, was a frequent visitor to the White House, and was named to several administration advisory boards, including one at the Pentagon. He said the only way to manage the challenges of the tech age is with "much greater transparency and no anonymity." According to Schmidt, "True anonymity is too dangerous."[12] These were catchwords, clichés—Schmidt did not believe them or that they applied to people like him. In fact, he asked Google colleagues to remove information from the search engine showing that he had donated to Obama's campaign.[13]

He resigned as Google CEO in 2011 to become executive chairman, which gave him more leeway to assist Obama's re-election efforts. Schmidt, according to reports, "was intimately involved in building Obama's voter-targeting operation in 2012, recruiting digital talent, choosing technology and coaching campaign manager Jim Messina on campaign infrastructure. The system was credited with helping Obama achieve his unexpectedly large margin of victory."[14]

Google had paid little attention to D.C. politics until Obama came to office. Schmidt seized the opportunity, and the company became an aggressive insider throwing its weight around Washington.[15] During the course of Obama's administration, nearly 250 people moved from government service to Google or vice versa.[16]

The tech-government merger was something new, an Obama phenomenon. "In the first decade of the Global War on Terror, there was friction between Silicon Valley and the defense complex," says Jacob Siegel, the former Army intelligence officer. "The tech companies only reluctantly gave up their back ends, but that disappeared with the election of Obama."

Embarrassed by the Edward Snowden disclosures, tech executives feigned surprise that the NSA was using their platforms to spy on Americans. But they knew Director of National Intelligence James Clapper was lying when he said just months before the Snowden leak that the NSA was not spying on Americans. How could they not know when Obama aides were bouncing back and forth between jobs in the White House, Pentagon, NSA, CIA, and Silicon Valley? It was a team effort.

The President gave Big Tech cover with a December 2013 White House meeting where top executives were given the chance to put their concerns about internet privacy in the public record. Schmidt and Sandberg were there, as was Yahoo's Mayer, along with Tim Cook from Apple and Twitter CEO Dick Costolo, all Obama donors. Netflix co-founder and CEO Reed Hastings attended, too. He later filled Obama's coffers with a multimillion-dollar production deal.[17] It was a Shadow Network Christmas Party.

"The president made clear his belief in an open, free and innovative Internet," the White House said in a statement after the meeting, "and listened to the group's concerns and recommendations, and made clear that we will consider their input as well as the input of other outside stakeholders as we finalize our review of signals intelligence programs."[18]

Obama needed Big Tech—it was his shortcut around the Fourth Amendment. Unlike the government, tech giants did not need probable cause to search private communications. "Facebook's internal purpose," Snowden later told the press, "is to compile perfect records of private lives to the maximum extent of their capability, and then exploit that for their own corporate enrichment. And damn the consequences." This, he said, "is actually precisely the same as what the NSA does."[19]

The Snowden revelations pushed Big Tech closer to Obama. The big platforms were wounded, and their reputation as free-speech libertarians was exposed as a fraud. Obama broke their will and made them see who they truly were—company men with their eye on the bottom line. The leaks made public who was really in charge, the disruptor-in-chief. If they made trouble, he could crush them.

Their Achilles heel is the exemption that Obama could reverse any time he liked. Section 230 of the 1996 Communications Decency Act stipulates that "no provider or user of an interactive computer service shall be treated as the publisher or speaker of any information provided by another information content provider."[20]

That is, because social media platforms are defined as "interactive computer services" and not information content providers, companies like Twitter, Facebook, YouTube, etc. cannot be held legally responsible for the information published on their platforms. Revising Section 230 to hold them accountable for their content, as publishers are, would destroy their financial model. The millions spent on lawyers lobbying against regulation would become billions spent on lawyers fighting lawsuits.

Obama held their fate in his palm. And he needed them, too. It was a true marriage.

MR. FISA

Big Tech's financial model and social prestige required it to proclaim its independence from government and its commitment to protecting user privacy, even if the Snowden leaks revealed that the online town square was flooded with spies on a digital stake-out. Big Tech's non-partisan libertarianism was strictly performative.

For instance, in 2014 Twitter said it wanted to release a public report with the precise numbers of FISA warrants and national security letters the government had served the company to collect users' electronic communications. After FBI general counsel James Baker prevented Twitter from releasing the full report, the company took the government to court.

But, says former FBI agent Stephen Friend, "at that point the toothpaste was already out of the tube." Either there were no requests from the government and Twitter was just posturing or, says Friend, "the government's requests came in, and Twitter handed over the information. They could have taken a stand against the government to begin with."

To handle the lawsuit, Twitter hired Perkins Coie, a prominent Democrat-aligned law firm that had represented Obama's presidential campaign. The firm's lead attorney was former Justice Department cybersecurity expert Michael Sussmann. He had worked with Baker at DOJ, and they were friends.

Baker affirmed in a September 2014 letter to his former colleague that Twitter could disclose the number of warrants in broad, inexact ranges but not the exact number. Specific numbers, according to Baker, would reveal "properly classified information."[21] The feds were arguing that publication of even the most basic data about its surveillance programs would damage national security, an argument the courts ultimately upheld in a ruling against Twitter.

Baker had joined the Justice Department in 1990 and rose through the ranks. He won awards from the CIA, the NSA, and the DOJ for his work in counterterrorism and counterintelligence. He was an expert in FISA—"Mr. FISA," his colleagues called him. During a stint as Verizon's assistant general counsel for national security, he facilitated the government's access to material obtained through FISA and other surveillance programs.[22] He moved into the private sector again when Comey was made general counsel at Bridgewater Associates, a wealth management firm founded by investor Ray Dalio. Comey made Baker his deputy.

Dalio, a longtime apologist for the Chinese Community Party and with billions staked to the Beijing regime, runs Bridgewater like a Maoist outpost. He holds show trials to test employees' loyalties to his "principles." Comey and Baker oversaw the cadre of former FBI agents that staffed the security team. The duo fortified Dalio's mini-surveillance state, with employees snitching on each other and seemingly being monitored by cameras in real time.[23]

Baker had his boss' trust. When Comey was named FBI director in 2014, he made "Mr. FISA" the top lawyer at the Bureau.

FISA is the most intrusive surveillance program that U.S. intelligence services possess, but few had ever heard of it until the Trump era. It became part of the national lexicon in April 2017, when the *Washington Post* disclosed that the FBI had obtained a FISA warrant to spy on Trump campaign volunteer Carter Page.[24] Although the story was designed to put Page under public suspicion and further the Russia collusion narrative, it ultimately backfired when Devin Nunes unearthed the warrant application's falsehoods and deceptions, many of which were revealed via the Nunes memo.

"Baker authored the Page FISA and signed off on all of it," says Kash Patel, Nunes' lead investigator. "When I was at DOJ, Baker had a reputation of being a FISA guru. The Page FISA was crafted by someone who knew what questions not to ask, and how to use language to get it past a FISA court judge without fully disclosing facts they knew would have disqualified the warrant."

"Baker made a habit of exploiting his powerful position for political purposes," says Nunes. "He's a sneaky operator and a political partisan—he never should've been anywhere near the FBI, much less its top lawyer."

In effect, Baker laundered the Steele dossier. The Clinton campaign's law firm Perkins Coie paid the Washington communications firm Fusion GPS and its subcontractor, FBI informant Christopher Steele, to smear Trump. Mr. FISA's job was to turn Steele's dirt into a serviceable warrant to spy on the GOP candidate.

The dossier operation was the most prominent of three concurrent anti-Trump operations run by the FBI in coordination with Perkins Coie. There was also the DNC hack, for which Perkins

Coie hired former FBI official Shawn Henry's cybersecurity firm, CrowdStrike, to attribute the hack-and-leak to Russian military intelligence. Third was the Alfa Bank campaign, intended to build the narrative that Trump was getting paid by Russian officials through a clandestine cyber channel. And it was the Alfa Bank operation that reunited Baker and his former colleague, Perkins Coie lawyer Michael Sussmann.

Sussmann got help from a tech executive he represented, Rodney Joffe, a regular visitor to the White House who advised senior officials directly on cyber matters. Comey had awarded him in 2013 for helping the FBI solve a cyber case. Joffe held security clearances and, like Steele, was a long-time FBI informant.[25]

His firm Neustar was an intermediary between the intelligence agencies and the telecom industry, processing FISA requests and other subpoenas on behalf of smaller phone companies and internet service providers that cannot afford to keep their spy brokers on salary.[26] Joffe's work gave him access to large amounts of non-public internet and cybersecurity data, some of which had been supplied by the U.S. government.

By July 2016, he had assembled a team of researchers hunting for dirt on Trump to tie his campaign to Russia, and zeroed in on a Russian financial institution, Alfa Bank. Joffe gave the researchers, including two Georgia Tech academics, a crib sheet listing six Trump associates, with personal information including home addresses, personal email addresses, business names, business websites and email domains, suspected IP addresses for those domains, and information pertaining to the spouse of one of these associates.[27]

Joffe's private spy network exploited data provided to them by the government ostensibly for developing a program to defend the U.S. from cyberattacks. Instead, they used the information to fabricate a narrative that Trump organization computer servers were in contact with servers from Alfa Bank.

"Being able to provide evidence of *anything* that shows an attempt to behave badly in relation to this, the VIPs would be happy," Joffe wrote to his team. "They're looking for a true story that could be used as the basis for closer examination."[28]

That is, as with the Steele dossier, the job was to establish the pretext for an investigation of the Trump circle. Indeed, the dossier and Alfa Bank campaigns were designed to converge. Steele filed a report sourced to Sussmann alleging that Alfa Bank's ownership was close to Putin. Taken together, the two plot points suggested that Putin allies were paying Trump, through contacts between the two computer servers.

What Joffe's team invented, as even Joffe had to admit, was a "red herring." It would not pass muster with anyone who knew how to read the data that Joffe's team produced. Nonetheless, Sussmann worked with Joffe's group and Fusion GPS to write up reports for Sussmann to hand off to his friend James Baker and get the FBI to open an investigation.

As with the dossier, the FBI investigated the Alfa Bank reports and turned up nothing. In a classic case of the tail wagging the dog, false stories concocted by Clinton campaign contractors and clients justified national security investigations. And also like the dossier, the Alfa Bank narrative and leaks about the FBI's investigation of it fueled a media feeding frenzy that continued even after the narrative imploded.

It also seems increasingly clear that attributing the DNC hack to the Russian hacking group Fancy Bear was a fraud. CrowdStrike president Shawn Henry later admitted to Nunes' House Intelligence Committee that the firm did not find any actual evidence that Russians had stolen the DNC's emails.[29] Moreover, the government's analysis of the DNC hack relied, in part, on researchers belonging to the Joffe team that engineered the Alfa Bank hoax.[30]

The consequences of the DNC's Russia-hacking hoax are worth summarizing. On account of attributing the hack to Fancy Bear, Obama sanctioned Russian military officials and enterprises, while expelling dozens of Russian diplomats and shuttering two diplomatic facilities shortly before he left office.[31] The Russian hack-and-leak story was a pillar of John Brennan's CIA memo, the basis of Jeh Johnson's finding that designated elections as critical U.S. infrastructure, and one of the foundations of Robert Mueller's special counsel investigation—which also partly relied on research from Joffe's Alfa Bank hoaxers.[32] And political operatives left and right raised millions of dollars to fund outfits like Hamilton 68 based on the official U.S. government position that the Russians had hacked the DNC.

In sum, the 2016 election interference program, the subsequent delegitimization of Trump's presidency, and the justification for censoring Americans were based on the DNC's claim that it had been hacked by Russia. But there was no evidence to prove it was true. And the FBI's 2020 election interference campaign was based on the same fabrication.

REQUIEM FOR THE FIRST AMENDMENT

The censorship component of the Shadow Network campaign unofficially began with Obama scolding Zuckerberg right after the 2016 election. He had been betrayed by Big Tech oligarchs, the very people with whom he had mind-melded. Obama was hurt and angry.

Within a month Zuckerberg succumbed to a pressure campaign led by the Poynter Institute, a weaponized non-profit research organization funded by Shadow Network sources including George Soros' Open Society Foundations and Big Tech oligarch Pierre Omidyar, founder of PayPal.[33] With Poynter repeatedly pushing stories like "Facebook's fake news problem won't fix itself," the company signed on to Poynter's International Fact Checking initiative.[34] If Poynter's fact-checkers labeled a story as fake, it was marked "disputed" and ranked lower on users' news feeds—i.e., shadow-banned. Censorship was on its way to becoming an industry.

First came propaganda, via the media, then surveillance, thanks to Big Tech and the spy services. Now, however, the Shadow Network leaned heavily on censorship. "It takes a while to build capacity for mass-automated censorship," says Siegel, "but the rudiments of the censorship apparatus get put in place as soon as Trump starts to rise."

Obligingly, Shadow Network mouthpieces began making the case for speech suppression.

According to former *Time* magazine editor and Obama State Department official Richard Stengel, "the intellectual underpinning of the First Amendment was engineered for a simpler era."[35] Freedom of speech is an anachronism, according to the Obama propagandist. The First Amendment, he wrote, "rests on the notion that the truth will win out in what Supreme Court Justice William O. Douglas called 'the marketplace of ideas.'" But on the internet, wrote Stengel, "truth is not optimized. On the Web, it's not enough to battle falsehood with truth; the truth doesn't always win."

Of course, no one in their right mind could argue the First Amendment guarantees the ultimate triumph of truth, because its purpose is to break the state's monopoly on speech by giving everyone a chance to speak, even if they are wrong.

But the real point of Stengel's argument was that Trump and his supporters had to be silenced. In 2016, Stengel wrote, "Russian agents assumed fake identities, promulgated false narratives and spread lies on Twitter and Facebook, all protected by the First Amendment."

In other words, Stengel would have us believe that the greatest threat to America is the Constitution. What Stengel and his class of propagandists describe is a new covenant for the internet age, one in which national security professionals and their private-sector partners censor Americans to protect democracy, a political system anchored by free speech.

According to Siegel, the roots of the Big Tech's spy service connection go back to the Global War on Terror. "Rebranding the GWOT as a mission of de-radicalization normalized the spy-tech exec pipeline, as both could now see themselves as contributing to the same larger civic mission of public safety," says Siegel. "With Trump's election, this latent vehicle of state-tech collusion built under Obama went into overdrive."

At the same time Wray was standing up the Foreign Interference Task Force, former FBI agents and other government officials (including ones from the CIA, DHS, State Department, and Pentagon) began migrating to jobs at Big Tech firms and social media platforms, just like Obama's aides. In the rare cases when social media companies pushed back against the government, the agencies just went around the civilians and worked with their people on the inside.

"New units like the FITF formalized an architecture that already existed under Obama while vastly increasing its size and visibility under the pretext of a state of emergency," says Siegel. "But once you had the FITF that meant you also now had the need for a whole new cadre of former security officials working at the tech companies as 'liaisons.' Essentially, the bigger and more overt the security agencies' presence inside the social media platforms, the more support staff was required to service it, which ended up drawing from the same incestuous pool of public-private bureaucrats."

A researcher who uses the pseudonym "Name Redacted" scoured LinkedIn for past employment records and found that after 2018, Facebook brought on a legion of former intelligence employees, including twenty-six from the FBI, sixteen from the National Security Agency (NSA), twenty-nine from Department of Homeland Security, thirty-two from the State Department, forty-nine from the Pentagon, and fourteen from the CIA.[36]

In the same time period, Google, according to the researcher, onboarded more than 165 former spooks—twenty-seven from the CIA, fifty-two from the FBI, thirty from the NSA, fifty from the DHS, and six from the DNI. The company's Trust & Safety team, which is responsible for deciding what constitutes "disinformation," is managed by former CIA agents.[37]

As for Twitter, prior to the 2020 election, dozens of FBI officials joined the company.[38] They called themselves "Bu alumni" and created their own private Slack channel with a crib sheet to give new FBI arrivals a head start.[39] The company's own director of strategy was Comey's former deputy chief of staff, Dawn Burton, another Russiagate activist, who later moved to Google to become its Director of Staff Privacy and Safety.[40] Twitter also employed former CIA targeter Nada Bakos, who played an active role in the agency's leg of the Protect Biden campaign. But far and away the most significant former intelligence official who dropped into social media was James Baker, named Twitter's deputy general counsel in June 2020.

Previously, Baker had embarrassed Wray's FBI with damaging attention from Nunes' team and other GOP-led congressional probes. Even the Department of Justice was investigating him for leaking to the media.[41] Wray reassigned him out of the FBI's general counsel office, and in 2018 Baker left the FBI. He was rewarded for his anti-Trump service with a job as a CNN legal analyst, where he demanded Trump apologize to him and the Bureau for challenging their integrity.[42] And then, having become Twitter's general counsel with the 2020 vote closing in, Baker was once again in place to interfere in a presidential election.

"Under normal circumstances," says Nunes, "Baker would be held accountable for the Carter Page FISA warrant and for his outrageous leaks. But as was typical for Russiagate perpetrators, Baker fell upward and became one of Twitter's top lawyers. And Twitter knew exactly what they were getting when they hired him."

Twitter brought on Baker because of the badge. "People like Baker, who go to high-level tech firms where merit actually matters, don't have a skill set that justifies their position," says former FBI agent Stephen Friend. "What they have is a Rolodex that allows them to reach back to contacts from their federal service and use the processes to get information." Baker serviced the FBI by passing on information collected from his new employer.

When Baker's employment at Twitter became public, Nunes warned users to stay away from the site, and in particular to avoid using the platform's direct message feature. It's not just the NSA that uses social media platforms to spy on users—the companies do it themselves, and send their collection to federal law enforcement authorities, which then get a warrant to read them lawfully.

For instance, when the DOJ subpoenaed Twitter for information on the accounts of Tara Reade, the former Senate staffer who alleged that Joe Biden had sexually assaulted her, the company gave up the information without a fight.[43]

At Facebook, meanwhile, the FBI was using a confidential human source to spy on users. This operation was known as Bronze Griffin, says Friend. "Social media users have been assured their communications are private and not subject to any sort of monitoring," Friend observes. "But that's not true. They turn them over to the FBI, and then the FBI works backwards to justify having them by getting a warrant to look for what they will inevitably find. It's like the parable of the man who knows there's gold in the field, so he buys the field."

Friend says he saw some of Operation Bronze Griffin's tips come in. "It was, 'Bronze Griffin reports that this account is saying X, Y, and Z.' The tip comes in and you're going to work backwards to develop some sort of probable cause for some kind of crime to send the search warrant off to justify having the information to begin with. And the information could be completely out of context. It could be something to the effect of, 'we got to go out there and fight.' So it looks like a call to violence. But then you get the full context and it's 'we got to go out there and fight to win the next election, so let's go knock on doors.' But once you have the investigation opened, it's a counterintelligence investigation and you can keep it going to develop further information, maybe develop who their contacts are so you can open investigations on them, too. I mean, it's never-ending."

For the FBI, the Shadow Network's praetorian guard, social media was just another perch to target political opponents.

PROTECTING BIDEN

In fall 2019, Congress impeached Trump after he asked the Ukrainian president to help investigate the Bidens' financial arrangements with the Ukrainian energy industry. Hunter Biden's laptop contained evidence that appeared to corroborate Trump's suspicions that the Biden family had used U.S. taxpayer resources to blackmail a foreign government and enrich themselves. So the owner of the repair shop where Hunter had abandoned his laptop, John Paul Mac Isaac, notified federal law enforcement.

In December, the FBI took possession of the laptop and formulated a plan to shape news of its contents. It was patterned after how they had shaped reception of Hillary Clinton's emails—blame it on Russia.

Twitter's then head of site security, Yoel Roth, said that throughout 2020, the FBI's FITF declared that it "expected that individuals associated with political campaigns would be subject to hacking attacks and that material obtained through those hacking attacks would likely be disseminated over social media platforms, including Twitter."[44]

The prime suspect was once again Fancy Bear, the Russian military intelligence cyber-unit that was alleged to have infiltrated Facebook and hacked the DNC.[45] And again, the story the FBI and its accomplices told about Fancy Bear was untrue. The Hunter Biden laptop was authentic, and Russian intelligence had nothing to do with it.

Tech executives later complained they were bamboozled by the FBI into censoring news of the laptop. But these executives may have realized the FBI was lying if they had not limited the reach of those who could lead them to the truth, like Nunes.

"I could see the suppression was happening across the board to anyone who challenged the narrative about Russiagate—or anything else for that matter," says Nunes. "The censorship and false discrediting of the Hunter Biden laptop story was clearly part of a wider pattern."

Big Tech executives told the FBI they found no evidence the Russians were infiltrating their platforms. Reminiscent of Russiagate, the Bureau badgered them to corroborate the cover story anyway.[46]

FBI agent Elvis Chan was in regular contact with Twitter executives. As a cyber specialist based in the San Francisco office, he coordinated communications between the FITF and social media companies. In July, he offered to get temporary security clearances for a group of Twitter employees in order to share information on threats to the upcoming election.[47] The FBI was sweetening the pot.

Friend explains, "If you go to a Big Tech firm and say, 'hey, we're going to set you up with a private backchannel to communicate with us, you'll have your own credentials, you have your own login, so you're kind of a fed too.' And that credentialing, that sort of informal deputization goes a long way. It makes things exciting. 'Hey, I'm meeting and regularly talking to the FBI.' It's a nice thing to offer to people like, 'you're a patriot and you're on Team America.'"

And security clearances, even temporary, are worth money.

"If you give people clearances, that's something that can enhance their future earnings," says Friend. "That's why FBI internships are huge. You're not making any money, but you have a security clearance. When you get out, you can basically write your ticket to go into federal service or a private sector industry where clearances are worth a lot."

In effect, Chan was offering Twitter employees a bribe.

Crunch-time was approaching. It was only a few months before Election Day, and it seems the FBI knew, via Rudy Giuliani, that the laptop story was going to go public. They had kept Giuliani under surveillance since spring 2018, when the former Mayor of New York City became Trump's attorney.[48] Repair shop owner Mac Isaac had reached out to him in August and passed the former mayor a copy of Hunter's hard drive. Giuliani told the press he thinks it was likely the FBI intercepted his communications regarding the laptop with journalists John Solomon and Miranda Devine, a columnist at the *New York Post*, which eventually broke the laptop story.

The FBI could not tell social media executives they had been spying on Giuliani or that they knew the laptop was authentic. That would have exposed the government's election interference initiative. So the FBI went around the civilians and spoke to their man on the inside.

In mid-August, Chan emailed Twitter executives. "FITF," he wrote, "asked us to work with you to identify if there is anyone at Twitter who currently holds a TS [Top Secret] clearance so they can get a briefing on something." When a company executive mentioned Baker, Chan replied, "I don't know how I forgot Baker is there now. Yes, he would be perfect." The next month, Chan and FITF head Laura Dehmlow invited Baker to a classified briefing.

When the *Post* published the laptop story in its October 14 edition and the article began circulating on social media platforms, Twitter leadership said it was not "clearly violative of our Hacked Materials Policy, nor is it clearly in violation of anything else."[49] But Baker said it was. The laptop was "faked, hacked, or both," he claimed. The allegation was spread by 51 former intelligence officials who signed a public letter denouncing the laptop's contents as Russian disinformation. This pressure set the stage for Twitter to block countless posts related to the laptop, including the original *New York Post* story and the *Post's* entire Twitter account.

It was a shocking, desperate, and anti-American act of censorship to protect Biden just three weeks before the presidential election. It demonstrated, beyond any doubt, that Big Tech was now in the pocket of the Shadow Network.

5

HOW TO COUP

"I've spent a lot of my career reminding people that the CIA is a foreign intelligence organization," says former CIA officer Peter Theroux. "It does not touch the United States."

After more than twenty years in government service, Theroux was awarded the Career Intelligence Medal. In addition to being fluent in Arabic, and the most prominent English translator of modern Arabic literature, much of his CIA work focused on the Middle East, where he targeted terrorist threats to the United States, especially from Iran and its Lebanese proxy Hezbollah.

"The CIA does joint investigations and joint cases with the FBI," says Theroux. "For instance, if there's an Iranian or an Iranian-American in whatever state who is illegally procuring components for the Iranian nuke program. The FBI is following him around and surveilling him and tapping his phone because they have a FISA warrant. And the agency's role is following the foreign connections, like his handlers back in Tehran or the way he's being paid or the way he's been tasked. So, I explain to people, 'look, that's the way we work. We're forbidden from touching the domestic United States.'"

Before joining the CIA, Theroux was a journalist and a member of one of America's most famous literary families—his brothers Paul and

Alexander are both novelists, and his nephew Justin is a screenwriter and movie star. Peter Theroux's recent book, *In Obscura*, describes how he rubbed elbows with Hollywood starlets before being shipped off to Iraq to work in the CIA's Baghdad station. He is used to fending off hostile questions from a conspiratorial, leftwing cultural establishment accustomed to portraying itself in heroic terms and the CIA as a reckless machine laying waste to foreign countries.

"Even when we are acting operationally overseas to thwart communists or something, that takes a very high degree of direction from the executive branch, of which the agency is a part," says Theroux. "The CIA can't freelance stuff like that. For ops like those in NATO countries that involve our allies, you need a presidential finding. Yes, we're going to manipulate. We're going to get our little hands into the workings of foreign governments, even in friendly countries. We're empowered to do that in the following limited way. It's very closely bounded."

But all that, he says, "is blown apart when this is done domestically. Goodbye to the argument that we're so clean and honest."

During the Obama era, America's foreign intelligence service made a habit of interfering in U.S. elections—most notably when then-CIA Director John Brennan sent the FBI false information to kickstart the Russiagate investigation. The foreign base of operations for the anti-Trump plot was London, where one of Brennan's deputies was station chief at the U.S. embassy.

In early August 2016, just after FBI agent Peter Strzok opened the Trump campaign investigation, Strzok visited the embassy in London to speak with Alexander Downer, an Australian envoy to the United Kingdom. Downer had informed U.S. officials about rumors he had heard second-hand from a Trump advisor that Russia had compromising information on Hillary Clinton. Strzok's visit, however, was more complicated than it appears. "The FBI can't just go overseas and run an operation on foreign soil," says Kash Patel. "That would violate that country's national sovereignty."

Before running operations abroad, Patel explains, law enforcement and intelligence officials must seek the approval and authorization of the top U.S. intelligence official stationed in that country. "And at the time when Strzok and James Comey and Andrew McCabe were lining up assets to take out Trump," says Patel, "they went to the CIA station chief in London, and that was Gina Haspel." She would later become Trump's CIA director.

"The FBI was running an undercover operative on foreign soil," says Patel. "Haspel would have been read in and known all about it."

The undercover operative was working with FBI informant Stefan Halper—a Cambridge University professor who enticed Trump campaign volunteer George Papadopoulos to London to spy on him. Halper brought along a female undercover U.S. government operative posing as his research assistant. He recorded his conversations with Papadopoulos and asked him if the Trump campaign had colluded with Moscow to steal and then leak Hillary Clinton's emails for an October surprise. Papadopoulos denied it, but the FBI edited his exculpatory statements from the transcripts and used the forged evidence to obtain the FISA warrant to spy on the Trump team.

That this happened on Haspel's watch, says Patel, "made her a core part of Russiagate. We sent her subpoenas. And not once did she respond."

"Haspel tried to bury Russiagate," says Devin Nunes. "She fought every attempt to get information about what the CIA, as well as the FBI and DOJ, had done. We were on to the CIA's maneuvers, and we knew exactly what tradecraft tricks Brennan used to develop their bogus intelligence community assessment that Russia meddled in the 2016 election specifically to help Trump win. But like Comey, McCabe, and the rest of them, Haspel was a real pro at obstructing investigations and hiding information."

Haspel claimed, says Patel, that providing documents "would destroy relationships with foreign allies and harm sources and methods." But foreign allies never collected any real intelligence on the Trump circle, no one did. U.S. spy services had simply used London as a listening post to spy on a presidential campaign, and Haspel had approved it. Haspel, says Patel, "covered up the corruption of the DOJ and FBI and her involvement in Russiagate."

It was during Haspel's tenure as director that CIA official Eric Ciaramella spearheaded the 2019 impeachment of Trump. And it was Haspel who greenlighted the campaign to shield Joe Biden with a letter signed by 51 spies claiming that the laptop was Russian disinformation.

"These people have permanently damaged the prestige of the institution," says Theroux. "After all this, people are going to think, 'what isn't the CIA capable of doing?'"

SHADOW DOCTRINE

The CIA was created in 1947 with the mission of collecting intelligence and waging covert actions tailored to the Cold War struggle—to blunt the Soviet Union's ability to project power without dragging the world into a nuclear exchange. The policy was called "containment" and its architect was George Kennan, a U.S. diplomat and expert in Russian affairs.

The "long-term, patient but firm and vigilant containment of Russian expansive tendencies" that Kennan counseled was primarily *political* containment to restrain a *political* threat. Accordingly, the bulk of the fighting was to be done not by armed forces but by political cadres. The problem was that Washington, unlike the highly ideological communist power in Moscow, did not have political cadres, yet. The leader of the free world was starting the superpower struggle short-handed.

In a 1948 memo called "The Inauguration of Organized Political Warfare," Kennan explained that "political warfare is the employment of all the means at a nation's command, short of war, to achieve its national objectives." Operations "range from such overt actions as political alliances, economic measures . . . and 'white' operations to such covert operations as clandestine support of 'friendly' foreign elements, 'black' psychological warfare and even encouragement of underground resistance in hostile states."[1]

America's national security establishment needed its own doctrine of political warfare and the infrastructure to sustain it, for Moscow had already mastered the dark art. "Lenin so synthesized the teachings of Marx and Clausewitz," argued Kennan, "that the Kremlin's conduct of political warfare has become the most refined and effective of any in history." The U.S. had to keep up. "Having assumed greater international responsibilities than ever before in our history and having been engaged by the full might of the Kremlin's political warfare, we cannot afford to leave unmobilized our resources for covert political warfare."

America, wrote Kennan, was handicapped "by a popular attachment to the concept of a basic difference between peace and war, by a tendency to view war as sort of sporting contest outside of all political context, by a national tendency to seek a political cure-all, and by a reluctance to recognize the realities of international relations—the perpetual rhythm of struggle, in and out of war."

It is true that Americans saw a clear line between peace and war, and that is a good thing. Without that distinction, U.S. statesmen would have found it difficult to send the citizens of a republic to kill and die without a vision of postwar peace. The Americans who had survived the cauldron of World War II were rewarded with the fruits of victory won by the greatest industrial power in history—access to college education, good jobs, new homes in newly created suburbs, new cars, household appliances for their wives, and free public-schooling for their children. Peace was not a concept but something real and tangible. The peace of Americans was an updated version of the Bible verse that George Washington made a personal motto—everyone sitting in safety under their own vine and fig trees, without anyone making them afraid.

Erasing the line between peace and war not only marked a shift in how to advance U.S. interests abroad but also a transformation of the character of American foreign policy. The USSR was a totalitarian regime that believed all human relations are based on power and thus everywhere was a permanent battlefield. The U.S. was promoting democracy and its consequent liberties, like self-government. The ideological content of U.S. political warfare was different but the form was the same: by mirroring the tactics of a rival that saw conflict as the core condition of existence, the wards of post-World War II U.S. foreign policy were suborning disaster. Tasking men to see the world as psychopaths do and to counter their moves by reflecting their actions back to them is to induce psychopathology on a societal scale. Seeing peace and war as indivisible could not help but lead to a state of permanent war.

The frontline of the superpower struggle was Europe, where the CIA built and funded opposition movements, trained activists, supported dissident media outlets, and pushed propaganda against communist targets. In the late 1940s, the CIA funded center-right parties to ensure the defeat of communist parties and communist labor unions in France and Italy. The bags full of money that operatives passed to Italian centrists to win the 1948 election was the CIA's first covert action and a great success.

"It was a very good thing and it helped advance American interests for a long time," says J. Michael Waller, a former operative for the CIA and author of *Big Intel: How the CIA and FBI Went from Cold War Heroes to Deep State Villains*. It's become fashionable with parts of the right to see the CIA as a net drag on U.S. peace and prosperity, but Waller says that this view is wrong: "People want to portray the CIA as an out-of-control entity trying to overthrow the world, when in reality we were in a Cold War with communism, and we prevented Italy from becoming communist. Can you imagine if Stalin had taken control of Italy? What would the world be like if Stalin had taken the whole Mediterranean, the center of Western civilization?"

Operations like those that kept Italy out of the red column saved lives and advanced American interests. "And we can see where our failure to intervene has had global and strategic effects that that are harming us today," says Waller. "China is at the top of the list."

As Waller, a Senior Analyst for Strategy at Center for Security Policy, details in *Big Intel*, America's World War II-era intelligence agency that preceded the CIA, the Office of Strategic Services (OSS), was riddled with communists and communist sympathizers and infiltrated by Soviet agents. "Can you imagine if the OSS had not been penetrated by the communists and had had not been sympathetic toward Chairman Mao and not been biased against Nationalist leader Chiang Kai-shek? Can you imagine how different the world would be today?"

In the 1950s, the CIA meddled in elections in, among other countries, Lebanon, Nepal, and the Philippines, often with support from private industries that had business interests in target countries.[2] In the 1960s, according to a 1975 U.S. Senate select committee report, the CIA manipulated Chile's political system by financing activities "from simple propaganda manipulation of the press to large-scale support for Chilean political parties, from public opinion polls to direct attempts to foment a military coup. The scope of 'normal' activities of the CIA Station in Santiago included placement of Station-dictated material in the Chilean media through propaganda assets, direct support of publications, and efforts to oppose communist and left-wing influence in student, peasant, and labor organizations."[3]

Some of the most famous coups the CIA was blamed for never actually happened, like the 1953 coup that supposedly toppled the democratically elected prime minister of Iran, Mohammad Mossadegh.

But Mossadegh was not elected. Rather, in accordance with the country's constitution at the time, he was appointed by the Shah. When the Shah asked him to step down after a tumultuous tenure, Mossadegh refused. The various Iranian constituencies that Mossadegh had alienated, including the military and religious leaders, joined forces to remove him from his post and replace him with the Shah's new prime minister. The main role U.S. officials played was to counsel the Shah to steel his spine and fire the troublemaker.

So how did the CIA get stuck with the damaging fiction that they had brought down Mossadegh? Kermit Roosevelt, President Teddy Roosevelt's grandson, was the CIA station chief in Tehran and spun an elaborate, fake story about how he had single-handedly toppled Mossadegh.

For Theroux, who has written on the Mossadegh affair, Roosevelt was a Cold War-era version of John Brennan, another arrogant bureaucrat whose need to be in the spotlight hurt the agency's reputation.[4] "The CIA's supposed role in the Mossadegh story is a real source of hostility among Iranians," Theroux says. "Because of Roosevelt's ego, we've taken the heat for something that the Iranians did themselves." And the story has fed the clerical regime's paranoid narrative holding the "Great Satan"—America—responsible for all the world's evils.

"I think it's perfectly fine that we mess up our enemies," says Theroux. "We've screwed up communists and terrorists, including the Islamic Republic of Iran, in a lot of ways. And that's a good thing. When I was serving in South America, some of the officers were complaining about how they needed permission to do something, and started reminiscing about the good old days, and a station chief directed covert action to mess with the Russians. They placed an ad in a Spanish newspaper in the name of the Soviet ambassador in that country saying we are having an experimental rescue and research program on small animals, and we will pay you the equivalent of $5 for every chicken, rabbit, cat, puppy, snake, and iguana that you will bring to the Soviet embassy. So they had hundreds and hundreds of South Americans with hens and roosters and baby pythons and cats and iguanas, ten deep around this Soviet embassy demanding money."

The Soviets were furious and threatening revenge, says Theroux. "The people who told me this story were laughing and lamenting the fact that we don't get to do that sort of thing anymore."

Jacob Siegel says he admires that version of the CIA—anti-Soviet and creative. "Some of the covert stuff that people now hold up as an example of how evil the CIA is have it wrong. Funding *Encounter Magazine*, Jackson Pollock exhibits, modernist jazz concerts abroad—that was incredible. That stuff was great, Cold War liberalism at its best. This is the best of America."

Those are what Kennan referred to as white operations, using the CIA to promote American values and virtues. And America's creative talent and technology gave it a decisive advantage in information warfare. The U.S. pioneered and then dominated twentieth-century media, from magazines to motion pictures.

"No one else in the world could compete with the West when it came to influencing hearts and minds through media," says former State Department official Mike Benz. "And there's been an open door between the national security state and private media that lasted for the entirety of the twentieth century up until the present day."

The problem is when you manipulate your own side. "Whenever you're covertly influencing the news, you're running an operation against your own public," says Waller. "You're manipulating what they think and how they understand the world, without them having any idea that you're doing it."

REBRANDING DESTABILIZATION

The CIA pursued its broad mandate to disrupt communist partisans into the 1970s, when revelations of assorted CIA and FBI abuses gave Senate Democrats a pretext to halt activities disrupting causes favored by the American left. The United States Senate Select Committee to Study Governmental Operations with Respect to Intelligence Activities was established in 1975 under the chairmanship of Idaho Senator Frank Church to investigate and curtail controversial intelligence agency programs, including the CIA's foreign interventions going back to the earliest days of the Cold War.

Waller says the significance of Church's investigations is widely misunderstood. "People have made Church out to be the patron saint of American freedom when he was really doing it because he was a left-wing nut," says Waller. "He was taking advantage of the collapse of Vietnam and Watergate and the rise of George McGovern and the Saul Alinsky cadres behind that. He did the right thing but for entirely the wrong reasons. And he wouldn't have gotten very far had then-CIA director William Colby, who was active from the beginning with these covert operations, not cooperated with the committee. Colby testified dozens and dozens of times before Congress in his short tenure as CIA director. He was completely cooperative. He knew that the CIA needed housecleaning, and he knew that anything that's so insular takes on a life of its own. He knew the CIA needed to be cleaned up and he knew the public was demanding it. It's important to rein in any government agency that doesn't have checks and balances. And for all the good that the CIA did, it also made a lot of terrible mistakes."

The Church Committee's findings led to many reforms of the CIA, including those limiting its ability to undermine foreign governments. U.S. officials, however, created a work-around: they realized that the same operations could be more safely conducted in plain sight, so long as they had no apparent connection to the CIA.

In 1983, the National Endowment for Democracy (NED) was established to build networks of pro-democracy dissidents around the world and support foreign media organizations—that is, train assets and push propaganda to subvert target regimes, just like the CIA had done, except it was all out in the open.[5] Ronald Reagan's CIA director, William Casey, was advocating behind the scenes for the U.S. taxpayer-funded public diplomacy organization but was convinced the agency should not appear to sponsor it.[6]

"It would be terrible for democratic groups around the world to be seen as subsidized by the C.I.A.," NED president Carl Gershman told the media at the time. "We saw that in the 60's, and that's why it has been discontinued. We have not had the capability of doing this, and that's why the endowment was created."

NED officials acknowledged that "democracy promotion" was just a re-branding of one of the CIA's jobs. "The biggest difference is that when such activities are done overtly, the flap potential is close to zero," said one NED executive. "Openness is its own protection."[7]

That is because, says Waller, "when you do it as a CIA op, you're causing people to commit treason against their country by working for a foreign intelligence service. But NED, on the other hand, is just a straight, transparent entity. It's not secret. There's nothing classified about it."

Using civil society activists rather than covert operatives to undermine foreign governments also made the mission more palatable to elite U.S. opinion-makers who had come to distrust the CIA after the Church committee disclosures. But target regimes understood that the NED's mission to promote democracy was just a screen behind which U.S. operatives were building out coup infrastructure.

Until the George W. Bush administration, democracy promotion was little known outside the Beltway. But after failing to find weapons of mass destruction in Iraq or Osama bin Laden in Afghanistan, the White House turned to democratizing the Middle East as its rationale for continuing its wars in the Middle East. The theory behind Bush's "freedom agenda" was that people turn to terrorism because their despotic regimes give them no voice in their own political system. Accordingly, overthrowing those regimes and democratizing the Middle East would keep America safe from another 9/11. But after Saddam Hussein was toppled in Iraq, the regimes most vulnerable to U.S.-backed coups were allies—foreign aid recipients like Egypt, which had to host coup activists or risk losing aid.

According to a 2007 U.S. diplomatic cable, then Egyptian president and longtime American ally Hosni Mubarak became "deeply skeptical of the U.S. role in democracy promotion."[8] Egyptian activists were brought to the U.S., where they were trained to use social media and mobile technologies. Sponsors included the State Department, Facebook, Google, and even MTV. "We learned how to organize and build coalitions," said one Egyptian activist. "This certainly helped during the revolution."[9]

The "revolution" that finally did bring down Mubarak was part of the 2010–2011 Arab Spring uprisings. Obama lit the match. He came to office determined to shake up the status quo at home and abroad, and in June 2009, he delivered a speech in Cairo that would undercut the traditional order of the Middle East—the U.S.-led order. He invited members of the Muslim Brotherhood, an anti-U.S. organization that was the intellectual and cultural wellspring of al-Qaeda, to attend his speech. Mubarak stayed away.

"The NED was giving money to Muslim Brotherhood front groups and training Muslim Brotherhood leaders," says Waller. "Why would we want to empower the Muslim Brotherhood against the leader of the most populous Arab country, who was friendly to us? Egypt under Mubarak was a colossal asset for us."

By the time Egyptians took to the streets of Cairo in January 2011, the Obama White House had budgeted $50 million to train tens of thousands of activists in communications, logistics, and evading security forces—i.e., coup technology—using Twitter, Facebook, and YouTube.[10] The coup, said Secretary of State Hillary Clinton, reflected "the power of connection technologies as an accelerant of political, social and economic change."[11] And it also brought the Muslim Brotherhood to power.

"There are instances where U.S.-led coup attempts went bad, but the plan at least was to ensure U.S. interests," says Waller. The only situation analogous to the coup that toppled Mubarak, he says, goes back to the "who lost China" debate of the 1950s. Waller says that "the sellout of the nationalist Chinese and assistance to Mao during and after World War II was precisely due to the influence of controlled Soviet agents and their communist assets in the State Department and the OSS."

So why did the White House push out a foreign leader in Egypt who defended U.S. interests to make way for a pillar of anti-U.S. resistance? Because, says Waller, "Obama was a different creature."

So was Brennan, Obama's fourth CIA director, serving from 2013 to 2017. He had been with the CIA for 25 years when he left in 2005 to start his own consulting firm, The Analysis Company. He joined Obama's 2008 presidential campaign as an adviser and briefed the press on intelligence and national security matters. In March 2008, one of his employees was caught breaking into the State Department's data bank to spy on Obama's passport file. At the time, allies of Obama's rival for the 2008 Democratic nomination, Hillary Clinton, alleged that Obama was not born in the United States. But State Department officials said there was no indication Brennan's employee was motivated by anything but curiosity.[12]

After Obama's victory, Brennan withdrew his name for consideration as CIA director and Obama named him homeland security advisor. In 2013, Obama made him head of America's foreign intelligence service.

"The CIA hasn't acknowledged, except for internally, how bad Brennan was," says Theroux, "or is. He's still alive. He's part of the swamp, the people who serve on boards with each other and publish each other's stuff and go in and out of the swinging doors between Brookings and Harvard Kennedy School of Government, and all the private LLCs and security organizations that they found. Informally, yes CIA people acknowledge it. Because Brennan is one of the most despised directors in modern times."

Like Theroux, Waller says he was surprised to find the CIA interfering in U.S. elections. "It wasn't something the CIA did," says Waller, acknowledging that for decades the CIA did work the American news media. "It took someone like Brennan and then a president to be the way Obama is and who surrounded himself in the White House with people like Valerie Jarrett with her Chicago Communist Party background.

It's really amazing. If you just look at those particular elements, then you think, 'well, of course, if people like this take power, they're going to abuse the instruments of control.' And it stands to reason that they would order this. And a bureaucracy is going to do what the people at the two levels above them tell them to do."

The bureaucracy itself is a problem. "There's been a generational shift," says Waller. The CIA is recruiting out of the same pool as the FBI, college graduates propagandized to hold their country in contempt. "Elements of society no longer go into intelligence because they are not welcome. If you look at the public recruitment, advertising, and promotional materials, the intelligence services are looking at only the weakest of the wolves as recruits." But the fundamental issue is not the bureaucracy but rather the Shadow Network deploying it to accomplish its aims.

FROM UKRAINE TO RUSSIAGATE AND BACK

Brennan believed that his moral compass was the same as Obama's. He told the press that he saw America's role in the world the same way the president did. The U.S. should act as the "world's organizer of support to countries that are in desperate need," said Brennan, but "recognize that our influence and power over the course of events is limited."[13] When it came to Ukraine, Obama and his CIA chief plotted like messianic cult members.

In September 2013, NED president Carl Gershman identified Ukraine as "the biggest prize" in the fight for Russia's periphery.[14] Between 2007 and 2012, NED spent $16.8 million in Ukraine on election watchdogs, independent media, and media watchdogs. These organizations had played a role in the 2004 Orange Revolution, which reversed the outcome of a run-off election alleged to be marred by corruption.[15]

The U.S. foreign policy establishment on both sides is united in its conviction that Ukraine is a U.S. ally, a democracy, and a beacon of freedom. But to understand what Ukraine truly is, it is important to start where all geopolitics begins: by looking at a map.

Ukraine is situated between two greater powers, Russia and the European Union. That makes Ukraine a buffer state. Geopolitical logic dictates that buffer states cultivate and maintain cordial relations with the greater powers that surround them, since siding with one great power against another often leads to catastrophe.

In 2013, the European Union offered Kyiv a trade deal, which many misunderstood as a likely prelude to EU membership. Young Ukrainians want to join the EU so they can flee Ukraine, one of the poorest countries on the continent.

The trade deal was an ill-conceived EU project to take a shot at Vladimir Putin with what seemed like little risk. The idea was to flood the Ukrainian market, and therefore also the Russian market, with European goods, which would have harmed the Russian economy—leading, the architects of this plan imagined, to popular discontent against Putin. Putin understandably saw this stratagem as a threat to his country's stability and his own position, so he gave Ukrainian President Viktor Yanukovych an ultimatum: either reject the deal and accept Moscow's $15 billion aid package in its place, or suffer crippling economic measures.

When Yanukovych duly reneged on the EU deal, the Obama administration helped organize street demonstrations for what became history's most tech-savvy and PR-driven regime change operation, marketed to the global public variously as Maidan, EuroMaidan, and the Revolution of Dignity.

In December 2013 the late Senator John McCain, chairman of the NED-funded International Republican Institute, visited Kyiv alongside senior State Department official Victoria Nuland to exhort the U.S.-backed protestors. Additional support for the coup came from, among others, George Soros' Open Society Foundation, which paid for cell phones, public relations firms, and drones to capture images of the protest zones.[16]

The coup was born on social media, just like the operation that toppled Mubarak. Social media was used to brand, organize, and recruit members into militia units to fight the security forces. Facebook and Twitter directed activists to protests. YouTube instructional videos showed protestors how to make incendiary devices. A new TV network called Hromadske emerged to cover the uprising.[17] It was funded by the U.S. Embassy in Ukraine and Shadow Network oligarch Pierre Omidyar, founder of eBay and billionaire sponsor of leftwing U.S. media and other activist organizations.[18]

In February 2014, the protests forced Yanukovych into exile in Moscow. Consequently, Nuland and other Obama administration officials worked to assemble a new Ukrainian government friendly to the United States and hostile to Russia.

In late February, the Russians responded to the American soft coup in Ukraine by invading Crimea and eventually annexing it while creating chaos in Eastern Ukraine. The Obama administration declined to arm the Ukrainian government, understandably anxious to avoid direct conflict with Moscow. By leaving Kyiv defenseless, however, the White House showed it had never fully gamed out all the possible scenarios that might ensue from setting a client state on course for conflict with a great power. Instead, Obama and the Europeans highlighted their deadly miscalculation by imposing sanctions on Moscow for exploiting the conditions that Obama and the Europeans had created.

The White House seems to have taken a perverse pride in the death and destruction it helped incite in Eastern Europe. In April 2014 Brennan went to Kyiv, and with no public rationale for his visit, he appeared to confirm the agency's role in the coup. Shortly after came Vice President Biden, who took his own victory lap and counseled the Ukrainians to root out corruption. Naturally, a prominent Ukrainian energy company called Burisma, which was then under investigation for corruption, hired Biden's son Hunter for protection.

By tying itself to an American administration that had proved to be reckless and dangerous, the Ukrainians made a geopolitical blunder that statesmen will study for years to come: a buffer state had staked its future on a distant power that had simply seen it as an instrument to annoy its powerful neighbor with no attachment to any larger strategic concept.

Ukraine then made a bad situation worse. When the same people who had left them prey to Putin asked them to take sides in an American domestic political conflict, the Ukrainians enthusiastically signed on.

In 2016, the Hillary Clinton campaign came calling on Ukrainian officials and activists to lend some Slavic authenticity to its Russia collusion narrative targeting Donald Trump. Indeed, Russiagate's central storyline was about Ukraine: according to the memos written by FBI informant Christopher Steele, Putin's ostensible reason for helping Trump win the presidency was to get him to drop Ukraine-related sanctions. For Ukraine, it was another chance to stick it to Putin and gain favor with what it imagined would be the winning party in the American election.

With Brennan and a host of senior FBI and DOJ officials pushing Russiagate into the press—and running an illegal espionage campaign against the Trump team—Ukrainian political figures gladly joined in. Key participants included Kyiv's ambassador to Washington, who wrote a Trump-Russia piece for the U.S. press, and a Ukrainian journalist and one-time parliamentarian who contributed to the Steele dossier. The collusion narrative was also augmented by Ukrainian American operatives like Alexandra Chalupa, who was tied into the Democratic Party's NGO complex.

The thought that playing political games in Washington might have consequences for Ukraine's relations with its more powerful and immediate neighbor did not seem to enter the heads of either the Ukrainians or the American political operatives cynically using them.

Ukraine had no existential or geopolitical reason to participate in the anti-Trump operation, which allowed it at best to curry favor with one side of the D.C. establishment while angering what turned out to be the winning party. Russiagate was the kind of vanity project that a buffer state with a plunging GDP and an army equipped with 40-year-old ex-Soviet weapons in a notoriously risky area of the world can ill afford.

Just as Russiagate seemed to be coming to a close in July 2019, U.S. national security officials injected yet another Ukraine-related narrative into the public sphere to target the American president. This one appears to have been initiated by Ukrainian American White House official Alexander Vindman and his colleague Eric Ciaramella, a CIA analyst who had served as Vice President Biden's point man on Ukraine during the Obama administration. When Vindman told Ciaramella about a phone call in which Trump had asked the Ukrainian president for information regarding allegations about the Biden family's corrupt activities in Kyiv, they called on help from U.S. intelligence services, the State Department, the Pentagon, Democratic Party officials, and the press. *Quick, scramble Team Ukraine—Trump is asking questions!*

They feared that Trump would find out that Joe and Hunter Biden had demanded $5 million each from Burisma's owner to make his problems go away.[19] In exchange, Obama's Vice President used a $1 billion U.S. loan guarantee as leverage to force the Ukrainian government do his bidding. Biden told the Ukrainians that if they did not fire the prosecutor investigating the energy company paying his son $80,000 per month, they would not get the money.

To cover up for the Bidens, a Democratic-led Congress impeached Trump for trying to figure out what American policymakers had been doing in Ukraine over the past decade. For the U.S. national security establishment, a Biden victory over Trump would ensure that its actions in Ukraine would stay hidden.

Days after the *New York Post* had broken the news about the laptop that gave evidence of the Biden family's record of corruption in Ukraine, Biden campaign adviser Anthony Blinken asked former deputy CIA director Michael Morrell for talking points about the laptop. Blinken knew Trump would raise the subject in the second presidential debate only days away. Morrell was eager to help.

Morrell had a history of mixing politics with intelligence to advance his career. It seemed he popped up every election cycle to help out Democrats in a jam, in hope that his efforts would be recognized and he would be named for the top job at the agency.

After the 2012 terror attacks on U.S. government facilities in Benghazi, Libya, Morrell edited talking points that portrayed the attack as a spontaneous protest against an anti-Islamic internet video. The truth was that it was a planned assault by al-Qaeda-linked terror groups, but that undermined the Obama administration's claims to have decimated al-Qaeda—and the election was just under two months away.

"Morrell showed his true colors in the scandal over the Benghazi talking points," says Devin Nunes. "He's a dishonest shill who played a major role in politicizing, discrediting, and corrupting our intelligence agencies."

Anticipating a Clinton victory in 2016, Morrell auditioned for the CIA directorship by endorsing her candidacy in an August 2016 op-ed and pushing the collusion campaign. "Mr. Putin had recruited Mr. Trump as an unwitting agent of the Russian Federation," Morrell wrote.[20]

For 2020, he wrote a letter with another retired CIA official, Marc Polymeropoulos, claiming that, in their expert assessment, the evidence of Biden family corruption found on Hunter Biden's laptop bears "all the classic earmarks of a Russian information operation."[21] Morrell had arranged for 49 other former intelligence bureaucrats to sign the letter, which Biden cited when Trump brought up the laptop in their October 22 debate.[22]

"These intelligence officials had spent the entire Trump presidency running ops like this," says Nunes, "dismissing problematic facts as Russian disinformation. The only thing unique about the letter was that they put their names on it—they typically operated anonymously. I guess they figured—correctly—that the media would rally around the letter, it would do the intended damage, and once it was discredited, none of the reporters would hold them accountable because the reporters themselves were their partners in this operation."

Of the 51 signatories, 42 had been employed by the CIA. One official at Langley recruited former agents to sign the letter.[23] A few of the former agents who signed, like Morrell, still had active contracts with the agency. Three former directors signed the letter, Brennan, Leon Panetta, and Michael Hayden, along with two former acting directors, Morell and John McLaughlin.

CIA Director Gina Haspel saw the letter before it was released and did nothing to stop its publication or even distance the CIA from a letter virtually printed on CIA stationery. But it was not her job to stop a propaganda campaign devised to influence a presidential election, for she was just a bureaucrat controlled by higher powers.

"The letter was a huge intrusion into domestic politics," says Theroux. "It was crooked and it was corrupt. They abused their credentials and their resumes to damage national security, to corrupt the electoral system, and to swing an election. And what angers and worries me deeply is that this plays to every conspiracy theory and every stereotype of the CIA as a dark, slimy institution that is corrupting the world and corrupting our national politics. And I wish it were fictitious, but the fact is, anyone who now wants to say the agency is crooked and partisan and runs black ops and goes rogue against our own population, they have much more than a talking point."

From Russiagate, to Brennan's intelligence community assessment delegitimizing the Trump presidency, to the first impeachment of Trump quarterbacked by Ciaramella, to the 51 spies letter, the CIA has left its indelible mark on contemporary American life. Under Obama, the permanent war Kennan designed to stop the communist threat was turned against the American public.

6

CENSORSHIP KILLS

The terror of Covid—commonly described as the most dangerous respiratory illness since the 1918 Spanish Flu—was driven by the notion that the disease could be spread by those who did not show symptoms yet might still be infected. Therefore, because sickness, perhaps even death, was lurking behind every corner, even when one least expected it, the people had to be locked down en masse, and those without signs of the disease had to be tested regularly to discern whether they were silent carriers.

It sounds like the plot of dystopian novel about an occupation regime breaking a country's spirit by shutting down public spaces and turning neighbors, friends, and family against each other until they feared the invader less than their loved ones who might unknowingly bring death home.

But it wasn't fiction. It was real. It was the Democratic Party's electoral strategy to get Joe Biden over the top. Selected by the Shadow Network as the most suitable avatar for Barack Obama's return to the White House, the candidate, already showing clear signs of the mental frailty that would derail his re-election campaign, needed help. The lockdowns were designed to collapse the most obviously indisputable success of Donald Trump's presidency, the economy.

Masking and social distancing alienated Americans from each other, and perpetual testing reminded a fearful public that anyone could transmit the disease. There was no way out. And thus, a quarantined and terrorized electorate had been convinced that it was too dangerous to vote in person, and readily accepted new voting procedures that would not only change the character of presidential elections, but also facilitate fraud on a scale unparalleled in American history.

The true damage done during the 2020 election cycle may never be tallied in full, for the Shadow Network squandered Americans' faith not only in elections but also in the medical profession and public health industry. In order to rationalize the new procedures, medical practitioners from family doctors to government bureaucrats lied to the public, and those who tried to tell the truth about the virus were silenced. The censorship that drove the largest mass-casualty event in U.S. history also gave Americans their first taste of totalitarianism.

OBAMA DICTATES THE PARTY LINE

After implementing the Fifteen Days to Slow the Spread on March 16, President Trump urged the country to reopen as soon as possible. Barack Obama was pushing in the other direction. He called for paralyzing the system, which would naturally cripple the economy.[1] On March 25, tweeting an article about healthcare workers in New York, he wrote, "These are the burdens our medical heroes already face in NYC. It's only going to get harder across the country. Another reason to maintain social distancing policies at least until we have comprehensive testing in place. Not just for our sake—for theirs."[2]

Marching to his beat, the media announced the purpose of Obama's campaign. "Obama urges Americans to continue social distancing despite Trump's wishes to reopen economy," read a CNN headline.[3] Broadcast news was awash with experts celebrating the Covid regulations and demanding more testing. The global supply shortage "is a huge problem," one public health professional told the media. "I'm really concerned that we are not going to have the capabilities to test those who really need and should get a test."[4]

Anyone who asked why testing was so important was pushed to the margins and silenced. "We don't go and test everyone for influenza," says Dr. Scott Atlas, a health policy scholar at the Hoover Institution at Stanford University, who joined the Trump administration in August 2020 as the President's coronavirus adviser. "If you're sick, the general recommendation is stay home because the sick people are the ones infecting people," Atlas tells me. "The idea that we'd test everyone for flu and keep those not showing symptoms out of work or school is absurd."

Testing to see if asymptomatic people were carrying Covid was a fear tactic unrelated to public health. There has never been any conclusive evidence that asymptomatic carriers spread flu-like respiratory diseases. A 2009 study published by the National Institute of Health (NIH) reviewed the literature and "found that there is scant, if any, evidence that asymptomatic or presymptomatic individuals play an important role in influenza transmission."[5]

Even Anthony Fauci acknowledged as much—at first. "In all the history of respiratory viruses of any type, asymptomatic transmission has never been the driver of outbreaks," the head of the National Institute of Allergy and Infectious Diseases (NIAID) said in a January 28 press briefing (the YouTube video documenting Fauci's statement has since been removed).[6] But by early spring, Fauci was reading from Obama's script. In an April 5 briefing, he expressed concern that between twenty-five and fifty percent of those infected could be asymptomatic and were likely spreading Covid.[7] Now Obama's message was being relayed from inside the Trump administration as the President and the Shadow President contested for control of the public sphere.

Fauci was the ideal Shadow Network validator. He was a public health expert with nearly a half century's worth of experience manipulating the federal bureaucracy. He learned how to manage the media in the 1980s when he was the government's point-man on AIDS. At NIAID, a subagency of NIH, he built his career on the still unfulfilled promise of a vaccine to end AIDS. Just as HIV treatments like antiretroviral medicines appeared and threatened to make him irrelevant, two planes collapsed the World Trade Center, ushering in the Global War on Terror. The September 11 attacks were followed by a brief but deadly bio-terror campaign that left five Americans dead and dozens more seriously ill.[8]

So Fauci was given the biodefense portfolio, one of the most sensitive in the national security establishment, and was rewarded for his work when he was made America's highest-paid bureaucrat. He augmented his enormous U.S. taxpayer-funded war-chest with donations from Shadow Network oligarchs like Bill Gates to build an empire consisting of scientists and researchers around the world bent on impressing Fauci to advance their careers. With Fauci in front, Obama could count on a global response to Covid buttressing his electoral strategy—more lockdowns, more testing, more fear and panic and terror.

Moreover, Obama and Fauci shared a secret. As some scientists contended that Covid was engineered in a lab, now the consensus opinion, the Obama administration was credited for imposing a 2014 moratorium on research designed to increase the transmissibility and/or virulence of pathogens, known as "gain-of-function" research, after a few near catastrophes at U.S. government labs. However, a footnote in the moratorium announcement shows that "an exception from the research pause may be obtained if the head of the USG [United States Government] funding agency determines that the research is urgently necessary to protect the public health or national security."[9]

In other words, there was no moratorium if Fauci was allowed to claim exceptions for work he was funding. Obama had not stopped anything. In fact, the gain-of-function research that led to the Covid outbreak started on his watch, when the NIH funded a 2015 Wuhan Institute of Virology project on bat viruses.[10]

Nonetheless, to distinguish Obama's public health record from Trump's handling of Covid, the former was credited for stemming an outbreak of the H1N1 flu virus and preventing Ebola from becoming a pandemic. In an early April video conference for U.S. mayors hosted by former New York Mayor Michael Bloomberg, Obama said, "I suspect many of you are already doing the things we would have done and did do when we were in the White House."[11] In other words, the former President was using a crisis that his administration had failed to prevent to score political points against the current White House. As CNN framed it, "Obama has repeatedly weighed in on the response to the virus, largely offering a more cautious message than that of President Donald Trump and advocating for protecting public health over re-starting economic activity."[12]

In an April 8 tweet, Obama wrote, "Social distancing bends the curve and relieves some pressure on our heroic medical professionals. But in order to shift off current policies, the key will be a robust system of testing and monitoring—something we have yet to put in place nationwide."[13]

Trump pushed back against Obama's efforts to break the economy. Within an hour, he tweeted, "Once we OPEN UP OUR GREAT COUNTRY, and it will be sooner rather than later, the horror of the Invisible Enemy, except for those that sadly lost a family member or friend, must be quickly forgotten. Our Economy will BOOM, perhaps like never before!!!"[14]

In June, the head of the World Health Organization's emerging diseases and zoonosis unit, *Dr. Maria Van Kerkhove,* inadvertently challenged the premise of the universal testing regime when she told reporters, "From the data we have, it still seems to be rare that an asymptomatic person actually transmits onward to a secondary individual."[15] Fauci moved quickly to check her. Kerkhove's assessment, said Fauci, was "not correct."[16] Kerkhove quickly retracted her statement. "I used the phrase 'very rare,'" she said, "and I think that that's [a] misunderstanding to state that asymptomatic transmission globally is very rare. I was referring to a small subset of studies."[17]

Fauci and White House Coronavirus Response Coordinator Deborah Birx ignored common practice and inverted basic knowledge about the most elementary issues like immunity after a viral infection. "When you recover from a viral infection, you typically have long term biological protection against serious illness or death," says Dr. Atlas. "That's basic immunology. That's not Ph.D. level immunology, or medical school virology, that's high school level biology. But Fauci and Birx rejected that."

And to implement lockdowns, they had to throw out the U.S. government's own pandemic playbook. "The known pandemic management for more than a decade showed that lockdowns don't work to stop the spread of viral respiratory infections and are extremely harmful," says Atlas. For example, according to a 2006 study on pandemic preparedness commissioned by the George W. Bush administration, "Communities faced with epidemics or other adverse events respond best and with the least anxiety when the normal social functioning of the community is least disrupted." The paper argued, "Strong political and public health leadership to provide reassurance and to ensure that needed medical care services are provided are critical elements. If either is seen to be less than optimal, a manageable epidemic could move toward catastrophe."[18]

Atlas' position was simply to use what years of cumulative human experience, common sense, and high-level research had taught public health experts about respiratory diseases and pandemics. "Starting in March 2020, I was calling for targeted protection, meaning increasing protection of high risk people—because lockdowns weren't protecting them—and opening up schools, and ending lockdowns," he tells me. "I had been doing interviews and writing about the pandemic for months before I went to Washington."

But returning to normal was precisely what Fauci's clients in the scientific community and media were trying to prevent. Social media stepped up to help. In August Trump posted a video in which he said that children are "almost immune" from Covid, and he was censored by Facebook and Twitter for violating Covid "misinformation" rules.[19]

"It was the general statement of a layman," says Atlas. "It was reasonable, because healthy children had minuscule risk of serious illness from Covid, but they blocked it. And it's the President of the United States—no matter what he says, it should be visible. It's supposed to be a free society."

Trump introduced Atlas at an August 11 press conference. "He has many great ideas," said the President.[20] Atlas was there to repair the damage done by Fauci and his Covid task force colleague Deborah Birx. And that meant FauciWorld could only see Atlas as an enemy. "As soon as I got to Washington, the press started with the hit pieces," says Atlas. "They claimed that I was calling to let the virus spread, to let it rip. I never said anything like that. That's not targeted protection"

But no one misunderstood Atlas' skepticism of mass testing and lockdowns. They just recast it to isolate him, the carrier of a message deadly to Obama's political project. The physical and mental health of Americans and the country's spiritual ballast required a return to normalcy, but Biden's path to victory depended on the ruin of the economy and the menu of new voting procedures designed to facilitate fraud.

GAGGING THE HERETICS

Censorship, says Atlas "is multifactorial, and there is a nuance to how you censor someone. There's explicit, overt censorship, and there are subtler forms of censorship that delegitimize you to undermine and destroy your credibility." Atlas was both censored directly and delegitimized.

In mid-September, YouTube pulled down a long interview he had done months before. "I was going through the data on what percent of children die, and what percent of children have severe enough infection from Covid to be hospitalized," says Atlas. "YouTube pulled it down because at that point I was in the White House. They said it was misinformation. The *Wall Street Journal* noted that it's no coincidence that YouTube pulled down a several-month-old interview once I became an adviser to the president. That's overt censorship."

At the same time, his academic colleagues organized a campaign to delegitimize him. In a September 9 public letter, seventy-eight Stanford Medical School doctors and researchers excoriated Atlas. "Many of his opinions and statements run counter to established science," according to the letter, "and, by doing so, undermine public-health authorities and the credible science that guides effective public health policy."[21]

"The authors of this letter were very politicized in an attempt to censor me," says Atlas. "They apparently had little understanding about the pandemic, and no facts to support their claims that I was wrong. They just wanted to delegitimize me. When I got lawyers involved, they immediately pulled the letter down from their website. But in my view, they caused a lot of the death threats that I had. And I had to hire 24/7 security surrounding my home. I had to install thousands of dollars' worth of security equipment."

The lead signature was Philip Pizzo, former dean of the Stanford Medical School who had worked at the NIH for two decades. He began his NIH tenure in pediatrics and then added the HIV portfolio in the 1980s when Fauci made AIDS the cornerstone of his public health career.[22] It seems that Pizzo, like scores of scientists around the world, was indebted to Fauci for his professional advancement.

"Delegitimization is a form of censorship," says Atlas. "It's a form of filtering out the truth. And it causes others to self-censor. What happened to me was so visible. Medical professionals told me that they saw what was happening to me and were afraid. They urged me to keep speaking, but they were concerned about their own careers."

Yet other medical professionals were inspired by Atlas and stood with him, like Stanford colleague Jay Bhattacharya, a professor of health policy. "I was really naive about all of this," Bhattacharya tells me. "I just was a scientist. If you looked for me in 2019, you would never have heard of me because I published in scientific journals and wrote for seven people that read my scientific papers. It was a fun life. I was just naive. I just didn't ever anticipate something like this happening in science. I could see it happening in other realms of society and politics. People play dirty all the time. But in science? I was definitely naive."

Stanford administrators went after him, too. "It was nasty," he says. "But I had to choose. Effectively they told me that I could go back to my quiet, happy life or keep speaking up. And I just couldn't stand the thought of living with myself, having to back down, because this is my area. This is what I studied my entire life, epidemiology, social science. These lockdowns were having effects on poor people, on children. I couldn't stay silent while it was happening."

He was aware, of course, of the effort to silence him. "It was really clear from the earliest days of the pandemic that there was some effort to smear or censor alternate views," says Bhattacharya. "Not just on Twitter, but on all social media platforms. I would watch colleagues post things that were their interpretation of published data, and it was unlike anything I've ever seen as a scientist. If you said something that was against the official government narrative, you were going to get either labeled as a misinformation spreader or your posts were going to be taken down."

He mentions Mark Zuckerberg's March email to Tony Fauci inviting the public health bureaucrat to use Facebook as a platform to reach the world. Bhattacharya says that with the redactions in the email it was hard to know if Zuckerberg also asked him for direction on censoring "disinformation." "Facebook had already been under a tremendous assault for supposedly getting Trump elected in 2016," says Bhattacharya. "If I were in their business, I would try to be proactive to avoid this kind of thing happening again when there's a new threat."

Bhattacharya suspected that Twitter was suppressing him, too. And after Elon Musk bought the company in October 2022, he invited

Bhattacharya to come visit Twitter headquarters and find out. "It was kind of shocking," Bhattacharya says. "It says the word 'blacklist' next to my account name, and it turns out I was put on this blacklist the day I joined Twitter. I think I had two posts that day. One was a link to an op-ed I wrote arguing that testing young and healthy people didn't make any sense. And then I had a link to the Great Barrington Declaration."

The Great Barrington Declaration, a health freedom manifesto published in October 2020 that made the case for re-opening the world, was coauthored by Bhattacharya, along with Sunetra Gupta, an infectious disease epidemiologist at Oxford University, and Martin Kulldorff, a Harvard Medical School Professor of Medicine. "The most compassionate approach," the declaration reads, "is to allow those who are at minimal risk of death to live their lives normally to build up immunity to the virus through natural infection, while better protecting those who are at highest risk."

Atlas explains how the declaration came to be. "Gupta said she saw what was happening to me and wanted to come and support me in Washington. I got her a security clearance to travel and the American Institute of Economic Research in Great Barrington, Massachusetts, paid for her ticket. So she stopped off there, where she, Bhattacharya, and Kulldorff co-wrote a statement, which became the Great Barrington Declaration."

Since its publication in the first week of October 2020, the declaration has been co-signed by thousands of medical scientists and practitioners and millions of citizens around the world. It promoted what Atlas had been advocating since the spring of 2020, focused protection—end the lockdowns, protect the elderly, and set the children free.[23] It was a plan, or a plea, to return to normal life.

Its authors tried to correct mischaracterizations of focused protection "as a laissez-faire approach to let the virus rip through society."[24] But, again, the issue was not that critics failed to grasp the true meaning of the argument. Rather, they were playing their role in a campaign to prolong lockdowns and continue terrorizing the American public. And it led directly back to Fauci.

Emails between him and NIH director Francis Collins show a coordinated effort to degrade the declaration and its authors. "This proposal from the three fringe epidemiologists," Collins wrote to Fauci, "seems to be getting a lot of attention – and even a co-signature from Nobel Prize winner Mike Leavitt at Stanford. There needs to be a quick and devastating published take down of its premises. I don't see anything like that on line yet—is it underway?"[25]

The first salvo was launched within a week of Collins' October 8 email. "Great Barrington Declaration is not grounded in science and is dangerous," according to an October 14 press release coordinated by twenty public health organizations, including the Johns Hopkins Center for Health Security at the Bloomberg School of Public Health, the Los Angeles County Department of Public Health, and the New York City Department of Health and Mental Hygiene. Yale epidemiologist Gregg Gonsalves tweeted, "This is not mainstream science. It's dangerous." "Allowing a dangerous virus that we don't fully understand to run free is simply unethical," declared World Health Organization (WHO) Director General Tedros Adhanom Ghebreyesus. "It's not an option."[26]

Bhattacharya believes Fauci and Collins were motivated by personal and professional as well as political considerations. "When three prominent scientists, from Stanford, Harvard, Oxford, say, no, there's another way. You're doing something that's quite harmful to the poor, to the vulnerable, to children, and working-class people," he says. "It was a threat to the illusion that there was a consensus underlying the lockdowns, that every reasonable scientist agreed. We had tens of thousands of scientists and doctors signing on to the Great Barrington Declaration."

Fauci could only see it as a threat to his authority. "He's used to getting his way," says Bhattacharya. "Fauci sits on top of a huge budget at NIAID and people agree with him because they don't want to cross him because then their careers might get threatened. He's destroyed the careers of scientists who crossed him."

"PEOPLE DIED FROM CENSORSHIP"

Given Atlas' ties to the authors of the Great Barrington Declaration, it was open season on Atlas himself. "It was clear that people inside the administration had friends in the media and the health agencies who were delegitimizing me and what I said." And indeed, Fauci emailed Birx and briefed her on countering Atlas.[27] After Twitter removed an Atlas post detailing data on masks, Birx told associates that the move came as a "relief."[28]

Birx, as Atlas notes, was the official head of the task force's medical side. "Fauci wasn't in charge of anything, but he was the most visible in the media. Birx was the one who was in charge of the medical side and personally wrote all the official policies for the governors to follow."

Fauci, Birx, and Robert Redfield, then-Director for the Centers of Disease Control and Prevention (CDC), all knew each other from their previous work on HIV, Atlas explains. "They funded each other. Birx said she had a pact with Fauci and Redfield that if any of them were fired by Trump, they would all resign. That's the mark of a self-interested bureaucrat. That's not the mark of a public servant."[29]

Atlas acknowledges it would have been good had they all left government. "They were in place for five or six months before I got to Washington. Their policies were in place all over the country. Nothing changed. I tried. I educated the public. I educated the President. But basically, their policies were implemented. So they own the results. The policies were so destructive and wrong, complete pseudoscience. Their policies of censorship—censorship of correct health policy—killed people. They didn't just cause people to be hostile to each other. They were so wrong in what they said, and they denied the scientific evidence and they gave false information. They prevented the process of scientific debate, which is used to arrive at truth. By their censorship, they prevented that."

Censorship, says Atlas, "is not just blocking the speaker. It's also blocking the listener and preventing them from getting information that could inform their decisions." It didn't matter that his information was based on authoritative research, or that people were dying for lack of it—he was being silenced because his true information undermined the premise the Shadow Network's new voting procedures.

"I was quoting CDC and NIH documents, and studies that were done on masks and their lack of efficacy," says Atlas. "And Twitter deleted it and suspended my account as adviser to the president. There is no doubt that the American people should hear what the advisor to the president is saying about the pandemic during the pandemic. Yet Twitter thought it was their judgment about what American people should hear, even at the point of blocking visibility of what the president's adviser was saying."

What's most worrisome about the censorship regime and the Covid measures it protected, says Atlas, "is that Americans were by and large acquiescent. There are small instances of people protesting, but most of the protests against the lockdowns were outside the U.S. Americans were weak and showed a lack of courage. And what does that portend for the future? This is the United States. This is not a *potential* situation in our country. This is the current state of our country. People don't want to acknowledge it. This is what the Soviet Union did. This is what communist China does."

After the election, Atlas urged Americans to stand up for themselves. When Michigan Governor Gretchen Whitmer announced a three-week lockdown, closing colleges, high schools, workplaces, and in-person dining, Atlas tweeted, "The only way this stops is if people rise up. You get what you accept. #FreedomMatters #StepUp"—meaning "speak up for your rights," he later explained.

Defending himself against accusations that he was "pitting Americans against each other" and inciting violence, Atlas immediately posted on Twitter, "I NEVER was talking at all about violence. People vote, people peacefully protest. NEVER would I endorse or incite violence. NEVER!!"[30]

Nonetheless, Atlas' academic colleagues exploited the occasion to attack him, again, and the Stanford Faculty Senate voted to censure him.[31] "There was no defense of me at the leadership level whatsoever," says Atlas. "And in fact, there was some piling on—really claiming that I was doing something that was wrong, and I didn't do anything wrong. People were dying and I was asked to serve the country. And I was 100 percent right. The problem is that they've made people reluctant to serve the country during an emergency if the leadership of the country is somebody who is politically not in favor. I was stabbed in the back by people at the highest levels of Stanford University and Hoover Institution, my employer."

That included Hoover Institution Director Condoleezza Rice. Atlas' "Rise Up" tweet, said George W. Bush's former Secretary of State, was "offensive and well beyond the boundaries of what is appropriate for someone in a position of authority, such as the one he holds."

Rice, hounded by Democratic operatives during her own government service, had joined with her tormentors to attack Atlas. "They're blinded by their political hatred of Trump and their obsession with Covid," Atlas says. "They need psychiatric help."

At the time Stanford was smearing Atlas, it was also playing a central role in a broader censorship regime. The Stanford Internet Observatory (SIO) was the lead partner in the Election Integrity Project, a cutout used by a Department of Homeland Security subagency to monitor social media and censor critics of the novel voting procedures legitimized by Fauci and Birx's Covid policies. After the election, the mass-surveillance and censorship operation was rebranded as the Virality Project to focus on Covid-related information. The Stanford-led organization collaborated with government agencies, the CDC, Surgeon General's Office, and Health and Human Services to rigorously censor First Amendment-protected speech.[32]

"Stanford has become the poster child of censorship, of misguided public policy, of overt denial of fact for political reasons, of standing for impingement on guaranteed freedoms in this country," says Atlas. "It has harmed the public good. I think we all knew the universities were generally one-sided politically. But I never understood that the overt, explicit, and harmful imposition on our rights was commandeered by universities. Covid exposed these things that all existed beforehand but we weren't aware of. Or I wasn't aware. I was completely naive about how the press was not interested in the truth. Instead, they were interested in destroying people to get their personal political objectives in place. I was very naive about how government bureaucrats prioritize their own careers and their own opinions instead of trying to help the country. There is no end to what these people will do to get what they want."

Atlas cites a recent poll on censorship to show how quickly the public has embraced the censorship regime.[33] "In 2018," he says "Thirty-nine percent of Americans said the government should censor 'misinformation on the internet.' Today, it's up to fifty-five percent. And it's seventy percent of Democrats. When you censor correct health policy—which is my job, health policy—it's not just censoring free speech. You're not just attacking the concept of diversity of opinion. People die and people died from the censorship of the correct policy."

The Shadow Network's censorship regime is responsible for killing Americans. "They got away with it and they're going to do it again because the people in power are still the same," says Atlas. "They killed people by locking them inside the house, which is where you couldn't protect the elderly. They killed people by lying that masks protected you from serious illness if you were high risk and you were old. They isolated children by shutting schools down. And teenage suicides in girls went way up. Obesity went way up in kids. Self-harm spread. These things are all correlated to death. They killed children. They killed old people by isolating them. Many in nursing homes that were isolated from seeing their families, they dwindled and died from being alone. They killed people."

The Covid regime, argues Atlas, "has now left us a country that does not trust science, does not trust government health guidance, and public health. They have destroyed trust. They caused that by their lies, their censorship, their demonization, and their failure to admit error. They inflamed people against each other. They made a false consensus appear to be true about masks, about social distancing, about isolation, about the need for lockdowns, about the need for school closures. All those things were grossly wrong and they were known to be wrong for 15 years, according to the standard pandemic literature. And they didn't just fail to stop the death, but they also were extraordinarily harmful to the population, particularly the poorer families. And so they've left us with a very hostile country that has no trust in public health guidance."

And the consequences extend far beyond public health. "You have to be a fool," says Atlas, "to think that there's any limit to how the government will exert its power in the United States, especially when the people are willingly enslaved."

PROHIBITION OF QUESTIONS

"It was like how people lived under communist regimes," Dr. Aaron Kheriaty says of the Covid-censorship regime. "You had to develop a secret language and terms of irony to say what you wanted to say. So to me, the worst part of the censorship regime is the self-censorship that occurs when you see people around you being punished for saying certain things."

Now Director of the Bioethics and American Democracy Program at the Ethics and Public Policy Center, Kheriaty was a professor in the School of Medicine at the University of California, Irvine (UCI) when the Biden administration imposed mandates for the Covid vaccine. "I was in the Department of Psychiatry, but about half my time was spent as the director of the medical ethics program at the hospital in the medical school. I'd been at UCI for 16 years as a faculty member and had anticipated spending the rest of my career there."

As director of the medical ethics program, Kheriaty was involved in drafting pandemic-related policies for the entire University of California system. "Our committee drafted the ventilator allocation policy, the triage policy. We drafted policies to allocate other scarce resources like monoclonal antibodies. We drafted the vaccine allocation policy. But when it came to the vaccine mandate policy, our committee was never consulted. I was sort of shocked that there was no conversation about it. We were basically told, 'this is the policy, it's going to happen,' and my efforts to try to get a conversation going were met with stonewalling."

He published a piece in the *Wall Street Journal* in June 2021, arguing that university vaccine mandates were unethical.[34] "A few weeks after that, UC finalized its vaccine mandate policy and started implementing it," says Kheriaty. "And because I had come out publicly, there were a lot of people at the university reaching out to me. Nurses who had worked every day during the pandemic treating Covid patients and had been at the hospital for decades were losing their jobs. Students were being kicked out of school, and they were reaching out to me very, very desperate. And it seemed like there was not anything I could do to help them because the policy was so rigid. It was impossible to get a medical exemption in California because the medical board was threatening physicians with disciplinary action if they wrote exemptions. A lot of religious exemptions were being denied. So, I decided that given my position, it was important for me not just to say something publicly criticizing the policy, but to try to change the policy."

He filed a lawsuit in federal court challenging the policy on Fourteenth Amendment equal protection grounds. "The university immediately placed me on investigatory leave, and then a month later on unpaid suspension," he says. "And then a month after that, they fired me." Kheriaty continued to speak out against the mandates. "Soon after I was fired, I did an interview with a journalist named Alison Morrow. I was just talking about my ethical argument, which is grounded in the principle of informed consent, which is the first principle articulated in the Nuremberg Code following World War II. It requires that people be allowed to accept or refuse participation in research, or a medical intervention. It's a central principle of twentieth-century ethics that was being steamrolled. I was making an ethical, philosophical case that we shouldn't mandate this vaccine for competent adults. That we should respect the principle of informed consent. We can engage in persuasion, we can engage in nudging, we can incentivize getting the vaccine, but we can't fire people. The interview was posted on YouTube, and it was immediately taken down, with a notice that it violates YouTube's policy because it's promoting misinformation about the vaccines, which it wasn't. It was making an ethical argument."

Then it seemed to Kheriaty that he was being censored everywhere. "I was gaining new followers on Twitter, but my total number of followers was basically capped because as I would gain followers the algorithm would automatically kick off other followers, and they weren't bots. They were usually accounts that had a large following themselves. It happened two or three times, and I realized this isn't a glitch in the system. Then I figured out from colleagues who were getting kicked off Twitter what you could and couldn't say. So, you end up self-censoring and speaking in code so that you could try to communicate an idea without using the keywords that were going to get you booted."

Kheriaty remembers early in the Biden administration getting a phone call from the solicitor general of Missouri, John Sauer, who later represented Trump in his successful case against the Justice Department regarding presidential immunity. "He reached out to me when the attorney general's office in Missouri was thinking about challenging the federal government based on public statements that the Biden White House had made from the podium about getting social media to censor users. It occurred to John, 'hey, wait a minute, you can't do that. That's unconstitutional.' He asked if I'd had experience with censorship."

Kheriaty gave concrete examples of how he'd been censored. "And they wanted to attach some private plaintiffs to the case because presenting to the court specific instances strengthens the case. So, I said, yes, I'm happy to be a plaintiff. And he asked if I could reach out to some other colleagues who had been censored. So, I reached out to Jay Bhattacharya and Martin Kuldorff, who I'd been working with since they drafted the Great Barrington Declaration."

Jill Hines, co-director of Health Freedom Louisiana, and Jim Hoft, publisher of Gateway Pundit, were also added to the case, *Missouri v. Biden*, filed in 2022 by Missouri Attorney General, now U.S. Senator, Eric Schmitt alongside Louisiana Attorney General, now Governor, Jeff Landry. "What we found in the limited discovery that the court permitted at the pretrial phase is astonishing," says Kheriaty, "just the breadth and the scope of how many government agencies were involved in censorship."

Initially, the focus was on the White House and the public health bureaucracies, like the Surgeon General's Office, the CDC, and the NIH, behind the Covid-related censorship. "But then you've got the Department of Defense, and a Homeland Security subagency, CISA [Cybersecurity and Infrastructure Security Agency]. We found out that the Census Bureau was involved in censorship, probably related to the elections. The Department of Treasury was involved in censorship for criticizing the government's monetary policy." Nearly the entire federal government was working with private-sector partners to violate Americans' First Amendment rights.

The plaintiffs' request for an injunction against the government, later renamed *Murthy v Missouri*, was eventually denied on a technicality (standing) at the Supreme Court in a 6-3 decision, but the case continues. And in the process, Kheriaty and the others had uncovered the Rosetta Stone of government censorship.

"I had a theoretical basis for understanding that regimes like ours could go sideways," says Kheriaty. "But I was still surprised that it happened so quickly. I thought these are going to be slow developments over the next fifty years, and we have to push back against this, and cancel culture is kind of an early phase of this. We have to keep fighting these tendencies, otherwise, the society that my grandchildren live in is going to look very different than the one I grew up in. But the rapidity with which it unfolded under the declared state of emergency was a perfect fulcrum for getting people to do things that otherwise they wouldn't have done. That it happened almost overnight, in March of 2020, shocked me."

Kheriaty tells me that since he first took his stand against Covid regulations, he has been reading Eric Voegelin, a twentieth-century political theorist who fled to America from Nazi Germany and who studied totalitarian systems.

"He explains that the common feature of all totalitarian systems is not mass surveillance or concentration camps, or secret police, men in jackboots," Kheriaty says. "The common feature of all totalitarian systems is the prohibition of questions. So, the regime monopolizes what counts as rationality, based on their own ideology. And if you raise questions about that, they don't debate you. They don't try to persuade you. The Marxist just says you're infected with bourgeois consciousness and you obviously don't understand the dialectics of history, so you're not worth talking to. You're not a rational person who understands the direction of history, so we're going to ignore you."

That is, since totalitarian regimes set the terms for what constitutes rationality, unless you subscribe to the regime's ideology, you're not a real person. Your criticism of the regime, or refusal to repeat its lies, and insistence on speaking the truth are all irrelevant. It's not dissent, it's nonsense, and therefore you simply don't register as a rational being. You don't exist.

"A dictator rules externally through force and external threats as punishment," says Kheriaty. "So you fall in line so that you don't lose your job. The totalitarian regime uses external force and threats of punishment initially. But eventually, as the ideology becomes absorbed there's less need for that. Fewer secret police are needed because everyone is informing on their neighbors. There's less mass surveillance because people are surveilling one another and surveilling themselves in a sense. And in a perfect totalitarian regime, the ideology has been so internalized by individual citizens that there's no longer any need for those things. Because dissident thoughts and questioning the regime, those questions no longer occur to you."

Surveillance, censorship, and propaganda—key components of the totalitarian state—are vital Shadow Network projects.

7

THE FIXERS

The Attorney General played the bagpipes. He was affable and eloquent. He was modest. He said he did not see himself as a historical figure who would be sung about long after his death like a Greek warrior in the Homeric epics. He did not need the job—he had already served as attorney general in the George H .W. Bush administration. He came out of retirement because he was worried for the country. He said it was not fair how Donald Trump was treated.

He was the star of countless pro-Trump internet memes warning that there was no place left for the anti-Trump spies to hide. He and the prosecutor he appointed to probe the FBI's investigation of Trump traveled together in Europe to get to the bottom of Russiagate. They were taking names and soon the bad guys would be fitted for orange jumpsuits. But in the end, Bill Barr fooled the country and betrayed his boss.

It's not hard to understand how Barr must have seen it. He was not a leftwing operative or a Never Trump activist who counted his CNN and MSNBC hits as career highlights. He was a serious man with a long record of service to his country. Having worked on national security issues across the government for nearly half a century, he had a specialized view of the issue.

The fact that senior FBI, DOJ, and CIA officials abused intelligence programs and spied on a presidential campaign was bad. But Barr's bigger concern was that Obama officials had carelessly exposed these crucial intelligence capabilities and provoked public opposition to them. The additional abuses of the special counsel probe, nominally overseen by his old friend and colleague Robert Mueller but really driven by leftwing activists like Andrew Weissman, were further souring Americans on intelligence collection and government surveillance programs.

For Barr, fixing the problem meant first stopping Mueller, then Trump, the outsider likely to lash out and destroy the vital programs and resources deployed against him.

Some may have seen Barr's betrayal coming, but no one can deny that his tenure represents one of the most remarkable performances in U.S. history. The lawman hired to restore justice and hold government officials accountable for crimes against the republic instead insulated the spy services. It was his destiny to deliver the coup de grace and bring down Trump, for dating back to his first term as attorney general he was one of the main architects of the surveillance infrastructure that would later be employed by Obama's Shadow Network. As a telecom executive, he welded together the public and private sector to build the largest intelligence apparatus in world history. He came to detest Trump, but for the most part it was not personal. He was just protecting what he had created.

SURVEILLANCE STATE ARCHITECT

To some Trump officials, it was clear that Barr had infiltrated the administration. "Of course I was suspicious," says a former senior Justice Department official in the Trump administration who spoke to me only on condition of anonymity. "Barr is a former CIA guy in the Intelligence Directorate who ran damage control for the agency, blocking and tackling the Church committee. He also engineered a resignation pact at the Justice Department during the George H. W.

Bush administration to put David Souter on the Supreme Court and keep Ken Starr off it. So it's not surprising that he then maneuvered himself in the Trump era into position with his big Audition Memo attacking Mueller's obstruction-of-justice theories."

The official continues, "He comes in and talks a good game. I think he fooled President Trump for a time. Even so, I gave Barr the benefit of the doubt early on, thinking maybe I shouldn't be harboring this distrust. Maybe Barr has seen how bad the country has gone off the rails and as a grandfather wants to make sure the country gets back on track. But by the time of the 2020 election, it became clear that my fears were right. He got rid of the Mueller investigation to earn just enough credit to stick around until he could do maximum damage."

Barr was a CIA legacy. His father Donald Barr had served with the CIA's predecessor, the Office of Strategic Services, during World War II as an Italian interpreter in a prisoner of war camp and as a member of a "target team" in Germany.[1] He worked in Washington for a year as associate program director for the National Science Foundation, then moved backed to New York and became headmaster of the Dalton School.[2] In 1973, he published a science-fiction novel about a child-trafficking network catering to the sexual tastes of power-mad oligarchs. The next year he hired a young math teacher, Jeffrey Epstein, who would later become notorious for running a child-trafficking network that served presidents, prime ministers, princes, and the world's wealthiest and most powerful men. The manner of Epstein's death in federal detention under Bill Barr's watch fed speculation that the billionaire was collecting intelligence, or blackmail, on behalf of U.S. spy services.

Bill Barr started at the CIA as a China analyst in 1971 and was moved to the agency's Office of Legal Counsel. In 1976, he drafted a memo to lift the congressional order placed on the CIA to stop destroying records in the wake of the Church Committee hearings.[3] With the Trump administration, he buried evidence of the spy services' unlawful activities, except in this case targeting not foreign governments but our own.

Barr was fundamentally a DOJ man. He started the George H. W. Bush administration as an assistant attorney general and was named attorney general in 1991. He and Robert Mueller, then head of DOJ's criminal division, greenlighted a secret Drug Enforcement Administration (DEA) surveillance program to collect the records of drug dealers. But they wanted more. DEA subpoenaed phone companies for billions of records of calls made by Americans to 116 countries where drug traffickers were believed to be operating.[4] It was the first program to collect the records of Americans in bulk, regardless of whether they were suspected of a crime.[5]

An internal DOJ report later found that Barr had "failed to conduct a comprehensive legal analysis" of its authority to gather those records. Moreover, DEA had shared its collection with "non-DEA federal agencies that had no apparent connection to specific drug investigations."[6] Barr and Mueller's program gave federal agencies a backdoor to illegally spy on Americans.

Civil rights lawyers and first-amendment activists describe the DEA program as a blueprint for the even broader National Security Agency surveillance in the wake of the September 11 attacks. The breadth of Barr and Mueller's program suggests that the arguments made to justify the post-9/11 surveillance regime were largely window dressing. The intelligence agencies seized on a terrorist attack to justify and expand on what they were already doing.

In 1994 Barr joined the private sector, where he became general counsel for the telecom firm GTE, which was acquired by Bell Atlantic in 2000 and renamed Verizon. Doing its part in the Great War on Terror, the company handed over the contents of Americans' electronic communications to the NSA as part of the Bush administration's massive, warrantless surveillance program known as Stellar Wind.[7] Documents leaked by former NSA contractor Edward Snowden showed that Verizon had supplied the NSA with metadata on all calls within the U.S. and to other countries on an "ongoing daily basis."[8] A court order prohibiting Verizon executives from discussing the arrangement, or even the order itself, gave the telecom company cover in case customers discovered their own phone company was spying on them.

In 2003, Verizon along with rivals AT&T and MCI entered into contracts with the FBI to compensate the companies for working on FBI business, just as the FBI paid Twitter $3.4 million two decades later for its help spying on Americans.[9] The FBI's Communications Analysis Unit repeatedly violated the Electronic Communications Privacy Act when agents invoked nonexistent emergencies to collect records.[10]

After the Bush administration's illegal surveillance programs were disclosed and lawsuits multiplied against the telecom firms, Barr lobbied Congress to immunize the companies from suits and legalize the intelligence services' spying on Americans.[11]

Before retiring from Verizon in 2008, Barr hired another DOJ man as a deputy, James Baker, who would later play a starring role in the FBI's 2016 surveillance campaign against the Trump circle and the Bureau's joint censorship operation with Twitter to silence Trump supporters ahead of the 2020 vote. As much as anyone, Barr brought the private sector into alignment with the intelligence bureaucracy and shielded both from legal liability for spying on Americans. He was one of the architects of the surveillance state, building capacity inside and outside of government to normalize the indiscriminate bulk collection of the electronic communications of millions of law-abiding Americans.

To protect what he built, he needed to be back inside. To get Trump's attention, he flattered him in the media. He defended Trump's firing of Deputy Attorney General Sally Yates after she resisted Trump's executive order to suspend the entry of nationals from seven countries into the United States pending stricter vetting procedures.[12]

He also said Trump was right to dismiss Comey, on procedural grounds. Barr said that Comey had overstepped his role as FBI director in exculpating Hillary Clinton. "By unilaterally announcing his conclusions regarding how the [Clinton investigation] should be resolved," wrote Barr, "Comey arrogated the attorney general's authority to himself."[13]

Barr defended Trump when he called for a special counsel to investigate the Clinton Foundation's relationship with foreign officials. "There is nothing inherently wrong about a president calling for an investigation," said Barr.[14] And he thought there was a strong case to be made for investigating Clinton, stronger than the case for "collusion." "To the extent [the Justice Department] is not pursuing these matters, the department is abdicating its responsibility," said Barr, who himself declined to investigate Clinton once he resumed the post of attorney general.

Barr agreed with Trump that there were too many Democrats on Mueller's special counsel team. "In my view, prosecutors who make political contributions are identifying fairly strongly with a political party," said Barr. "I would have liked to see him have more balance on this group."[15]

Most important, Barr disputed the special counsel's case against Trump. In June 2018 he sent Deputy Attorney General Rod Rosenstein what Barr critics call the "Audition Memo." "Barr deliberately lied to plant himself into the Administration to make sure Trump was a one-term president," says the former DOJ official who worked under Barr. "Barr thought, 'how do I get in? I'll kill off Mueller, who's turning out to be a dud for the Democrats and not really the killer the Dems thought he'd be anyway.'"

In the memo, Barr argued that Mueller could not charge Trump with obstruction for asking Comey to leave alone his former National Security Advisor, General Michael Flynn. Under Mueller's theory, wrote Barr, "Simply by exercising his Constitutional discretion in a facially-lawful way—for example, by removing or appointing an official; using his prosecutorial discretion to give direction on a case; or using his pardoning power—a President can be accused of committing a crime based solely on his subjective state of mind." Barr noted that "this theory would have potentially disastrous implications"—namely, it would legitimize political prosecutions.

Six months later, Trump appointed Barr as attorney general, and Barr hit the ground running. First order of business was to rein in Mueller, and in March 2019 the special counsel filed its two-volume report. Mueller found no evidence of Trump colluding with Russia, and he declined to recommend either for or against charging Trump with obstruction. Barr promptly cleared Trump of obstruction, bringing the years-long collusion investigation to a close.[16]

In April 2019, he told a Senate committee that the Trump campaign was spied on. "Spying on a campaign is a big deal," he noted.[17] To find out whether the FBI's collusion investigation was "adequately predicated," he appointed a U.S. Attorney from Connecticut, John Durham, to run a special counsel investigation.

Durham had a reputation as a tough prosecutor, but the high-profile investigations he had led against U.S. security services were duds. His case regarding the FBI's handling of criminal informants in Boston led to the prosecution of only a single agent. He investigated the CIA's destruction of videotapes depicting the torture of terror detainees and declined to press any charges.[18]

Nevertheless, Devin Nunes and his team were optimistic. They sent numerous criminal referrals to the Justice Department and offered to assist Durham's office any way they could.

"Barr came in and asked me to sit down with Durham and unload the Russiagate investigation I had run," says Kash Patel. "I sat in the SCIF [sensitive compartmented information facility] with Durham, and we referred to him dozens of people who should be criminally investigated. Devin and I were John Durham's biggest cheerleaders."

"We passed on a slew of criminal referrals based on what our investigation had uncovered," says Nunes. "We knew there was no hope the

DOJ would do anything while Rosenstein was empowered there. But with Durham now in place, we really thought we'd finally see some accountability for all the malfeasance we'd documented."

Others were less optimistic about Durham's appointment. "New England doesn't breed a lot of hardcore populist conservatives," says the former senior Barr DOJ official. "I didn't understand appointing a U.S. attorney from Connecticut when there were lots of prosecutors from red states that could have been named. But for Barr, who was raised on the upper West side in New York City, it was par for the course."

Barr was saying all the right things about getting to the bottom of the FBI's 2016 election interference campaign—even as the FBI director who answered to him was building the infrastructure for its 2020 operation with the Foreign Interference Task Force.

But it was not just FBI and CIA leadership preparing to rig 2020. The Department of Homeland Security (DHS) was building out an enormous enterprise drawing in not just Big Tech but other private sector actors including federally funded centers at some of America's top universities.

As Attorney General, Barr was responsible for protecting Americans' civil rights," says the former DOJ official. "And yet right under his nose a censorship campaign was taking shape with no other purpose than to violate Americans' most precious right—to choose our own leaders."

BUILDING THE RED-MIRAGE BLUE-SHIFT NARRATIVE

The FBI's Foreign Intelligence Task Force protected the Joe Biden's candidacy by burying evidence of his family's corruption detailed on Hunter Biden's laptop. But other agencies were responsible for protecting the fraudulent premise of the Shadow Network's election strategy by censoring criticism of the new Covid-prompted voting procedures. That effort appears to have been led by a small unit operating inside DHS called the Cyber and Infrastructure Security Agency (CISA).

The predicate for CISA's authority to censor Americans was set with DHS Secretary Jeh Johnson's January 6, 2017 memo designating elections as critical national infrastructure. This directive was issued in support of an information operation delegitimizing the Trump presidency by claiming the election had been compromised by foreign interference. Thus, protecting election infrastructure was coded language for targeting Trump.

In short time, protecting critical infrastructure meant more than just polling places, voting machines, and computer systems—it applied also to "cognitive infrastructure," meaning the digital townsquare. CISA's job was to protect Americans from "disinformation," including domestic speech as well as foreign propaganda. Indeed, according to Chris Krebs, the subagency's first director, CISA "did not treat content on social media differently based on its domestic or foreign origin."

Krebs worked previously at DHS before becoming Microsoft's Director of Cybersecurity Policy and then rotated back into the national security bureaucracy. At CISA, he identified "monitoring disinformation" as a "core line of effort" and was eager to "work with social media organizations, as well as state and local governments to clarify and combat misinformation." For the 2020 election, CISA targeted speech critical of the new voting procedures.

The novel voting regulations were enabled by Covid, which Democrats recognized as a historic opportunity to permanently skew elections in their favor. As election expert Hans von Spakovsky put it, the Democrats were taking "advantage of COVID-19 to get the changes they've wanted for years into election rules."[19]

As late as 2005, Democrats and Republicans agreed that mail-in and absentee voting were recipes for voter fraud. A bipartisan report that year chaired by former President Jimmy Carter and former Secretary of State James Baker found that "absentee ballots remain the largest source of potential voter fraud."[20]

What changed was that Democrats had employed some of the new procedures with great success, starting in California. Devin Nunes had seen it up close in his home district in the Golden State's Central Valley.

"The Democrats systematically altered California's voting system," says Nunes. "There are now masses of mail-in and provisional ballots, resulting in vote counting that spans days and even weeks. The center-piece of their whole scheme was ballot harvesting—allowing people to turn in other people's ballots. All these measures increase fraud, but obviously the point of these changes is not to increase election security, it's to help Democrats win. They'd already engineered this in California, saw that it worked, and then Covid gave them an excuse to implement a lot of it nationwide."

Unsurprisingly, Barack Obama was a zealous advocate of the new voting regime. "Let's not use the tragedy of a pandemic to compromise our democracy," tweeted Obama on April 10, 2020. "Check the facts of vote by mail." It was part of a series of Obama tweets the same day pushing for new voting procedures.[21] Another tweet read, "Everyone should have the right to vote safely, and we have the power to make that happen. This shouldn't be a partisan issue."[22]

Meanwhile, Democratic Party operatives were working the court system to legalize voting procedures facilitating fraud. There were more lawsuits filed "before the election trying to change election rules than I've ever seen before," said von Spakovsky, "and I've been doing election stuff for three decades."

The effort was led by Marc Elias, a Shadow Network lawyer who had represented Obama's official campaign arm, Obama for America (OFA). In 2016, OFA paid law firm Perkins Coie $1 million, fueling suspicion that Obama had chipped in to the Clinton campaign's dirty tricks operation, led by Elias.[23] While Perkins Coie colleague Michael Sussmann was point-man for the Alfa Bank hoax, Elias was executive producer of the Steele dossier, having hired Fusion GPS to manufacture the evidence that the FBI used to spy on the Trump circle.

Four years later, Elias was back on the job. Party operatives appear to have been planning to turn Covid into a platform for voter fraud well before Trump declared a Covid national emergency on March 16. In fact, that same day, Elias published a *Washington Post* article promoting vote by mail.[24] According to the Democratic lawyer, no previous barrier to voting, not even foreign war, "posed the same threat that the novel coronavirus does for the 2020 election."

Elias claimed he was challenging laws "that unnecessarily restrict voting rights, particularly the rights of lawful voters to cast their ballots in the middle of a pandemic and have them counted." He was marketing fear. "The virus poses a health risk to voters in every state, city, town and village in the country," he wrote. Social distancing guidelines keeping voters six feet apart would make in-person voting impractical, but the alternative was too terrifying to contemplate. "Not only will voters not want to wait in line and file into schoolrooms in proximity to others," Elias wrote, "but election workers—many of whom are elderly—also may not eagerly sign up to staff polling places where they will come in contact with hundreds of strangers in a single day."

But merely allowing vote by mail and ballot harvesting was not enough. These practices had to be encouraged, with states paying for "the printing and distribution of millions of extra ballots," free postage, and the extra officials needed to process and count mailed ballots. Further, states had to "minimize rejections based on issues with voters' signatures." In other words, verifying signatures on mail-in ballots was now a thing of the past.

Because ballots were being sent out en masse, even to people who did not request them—like people who had changed addresses and dead people—counting all those ballots would extend elections beyond Election Day, by days or even weeks. The new procedures were designed to flood the system and create a long enough vote counting period to conjure up however many ballots were needed to put Biden over the top.

The Democrats exploited government officials as well as Big Tech to enforce a ruthless censorship regime against those criticizing or even questioning the new voting procedures. Social media posts doubting the integrity of those procedures, like mass mail-in ballots, early voting drop-boxes, lack of voter ID requirements, and forecasting potential tabulation issues on election night would be categorized as cyber-attacks on vital American election infrastructure.

"The problem," says former State Department official Mike Benz, "is that CISA knew they could not directly censor social media posts from Americans who expressed reservations about the new voting procedures. So they deputized outrageously biased institutions to censor upwards of millions of First Amendment protected tweets. This is the sort of thing that the Treasury Department sanctioned North Korea for in 2017."

The avatar CISA built to disguise its heavy-handed election interference was called the Election Integrity Partnership (EIP). It consisted of Stanford University's Internet Observatory (SIO); the University of Washington's Center for an Informed Public; the Digital Forensics Research Lab attached to the Washington, D.C. think-tank the Atlantic Council, and Graphika, a private analytics firm staffed by former intelligence and defense officials and funded in part by U.S. government agencies.

The SIO, chaired by former chief security officer for Facebook Alex Stamos, was lead partner. Stamos said he had come up with the idea to form a consortium to censor social media in conversation with CISA's chief Chris Krebs. Stamos made clear to social media platforms that EIP was a cutout for the federal government. He explained to a social media executive in a 2020 email that EIP was "a one-stop shop for local election officials, DHS, and voter protection organizations to report potential disinformation for [the EIP] to investigate and to refer to the appropriate platforms."[25]

CISA and the State Department's Global Engagement Center were the top federal agencies that submitted complaints to the EIP identifying social media posts as "misinformation," which EIP relayed to Big Tech with specific recommendations on how the social media platforms should censor the posts—shadow-ban them, remove them entirely, or even suspend the user's account.

CISA and the EIP targeted at least one Trump tweet. On October 27, the President posted, "Strongly Trending (Google) since immediately after the second debate is CAN I CHANGE MY VOTE? This refers changing it to me. The answer in most states is YES. Go do it. Most important Election of your life!" A local official incorrectly reported it as "misinformation," and the EIP notified Twitter with the aim of censoring the leader of the free world. The platform let it go at the time but would eventually banish Trump altogether.

Other Republican and conservative individuals and institutions targeted by the CISA-EIP censorship consortium included members of Trump's family; political figures like former House Speaker Newt Gingrich, one-time Arkansas Governor Mike Huckabee, Congresswoman Marjorie Taylor Greene; journalists and opinion-makers like Sean Hannity, Mollie Hemingway, Harmeet Dhillon, Charlie Kirk, Jack Posobiec, Tom Fitton, James O'Keefe, Benny Johnson, Sean Davis, Dave Rubin, Paul Sperry, Tracy Beanz, and Chanel Rion; and conservative media outlets including Fox News, the *New York Post*, the *Epoch Times*, the *Washington Times*, Breitbart, Just the News, and Newsmax.

The EIP-CISA consortium was not scouring social media just to punish individual infractions. Rather, they were looking to censor the larger story that the particular posts advanced—that the integrity of the 2020 election was compromised by the new election procedures.

"The public and private sector got together to control the public response and predictable outrage that would happen when you had one winner on election night and another winner the day or days after," says Benz. "They called this the 'Red-Mirage Blue-Shift' phenomenon."

What that described was an apparent Trump victory on election night followed by a Biden victory after the vote counting finished days, weeks, or even months later. Half a year before the election, Democratic Party operatives had fine-tuned the language to explain exactly what would happen the night of the election and afterward so that by the time the public watched the obvious fraud unfold in real time, they would believe the vote was wholly legitimate.

BALLOT FRAUD MANIFESTO

While CISA and EIP were protecting the "Red-Mirage Blue-Shift" operation, another group of political operatives, including former senior U.S. officials, were running scenarios to test reactions to it. Called the Transition Integrity Project (TIP), this collection of anti-Trump activists was apparently acclimating the public to massive election fraud and preparing the ground for how to deal with the ensuing chaos.

TIP was the brainchild of former Obama Pentagon official and Georgetown University Law School professor Rosa Brooks. Her mother Barbara Ehrenreich was once co-chair of the Democratic Socialists of America. "The idea is not that we will win in our own lifetimes," Ehrenreich wrote, "but that we will die trying."[26]

Dozens of articles and interviews about TIP in Democrat-allied media published in the summer and early fall, including a long *Washington Post* article by Brooks herself in September, taught Biden voters how to talk about the vast election operation undertaken on their behalf.[27] The TIP dossier, and the media reports about it, forecasted how Trump was likely to contest the election and what the Democratic Party and allied institutions—from the media and social media to the court system and Congress—were preparing in response to stop him and his supporters.

To wargame election scenarios, Brooks tapped numerous Trump enemies including former chairman of the 2016 Hillary Clinton campaign John Podesta, former Michigan governor and later Biden Energy Secretary Jennifer Granholm, former chair of the Democratic National Committee Donna Brazile, and, to play on the Republican side, Never Trump operatives Bill Kristol, David Frum, and Max Boot.[28]

The first thing Americans needed to know, according to TIP's August 2020 report, is that there is no such thing as election night anymore.[29] "The concept of election night is no longer accurate and indeed is dangerous," wrote Brooks.

In retrospect, it is easy to see why she alerted Democrat allies that election night was a thing of the past: with hundreds of millions of mail-in ballots indiscriminately sent to addresses across the country, it would take time to count how many Biden ballots were needed in battleground states to beat Trump. Accordingly, Brooks wrote, "We face a period of contestation stretching from the first day a ballot is cast in mid-September until January 20. The winner may not, and we assess likely will not, be known on 'election night' as officials count mail-in ballots."[30]

Brooks continued, "This period of uncertainty provides opportunities for an unscrupulous candidate to cast doubt on the legitimacy of the process and to set up an unprecedented assault on the outcome. Campaigns, parties, the press and the public must be educated to adjust expectations starting immediately."[31]

Naturally, TIP anticipated that Trump would doubt the integrity of the election since the exercise taught Democrats how to talk about an election fraud scheme. Party officials and auxiliaries, like the media, as well as Biden influencers were advised to propagandize the electorate by addressing "the two biggest threats head on: lies about 'voter fraud' and escalating violence."[32]

According to the report, "Voting fraud is virtually non-existent, but Trump lies about it to create a narrative designed to politically mobilize his base and to create the basis for contesting the results should he lose. The potential for violent conflict is high, particularly since Trump encourages his supporters to take up arms."[33]

These were key talking points, both untrue: mail-in ballots, especially without signature ID, guarantee voter fraud, and Trump never encouraged violence, not even as blue militias Antifa and BLM burned and looted American cities in the spring and summer of 2020. Notably, almost every TIP wargame scenario urged the Biden team to send millions of protestors into the streets to replay the spring and summer George Floyd riots, which enabled Biden's campaign "to gain momentum in the battle for public opinion."[34] Brooks was debuting the idea that there would be violence and bloodshed if the Democrats did not get what they demanded.

It is astonishing to read the initiatives proposed by Brooks' cohort. Even if Trump had won a clear victory, they argued, Biden should nonetheless hold the country hostage by urging California, Oregon, and Washington to leave the Union unless Republicans agreed to eliminate the Electoral College. Another proposal sought to secure a permanent Democratic majority in the Senate by granting statehood to Washington, D.C. and Puerto Rico, and dividing California into five states.[35]

Brooks' cadre also sketched a post-election agenda to counter Trump's potential countermeasures and then harass him after his coming loss:

- She suggested Trump might disrupt the transition by deploying the National Guard. In fact, then-House Speaker Nancy Pelosi ignored the White House's request to deploy guardsmen in anticipation of the January 6 protests even though her aides had been secretly preparing for violence for months.

- Brooks predicted that Trump would destroy documents "to preserve the President's legacy and thwart future criminal investigations." One of the DOJ's two cases against the former commander in chief deals with mishandling classified documents.

- Trump and his supporters, Brooks claimed, would "engage in an orchestrated disinformation campaign to shape the public's perception—in fact, misperception—of the 'facts' underpinning a dispute over electoral results." The DOJ's second case against Trump charges him with obstruction for spreading "misinformation" about the election.

- According to Brooks, "The period from November 4th to December 14th sets the stage for a potential fight in the Congress on January 6th, 2021." There was no fight inside Congress in part because the anticipated debate over electors was forestalled when a massive protest infiltrated by intelligence and law enforcement officials turned violent and the Capitol was evacuated.
- Brooks also predicted that Trump would initiate "a new media outlet" and "extend his norm-disrupting influence after he leaves office through an independent media company or partnerships." Maybe the government-led censorship consortium was already planning to banish Trump from social media as part of the post-election crackdown. But she was right—Trump created Truth Social in response to the Shadow Network's censorship of him, his supporters, and anyone who contradicted government narratives on a host of topics.

Brooks even speculated that Bill Barr would launch an investigation into "terrorist ties" of the Biden transition team "to justify surveillance." This speculation was just mirror-imaging. All Barr did was to clear Obama's spy chiefs who had launched a phony investigation of Trump to justify surveillance and then a show trial that undermined his presidency.

INCENTIVIZING ELECTION INTERFERENCE

Asked whether Durham was investigating Obama and Biden, Barr said no. "Whatever their level of involvement," said Barr, "I don't expect Mr. Durham's work will lead to a criminal investigation of either man. Our concern over potential criminality is focused on others."[36]

But why was he not investigating them? Their names were all over the documents chronicling the origins of the anti-Trump plots. There was Susan Rice's memo of the January 5 meeting in the White House—Obama and Biden were there, directing law enforcement's actions against the Trump team. The FBI documented the same meeting. Biden was one of forty Obama aides who had spied on General Flynn by unmasking his name in classified transcripts of foreign intelligence intercepts. And crucially, the spy services had John Brennan's handwritten notes of an August 2016 meeting with Obama showing that the president had been read into the plot against Trump.[37]

After the notes were declassified, the shocking news was out in the open—Obama had greenlighted the surveillance of Trump and sabotaged the incoming Trump administration via Brennan's Intelligence Community Assessment. And yet not only would Obama and his Shadow Network evade accountability for interfering in the 2016 race, but they would be given wide berth to fix the 2020 vote, too.

Barr said that Durham was "pressing ahead as hard as he can." He said that Covid had slowed the investigation, but that nevertheless he expected "some developments hopefully before the end of the summer."[38]

In August Durham indicted FBI agent Kevin Clinesmith for doctoring an email from the CIA attesting that Trump advisor Carter Page, a target of the FBI's Russia probe, had been a CIA source[39]—Clinesmith changed the email to say Page was "not a source" in order to obtain a warrant to spy on the retired Navy officer.

Clinesmith's actions were the clearest proof that the FBI had not merely been mistaken and over-zealous in pursuing leads about the Trump team's ties to Russia. Rather, these investigations were a setup from the outset. Optimists hoped Durham would use the indictment to corner Clinesmith and make him give up his superiors—at last, Russiagate would unravel with the conspirators turning on each other. Instead, Clinesmith pled guilty to a single felony false statement charge and got only twelve months' probation. Soon after, he even got his law license back.

When Barr announced in October that there would be no additional indictments or even a report from Durham before the election, it signaled to the agencies and individuals responsible for 2016 that the coast was clear to repeat their efforts to shape the 2020 election.[40] And so FBI agent Brian Auten, who had played a leading role in Russiagate, set about protecting Trump's 2020 rival by shutting down an investigation into Hunter Biden's laptop, labeling verified evidence as "Russian disinformation."[41]

It seems Barr, too, was burying evidence of the Biden family's crimes. When a confidential source claimed that Biden had demanded $5 million from the chairman of Burisma—the Ukrainian energy company paying his son Hunter $80,000 a month—Barr sent the information to the U.S. Attorney in Delaware.[42] As a DOJ man, Barr would know that no Delaware prosecutor would risk his career tangling with the political dynasty that had dominated the state's politics for nearly a decade.

"No rational person would send evidence of Hunter Biden's corruption to Delaware to be investigated and prosecuted," says the former senior DOJ official who worked in the Trump administration. "U.S. Attorneys in blue states have very close ties to Democratic senators, and that was true even under Trump. Hunter Biden was a sprawling crime spree from coast to coast. That evidence could have been sent to a red state U.S. Attorney to prosecute for some misdeed with a nexus to that jurisdiction."

When Biden cited the 51 spies letter to deflect attention from his son's corruption during the October debate with Trump, Barr said he was shocked. "To suggest it was Russian disinformation," he said later, "was just an outright lie to the American people."[43] But Barr said nothing publicly at the time.

His Justice Department had the laptop and Barr knew it was authentic. And yet the FBI was briefing the same lie about Russian disinformation to anyone who would listen. The Foreign Interference Task Force had been prepping social media companies for nearly a year to expect another Russian disinformation campaign. "There were eighty

FBI agents in that unit working on foreign disinformation," says Kash Patel. "It was about a presidential election, so it would require authorization from the FBI director and the attorney general. Barr knew."

Barr could not have missed the media reports. A *Washington Post* story published a day after the laptop story dropped claimed that it was the product of an "influence operation by Russian intelligence" and that U.S. officials had been briefing White House officials since December.[44] Where had Barr been all that time? How could he have been *shocked* Biden would use the same false narrative teed up by the FBI a year in advance and repackaged by the CIA as an ad hoc intelligence assessment? Director of National Intelligence John Ratcliffe said publicly that there was no evidence to support the claim the laptop was a Russian operation, but the attorney general kept silent.[45]

At the same time, the FBI was showcasing another anti-Trump instrument, one meant to color the election and shape the environment after it.

On October 8, Michigan governor Gretchen Whitmer announced the arrests of fourteen members of a local militia called the Wolverine Watchmen who had allegedly plotted to kidnap and assassinate her. Biden congratulated the FBI and turned the narrative against his opponent—"there is a through line from President Trump's dog whistles and tolerance of hate, vengeance, and lawlessness to plots such as this one," said Biden.[46]

Finally, evidence had materialized to support the claims made by TIP and others that Trump had urged his supporters to resort to violence. The timing, a month before the election, was perfect and so was the location, a swing state Biden needed for victory. In fact, it was too perfect—it turned out the FBI that had hatched the plot.

The evidence, as defense lawyers later wrote, "establishes that government agents and informants concocted, hatched, and pushed this 'kidnapping plan' from the beginning, doing so against defendants who explicitly repudiated the plan." And "when the government was faced with evidence showing that the defendants had no interest in a kidnapping plot, it refused to accept failure and continued to push its plan."

FBI whistleblower Stephen Friend was part of a SWAT team tasked to help the FBI's Detroit field office arrest suspects in the Whitmer plot.

"It was represented to us as a big domestic terrorism takedown," Friend tells me. "We had an informant in place who had brought this to us and we were told they're going to kidnap her, they're going to have a show trial, and they're going to execute her."

Friend remembers the briefing he got the night before the arrest. "It was unlike any other briefing we had—we didn't just get a picture of the subject, a driver's ID or something like that, which is what we usually got. We got video of these guys training, which was very odd. And the briefers were describing them as 'near-peer.' I'd never heard that term before, none of us had. It meant these guys have tactical abilities, tools, and they are squared away like they are equal in ability to us. Meaning, if we get into a gunfight, it's not like we're guaranteed to win. So that set a tone within the room because normally SWAT is a very locker-room type atmosphere with guys that give each other the business. But it got really serious and it was very quiet in that room."

The next day, Friend's team arrived at the scene and discovered the suspect had already been arrested. "The people who came out of the house," says Friend, "were an elderly gentleman and two teenagers. We pulled them out, secured them. Normally in the ops plan once the area is secure, we just turn it over to evidence teams. But they said we had to be there. They said that these guys were a huge network, they had encrypted communications, and if any one of them was apprehended by law enforcement or had any sort of contact with law enforcement, they would be able to send out a distress signal. And then these guys had arranged predetermined locations to respond to because this was like the final fight. And they said we had to maintain security outward bound from the house we were at because these guys were going to show up and engage us in a gunfight."

Of course, none of that happened. Instead, the case began to fall apart when one of the FBI's lead agents on the case was arrested for assaulting his wife after a swinger's party.[47] Another agent used news of the operation to drum up business for his side gig, a private security firm.[48]

Eventually it became clear that there were so many agents and informants prodding the Wolverine group that the entire Whitmer kidnapping was a set-up. But with a month before the election, the FBI had achieved its goal—to stage an operation showing that Trump supporters were violent extremists who kidnapped and killed their political opponents.

"I felt betrayed," says Friend. "I was like, you guys used me. You geeked me up worse than I've ever been in my entire SWAT career. I was 100 percent convinced that I was going to wind up shooting somebody. And I felt like they might have geeked us up to actually get into a fight that was completely unnecessary. I put that in my back pocket because it showed the FBI's willingness to operate outside protocols and procedures. And it was with the Whitmer case in the background that I got concerned about exactly what happened on January 6."

Indeed, the Whitmer kidnapping hoax was a dress rehearsal for the outrageous abuses and mass incarceration set into motion by the fateful January protest at the U.S. Capitol.

8

DISAPPEARING THE OPPOSITION

The Democrats were right. Through Rosa Brooks' Transition Integrity Project, party bosses messaged to the media and other operatives to prepare in advance of November 3 that there was no such thing as Election Day anymore. And, on the night of November 3, voters—especially Trump voters—learned this was true.

The ballot count lasted several days, with most media organizations declaring victory for Biden on Saturday after results from Pennsylvania put him ahead of Trump by more than 30,000 votes. The delay showed that the "Red-Mirage Blue-Shift" was real. What looked like a Trump victory in the late afternoon of Election Day 2020 melted into the autumn evening. And in short time, something like poison filled the American air.

What happened? Some Trump deputies and GOP influencers said it was the voting machines, but the main problem had been publicized by the Democrats themselves for more than half a year—it was the new Covid voting procedures. That is why DHS' cyberunit CISA was censoring social media posts questioning the integrity of mail-in voting, drop-off boxes, and other new procedures that facilitated ballot fraud. And it is why Brooks and TIP warned it might take days, maybe weeks, or even months before a winner would be declared. If the source of the problem was just the voting machines, there would be little if any delay, since presumably votes could be altered instantly. There was no more Election Day because of how long it takes for Democrats to assemble enough mail-in ballots to make their candidate the winner.

Only seventeen percent of Biden voters voted in person on Election Day, compared to thirty-seven percent of Trump supporters. A whopping fifty-eight percent of Biden's votes came by absentee or mail-in ballot, which means forty-seven million of Biden's eighty-one million votes were harvested before the election. Presumably most, or at least many, of those votes were genuine and lawful, but there was, and is, no way to know.[1] The new voting system was designed to make it hard, if not impossible, to prove fraud.

Before Covid, states required voters to file a request for a mail-in ballot and sign it. That signature was the baseline against which to check the signature on the final ballot. It was hardly a foolproof method, but it was something. The new voting procedures eliminated even that. Rather than requiring voters to submit their signed requests, state election officials just mailed out ballots to everyone registered to vote, which meant there was no baseline signature for comparison. And then, depending on the state, party operatives harvested the ballots, which could be added into the mix when needed.

Texas Attorney General Ken Paxton said he had warned Trump in May that he could lose the Lone Star State. Having won Texas by nine points in 2016, the president did not believe him. Paxton told him that if his office lost any of its twelve legal cases involving voting procedures, harvested ballots from any one of several large counties could give Texas to the Democrats.

In the end, Paxton won his cases, and Trump won Texas, but on election night Paxton saw how close his state had come to going blue by fraud. "For the first time in my life election counting stopped in numerous states," he said. "I knew immediately what they were doing, they were figuring out how many real votes they had, just like they would have done in Texas and they were just going to count as many mail-in ballots [as they needed], because you don't know where those mail-in ballots came from, there's no way to prove that they came from the person that supposedly signed it."

The nationwide 2020 iteration of the oldest dirty trick in the election playbook, ballot stuffing, was all done under the color of law. True, no one voted to compromise the integrity of presidential elections by eliminating signature verification, but state party officials across the country did it by fiat, sending out bushels of ballots indiscriminately. No one stopped them, and leftwing judges winked at it. The judges, as Paxton put it, "basically ignore our state law and say 'no, because of covid we're not going to follow state law.'" When there's no ballot security, Paxton said, "I can tell you what's going to happen—you're going to lose."[2]

And that is how it happened, just as the Democrats had been telegraphing for months. The one thing they got entirely wrong, however, was William Barr. It is true that he had said before the election that the new voting procedures were dangerous. "We're a very closely divided country," Barr told the media. "People trying to change the rules to this, to this methodology—which, as a matter of logic, is very open to fraud and coercion—is reckless and dangerous and people are playing with fire."

Maybe Barr feared he would be stoking the fire by investigating the many claims of ballot fraud, or he was scared of being impeached, or he was just protecting what he had built. Or it was all those reasons together. In any case, he ultimately refused to investigate the most controversial election in U.S. history.

EXIT, BARR

On November 9, the White House's liaison to the Justice Department, Heidi Stirrup, spoke with a Barr deputy to ask what efforts were being made to investigate potential election fraud. She was given two contradictory messages.

First, she was told that the DOJ was drafting a memo to give U.S. Attorneys authority to investigate election fraud. Barr's memo, drafted that same day, stressed the importance of maintaining public faith in the voting system's integrity. The memo authorized prosecutors "to pursue substantial allegations of voting and vote tabulation irregularities prior to the certification of elections in your jurisdictions in certain cases, as I have already done in specific instances. Such inquiries and reviews may be conducted if there are clear and apparently credible allegations of irregularities that, if true, could potentially impact the outcome of a federal election in an individual State."

And second, Stirrup was told that the DOJ "looked into every allegation that was brought forward and found no evidence of fraud."

There is little chance that less than a week after the election the DOJ had already investigated every voting fraud allegation. But if it had, what was the point of issuing a directive clearing the way for prosecutors to investigate what the DOJ said it had already investigated? Barr further confused matters when he told her that even if prosecutors found evidence of fraud, no investigation would take less than two years and the election would not be overturned. Stirrup said she was not interested in overturning the election but wanted to know what was being done to investigate the fraud allegations.

The point is that without investigations, without anyone held accountable for stuffing ballot boxes, the Shadow Network would keep using the new voting procedures to defraud the American electorate. But Barr was not budging. It seems the November 9 memo was generated to get Trump off his back and placate Trump voters while doing nothing to investigate fraud.

"Barr was afraid," President Trump tells me at Mar-a-Lago. "As soon as he heard he was going to get impeached, he became afraid."

The impeachment threats against Barr had begun earlier in the summer, growing more intense by mid-October.[3] A report filed by progressive groups claimed that Barr merited impeachment for, among other reasons, shutting down the Mueller investigation and intervening in the cases against Roger Stone and Michael Flynn. Running point on the anti-Barr campaign was Citizens for Responsibility and Ethics in Washington (CREW), co-founded by former Obama official Norm Eisen and funded by leading Shadow Network donor George Soros.[4]

"Barr was so afraid of being impeached," says Trump. "And how do you not get impeached? You don't investigate the election."

Some federal prosecutors did want to investigate, like the U.S. Attorney in Philadelphia William M. McSwain. He said it "was a partisan disgrace" how Pennsylvania Democrats ran the 2020 election. "The Governor, the Secretary of the Commonwealth, and the partisan State Supreme Court made up their own rules and did not follow the law," said McSwain. The State official responsible for enforcing election law, Attorney General Josh Shapiro, now Pennsylvania governor, said days before the election that Trump could not win the election. "It would be hard to imagine a more irresponsible statement by a law enforcement officer," said McSwain, "especially during a hotly contested election."

The DOJ could have investigated those rule changes, civilly or criminally, and at the very least filed *amicus* briefs or statements of interest in election contests in federal or state courts in Pennsylvania indicating the new rules were unconstitutional, suspicious, and one-sided in their impact. But the Justice Department never did.

According to McSwain, his "office received various allegations of voter fraud and election irregularities." He said he wanted to be transparent with the public, but Barr told him not to make any public statements or put out any press releases regarding possible election irregularities. He said the DOJ told him to pass along serious allegations to the same State Attorney General who said Trump could not win. That is, he was told it was useless to investigate.

In a December 1 interview, Barr declared, "To date, we have not seen fraud on a scale that could have affected a different outcome in the election."[5] He told his secretary he would probably be fired for saying it.[6] In a meeting in Trump's office, Barr offered his resignation, and the president accepted it.

Barr later rationalized his decision to ignore the president's concerns. "There's always *some* fraud in an election that large," Barr wrote in his memoirs. "But the Justice Department had been looking into the claims made by the president's team, and we had yet to see *evidence* of fraud on the scale necessary to change the outcome of the election."[7] But of course, the Department did not need to investigate the entire election, just irregularities in key cities in battleground states that turned the election in Biden's favor, like Atlanta, where ballot counting was stopped at 10:30 on election night.

"Barr was a bad guy," says Trump. "He came in, recommended by people that I respected at the time. He did nothing on the investigation of the election and he should have. And we learned that because numerous U.S. attorneys, like McSwain from Pennsylvania, said that Barr told them not to do anything. Bill Barr was a coward."

Barr defended his unwillingness, or inability, to hold anyone accountable for the election interference operations of 2016 and 2020. He said, "There's a growing tendency to use the criminal justice system as sort of a default fix-all, and people don't like something, they want the Department of Justice to come in and 'investigate.'"[8]

But this explanation was flatly dishonest. The problem was not that the public expected too much or that the opposition wanted federal law enforcement weaponized against those who had been hunting them. Rather, Americans had seen the corruption of Barr's own institution eat away at the republic even while he was in charge of it. All Americans wanted from the DOJ and FBI was impartiality and accountability for their interference in the 2016 election. By failing to do that, aside from the single conviction netted by the Durham probe, Barr incentivized the coup plotters to make another run at the 2020 race. It was on his watch that U.S. law enforcement agencies participated in the largest election interference operation in American history.

Barr's reverence for the systems he helped build over decades of government service, in tandem with his contempt for the president he served, had blinded him to an essential fact: the resources deployed to build an apparatus designed to interfere with elections, censor and spy on Americans, and prosecute political opponents, show that the Shadow Network's true goal was not to push out Trump, but to replace the republic.[9] By legitimizing blue vote fraud, Barr held open the gates of hell.

THE CRACKDOWN BEGINS

Those who questioned the integrity of the election put themselves in the Shadow Network's crosshairs. The offensive started with Trump aides, moved on to his supporters, and finally doubled back on the president himself. It was as though the battle plan was keyed to the Constitution, with one right after another under assault—including the right to legal counsel, free speech, and freedom of assembly.

Naturally, the Atlanta election still had the Trump team's attention. Broadcast media across the country had announced on election night the bizarre news that election officials at the State Farm Arena in Fulton County, Georgia, stopped counting votes at 10:30 p.m., ostensibly because of a watermain leak. But that was untrue—a single urinal had overflowed.[10] Under cover of the watermain story, however, vote counting was stopped and election monitors were sent home. When the count restarted a few hours later, Democrat ballot counters were left unwatched. There was also video of what appeared to be suitcases from an external source stuffed with ballots wheeled into the arena for ballot counters to process. This irregularity caught the eye of Trump lawyer and former New York City Mayor Rudolph Giuliani, who pressed for an investigation.

The U.S. Attorney for the Northern District of Georgia Byung Pak was formally put in charge of the probe, but there is no evidence he took any of his own investigative steps. Rather, the FBI fed its findings to Pak, assessing that Giuliani's concerns were unwarranted. Pak failed to investigate other irregularities at the arena like the false pretext used to stop ballot-counting, send poll watchers home, and keep Republican monitors from returning to where the ballots were being processed.

On December 4, Trump lawyers filed a lawsuit against Georgia Governor Brian Kemp and Georgia Secretary of State Brad Raffensperger to decertify the state's election results. The case was not moving, so to get the state legislature to act, Assistant Attorney General Jeffrey Clark drafted a letter that, if approved, would have gone to the leadership of the Georgia state legislature, with a copy sent to Governor Kemp. The letter apparently was shared with the president and debated with others at the Justice Department and the White House, mostly White House Counsel's Office lawyers.

"What the memo recommended to Georgia was very modest," Clark tells me. Regulations prevent him from speaking about his exchanges with the president, so he is limited in what he can say at this time. "Suffice to say, I would never propose a course of action that I believed to be a violation of the U.S. Constitution, a federal statute, or any source of federal law," he says of the letter. "Most claims by the left about the letter are entirely at odds with what the letter actually says."

The December 28 letter he drafted asked about the status of the lawsuit and recommended that the Georgia General Assembly convene to take additional testimony, receive new evidence, and deliberate on whether Georgia should make changes to the set of electors to Washington, D.C, with one set casting their votes for Biden and an alternate slate for Trump. The letter did not purport to order the Georgia legislature's Speaker and President of the Senate to change its electors but, after further investigation, to decide whether to do so themselves.

The memo was never sent. And yet the campaign to destroy Clark began less than a month later, just over a week after he left office. A January 21 *New York Times* article laid the groundwork for the attack by depicting Clark's efforts to give the president legal counsel as a Justice Department coup. Once again, Obama lawyer Norm Eisen took the lead, wrangling federal law enforcement authorities, the media, and Senate Democrats to zero in on the Trump appointee.

Illinois Senator Dick Durbin called for the D.C. Bar to investigate and sanction Clark. The former Georgia official was one of seventeen people, including Trump, charged by Fulton County, Georgia District Attorney Fani Willis for interfering in the 2020 election. Other Trump lawyers charged in the Fulton County case included Giuliani, John Eastman, Sidney Powell, and Jenna Ellis.

The point was not just to punish Trump's lawyers for 2020 and to scare other lawyers away from representing the president and America First causes. The prosecutions were also meant to send a warning for the future. Since Barr's failure to bring anyone to justice for 2016 ensured more election interference and fraud, ballot fixing and other corrupt practices were destined to become a standard feature of our steadily eroding representative government. Anyone who protested could expect to be punished to the full extent of the law, which was now largely a regime instrument to batter and coerce the opposition.

JANUARY 6: THE BIG SHOW

Next came the first large-scale operation targeting Trump supporters, not professional politicians or elected officials, but ordinary Americans whose involvement in politics typically went no further than voting. But then the rules were rewritten without them having a say in it, without them even knowing about it. What happened to Election Day? Why did it take so long to count the votes that had always been tallied in less than 24 hours? And what happened in the hours after they turned in for the evening that caused their candidate to go from being way ahead to way behind? Since they believed that their voices were not heard November 3, they came to the Ellipse, the park behind the White House, two months later to support their candidate and exercise their rights to speak and assemble.

Virtually every leading detail of what that the media reported about the January 6 "Stop the Steal" rally is false, even though they were repeated by top Democratic officials from Biden down.

The Stop the Steal protestors did not en masse storm the Capitol building. Of the hundreds of thousands of demonstrators who listened to Trump's speech at the Ellipse, only a fraction made the mile and a half walk to the Capitol. Of the estimated 800 who entered the Capitol building, most walked through open doors and were ushered into the building by police. Admonished by officers to behave respectfully, most of the protestors inside the building stayed behind the ropes designating where visitors are permitted to roam.

Contrary to what Biden himself repeatedly claimed, Capitol Hill police officer Brian Sicknick was not killed by Trump supporters. He died from a stroke on January 7. But the lie was essential since it was the foundation on which Democrats built the second impeachment trial of Trump. Without alleging that Trump's speech led to a murder, the Democrats would have had a hard time making their single article of impeachment, "incitement to insurrection," stick.

The two people who were killed on January 6 were Trump supporters. Ashli Babbitt, an unarmed Air Force veteran, was shot in the neck by U.S. Capitol Police officer Michael Byrd. After a cursory investigation by the D.C. Metro Police, the DOJ closed the case with no charges against him. Another Trump supporter, Roseanne Boyland, died as a result of excessive police force. Video documents Metro D.C. police officer Lila Morris beating Boyland while she was on the ground.

And it was not an armed insurrection. There were broken widows and scuffles with police, but no protestors brought firearms into the

Capitol, where only one shot was fired—the bullet that pierced Ashli Babbitt's throat.

"January 6 was used to launch a domestic war on terror against the right," says journalist Julie Kelly. "The targets include everyone from Donald Trump to his cabinet officials, his longtime allies, supporters in Congress, and, of course, voters across the country to use the national security state, and the law enforcement capabilities and tools that were created during the first War on Terror. We've seen this unfold much more rapidly than I think we could have ever envisioned."

Kelly is author of the definitive account of the day and its aftermath, *January 6: How Democrats Used the Capitol Protest to Launch a War on Terror Against the Political Right.* She says that when she first started reporting on January 6, it did not occur to her that it was an inside job. Indeed, at first, like most Americans outside the coastal bubble, the protest seemed to her like a milder variation of the leftwing demonstrations that had roiled American cities throughout the late spring and summer. Then, as she started to dig into what really happened that day, questions started to nag at her.

"Part of it was coming to the realization that the Capitol Police had played a bad role, including its involvement in feeding the lie about Officer Sicknick's death," says Kelly. "Then they withheld video, and I saw footage of them attacking and provoking protestors."

But the most convincing evidence that the FBI and other entities were fully engaged in setting up the "insurrection," says Kelly, "is the Gretchen Whitmer case. It was a practice run for January 6. In fact, the same FBI agent who masterminded the takedown of the anti-Whitmer conspirators, Steven D'Antuono, was later given charge of the January 6 investigations."

Planning to use an opposition protest to frame Trump supporters had clearly long been in the works. And the many federal informants and undercover agents who had infiltrated the Capitol Hill protest suggest the operation was supported by official channels. A week before the rally, Acting Attorney General Jeffrey Rosen summoned the FBI's hostage rescue team to Quantico to prepare for the event. But activating law enforcement's most elite team—the FBI's equivalent to the military's tier-one special operations units—also contradicts the official story that local and federal authorities were not prepared for the chaos. Rather, it appears they were ready to use overwhelming force against Trump supporters.

"The problem is not just with the FBI," says Kelly. "The D.C. Metro police had undercover officers at the protest. So did the Capitol Police. The Department of Homeland Security had undercover agents there. All these law enforcement agencies sent uniformed and undercover officers to the event as well as informants, so how did this get out of control the way it did"?

The Secret Service also had plainclothes officers present. "And there are still outstanding questions about the Secret Service," says Kelly. "January 6 records and text messages between top Secret Service officials, including the director, were deleted at the end of January 2021. They took Donald Trump to the White House instead of the Capitol, as he had planned and instructed them to do so. Did they know something was going to happen on the Hill? If they did, and he was in danger, why did they still let him give his speech?"

They had to let Trump deliver his speech because that was to be the evidence he had incited an insurrection. And his social media accounts had to be censored to erase exculpatory evidence that he had told his supporters to act peacefully.

On the morning of January 6, Trump posted several tweets urging Vice President Mike Pence not to certify the electoral college vote: "If Vice President @Mike_Pence comes through for us, we will win the Presidency. Many States want to decertify the mistake they made in certifying incorrect & even fraudulent numbers in a process NOT approved by their State Legislatures (which it must be). Mike can send it back!" He further exclaimed, "States want to correct their votes, which they now know were based on irregularities and fraud, plus corrupt process never received legislative approval. All Mike Pence has to do is send them back to the States, AND WE WIN. Do it Mike, this is a time for extreme courage!"

At 1:49 p.m. ET, the President posted a video from the rally at the Ellipse. As the crowd moved to the Capitol and violence broke out, he tweeted, "Please support our Capitol Police and Law Enforcement. They are truly on the side of our Country. Stay peaceful!" He added, "I am asking for everyone at the U.S. Capitol to remain peaceful. No violence! Remember, WE are the Party of Law & Order – respect the Law and our great men and women in Blue. Thank you!"

Two days later, Twitter announced it was banning Trump from the website permanently: "After close review of recent Tweets from the @ realDonaldTrump account and the context around them — specifically how they are being received and interpreted on and off Twitter — we have permanently suspended the account due to the risk of further incitement of violence."[11]

The platform cited two of Trump's tweets from January 8. The first was, "The 75,000,000 great American Patriots who voted for me, AMERICA FIRST, and MAKE AMERICA GREAT AGAIN, will have a GIANT VOICE long into the future. They will not be disrespected or treated unfairly in any way, shape or form!!!" The second post read, "To all of those who have asked, I will not be going to the Inauguration on January 20th."

The company's statement proclaimed, "Due to the ongoing tensions in the United States, and an uptick in the global conversation in regards to the people who violently stormed the Capitol on January 6, 2021, these two Tweets must be read in the context of broader events in the country and the ways in which the President's statements can be mobilized by different audiences, including to incite violence, as well as in the context of the pattern of behavior from this account in recent weeks." Then Twitter suspended the president.

Thinking back on it, Trump shakes his head in disbelief. "When you look at the tweets that I put out on January 6th, they were perfect," he tells me. "The reason I was canceled was because they were so good. Not because they were bad, but because they were so good. 'Go home.' 'Law enforcement is on your side.' 'The police are on your side.' They were perfect tweets. They didn't cancel me because they were bad. In fact, they said, how do we do this? They tried to get rid of all those statements and they canceled me because my statements were so good."

By banning Trump's account, Twitter erased evidence that he had urged calm amidst the chaos. If Trump had not incited a violent "insurrection"—worse than Pearl Harbor and even the Civil War, said Biden—then there was no basis to impeach him, as Congress did again in January 2021, or for standing up the January 6 committee designed to produce evidence to prosecute the president and exile him from public life forever.

January 6 made the left giddy with success. With Trump banished to the wilderness, his aides in legal jeopardy, and his supporters fighting to stay out of prison, the ruling party believed it was ushering America into a period of unstoppable leftwing rule, a permanent regime unafraid to exercise its power. Security services urged private sector partners to join the hunt, and the slaughter was on.

"The FBI issued a geofence warrant for Google and cell phone companies to get the user information from everyone within the Washington, D.C. area," says Kelly. It was effectively a general warrant that applied even to those who didn't attend Trump's speech or the subsequent demonstration at the Capitol.

"Google turned over that information voluntarily," says Kelly. "And as you see in FBI affidavits, when Google turned over information for this cell phone, it's tied to this Facebook account, and this Amazon account, etc. In other words, they get everything on the phone. Amazon turned over information about the clothes people were wearing on January 6. The coordination between the private sector and the government went far beyond what we saw with the Hunter Biden laptop. Corporations actively helped the FBI and DOJ investigate and prosecute their own clients, and mostly for nonviolent offenses."

Bank of America, for instance, volunteered the records of people who used their debit or credit cards in the Washington, D.C. area on January 6. "In some instances, they also handed over records of gun purchases during the previous years," says Kelly. "It's an invasion of privacy that signals a dangerous escalation of the private sector working with the intelligence and law enforcement apparatus to go after Americans whom they disagree with politically."

THE PARLER TAKEDOWN

While disappearing the leader of the opposition and masses of his supporters, the Shadow Network also went after what had quickly become one of the keystones of conservatives' communications infrastructure—Parler. Modeled after Twitter and co-founded by Trump donor Rebekah Mercer, the social media platform was launched in summer 2018. It started small, but as more users felt the heavy hand of Twitter and Facebook censorship, it began to grow. By late spring 2020, prominent conservative accounts, elected officials, journalists, and influencers began to migrate to Parler. They were shepherded there by former New York City policeman, secret service agent, author, commentator, and podcast host Dan Bongino.[12]

"Dan was one of the pioneers of podcasting," says Devin Nunes. "He was creative and was the first to really take Russiagate seriously and investigate it on his show. So when he talked about Parler on air, and then I saw what he was doing on the platform, I jumped on, and within only a few months in mid-2020 I had 400,000 followers."

"We were the first real momentum-building microblog platform that didn't mass censor conservative thought," Bongino tells me. "When I jumped on board, Parler had only a fraction of the user base it would have through my efforts to build this parallel communication system out in this parallel economy. We were closing in somewhere around 15 to 20 million users. It was becoming the go-to spot."

Bongino's relationship with Parler would eventually include an equity stake. The platform was shaking up the communications ecosystem, and the left panicked. "The one thing the left can't have is an honest debate because they'll lose," says Bongino. "So if the battlefield isn't tilted in their direction, they freak out, and Parler really scared the hell out of them. So it became their focus. I've never seen anything like it. The stuff that was happening to Parler was relentless. It seemed like a coordinated assault. Behind the scenes, it was a thousand times worse than what it looked like. It was like something you would see in a movie about gulags and the Soviet Union. We couldn't believe it was happening."

In the months leading up to the election, Parler had set itself apart. As Twitter and Facebook began censoring posts about, among other topics, Covid, the new voting procedures, and the Hunter Biden laptop, Parler stuck by its free-speech principles. In the week following Election Day, it was downloaded nearly a million times. After Twitter banned Trump on January 8, it was the most downloaded app from the Apple Store. That was enough for the Shadow Network.

The leftwing press and other activists accused Parler of breeding the culture that led to the January 6 "insurrection," and Big Tech giants stepped in to deny the company service. "We looked at the incitement of violence that was on there [Parler]," said Apple CEO Tim Cook, "and we don't consider that free speech and incitement of violence has [sic] an intersection."[13] He pulled Parler from the Apple Store, Google removed the app from its PlayStore, and Amazon Web Services, announcing that the company represented "a very real risk to public safety," pushed it off its servers and thus off the internet. Firms responsible for Parler's two-factor authentication, identity management service, and database also cut off the company.

Parler was finished. The platform would later return in various forms and under new leadership, but for all practical purposes it was gone. The Shadow Network showed it could not only censor speech on the platforms it controlled but could also destroy companies that did not abide by its demands to silence and censor the opposition.

Bongino says he was not surprised. "Other people at Parler didn't see it coming," he says. "We warned them about it repeatedly, and that it was only a matter of time before the guillotine came out."

He had known early on that Parler would come under attack. "I just didn't anticipate them to do it so publicly," he says. "You had people like AOC and Ro Khanna calling for Parler after January 6—despite us having nothing whatsoever to do with January 6—you had them openly calling for us to be deplatformed. And I thought to myself, 'In a republic, isn't that kind of dangerous? You're taking on risk.' They just didn't care because they knew they'd be protected by the leftwing media. And that was what disturbed me most. Not that liberals are commies. That's fairly obvious. It's that they're open commies and they suffered no ramifications for it whatsoever."

Nonetheless, the demolition of Parler showed the opposition what it needed to do going forward to harden its communications infrastructure.

"It wasn't good enough to just own a microblog that values free speech," says Bongino. "It told me you needed the servers, the financial processing backbone, the video capabilities, all of this, because the left—you have to understand that the modern left, they're actual communists—they don't believe in rights. They don't believe in free speech. They don't believe in debate. They believe in one thing, and that's power. They will always try to censor, to maintain power. They'll poke and prod until they find a weak point. And if they can't take down the microblog, they'll take down the servers. If they can't take down the servers, they'll take down the financial processor. If they can't take down the financial processor, they'll go for the bank. I think we underestimated how genuinely evil the left really is."

And that was the other unexpected benefit from January 6. With its quasi-orgiastic public celebration of power, the Shadow Network surfaced, if only briefly, nodes of power previously undisclosed—institutions and individuals, from Norm Eisen and Tim Cook to the Secret Service and Bank of America. Up until then, only those within its structures had understood their significance. But by openly joining in the war against the republic, they had inadvertently added detail to a map that would prove invaluable to the opposition.

NATION IN DISTRESS

FBI Director Christopher Wray wanted to assure Americans that his agency "had deployed every single tool at its disposal and its full arsenal of investigative resources" to target their families, friends, neighbors, and fellow citizens who exercised their right to free speech and free assembly on January 6. "This ideologically motivated violence," he told a Senate committee, "underscores the symbolic nature of the National Capital Region and the willingness of Domestic Violent Extremists to travel to events in this area and violently engage law enforcement and their perceived adversaries."[14]

The FBI's post-January 6 operations were intended to terrorize the opposition into silence. Dissidents would continue to be prosecuted, and anyone foolish enough to organize in the "National Capital Region"—that is, Barack Obama's center of operations—would have their lives ruined, just like January 6 defendants. Here, the Shadow Network's political program, to shatter the opposition, intersected with the professional ambitions of Washington's permanent bureaucracy.

As the U.S. had begun to downsize its presence in the Middle East, national security bureaucrats and their parasitical private sector partners saw that the industry that had made them rich was now at risk. Counterterrorism is a multi-billion-dollar Beltway business, filling a trough that feeds Republican and Democratic constituencies including the State Department, the FBI and other spy services, as well as defense contractors, NGOs and think-tanks. The "insurrection" reinvigorated the industry, easily adapting to the new model with counterterror experts plugging in the same keywords—radicalization, self-radicalization, lone wolves, etc.—for what is essentially the same enterprise, except that instead of fighting dangerous terrorists abroad, they are targeting Trump supporters. What Wray called "domestic violent extremism" is a fiction contrived to frame the political right as terrorists and increase FBI budgets.

"In our office in Daytona, for instance, there were no legitimate domestic terror threats," says former FBI agent Stephen Friend. "There were no active cases that were any good. The most that they were doing was like the Whitmer case. My first day in Daytona they gave me this case with these guys that just lived in the backwoods. They hadn't done anything. A tip came that these guys might be domestic terrorists, but there was nothing to it. And I wanted to close it, and then supervisors were insisting, 'no, we should get an undercover or an informant to go bump these guys and see if they'll sell us a weapon and then we could charge them with a gun crime.' And I said, 'that's entrapment, and I'm not interested in doing that.'"

For the FBI, January 6 was a bonanza. It let Wray and FBI leadership boost the nearly non-existent numbers of domestic terrorists to thousands in order to please their political masters and strengthen their hand in bureaucratic battles. With a live-action example of domestic violent extremism in the nation's capital playing out on broadcast media around the world, FBI leadership had what it needed to press Congress to cough up more money.

"January 6 happens in Washington D.C., so the Washington field office would have responsibility for that case," says Friend. "And then typically that office would open one case. And you investigate the subjects you want to investigate and if they don't live in Washington D.C., as most of the Jan 6 people didn't, it wouldn't make sense to hop on a plane to go interview them. You would cut a lead, and an agent in the office where the subject is located would go do the interview."

But that is not what happened with the January 6 cases, says Friend. "They stood up a task force in Washington, D.C. which was doing the investigative actions. So these tips would come in by the hundreds and the thousands with the directive to field offices to open a case on these people. And we did it for every single person."

By making the field offices open separate cases, the FBI turned January 6 into thousands of cases, one opened for every investigative subject. Spreading those cases around the country is how the FBI cooked its books so it could pronounce rightwing extremism as the number one threat to U.S. national security. The fact is that most of the January 6 cases were not even domestic terrorism cases.

"All the January 6 cases are either one of two things," says Friend. "They're either 266, which means domestic terrorism, but the lion's share of them are 176, which is a criminal charge, parading and rioting. But those riot charges are being investigated by joint terrorism task forces, and they're being called domestic terrorist cases for statistical reasons. They're juking the numbers. But people don't know that. They think, 'January 6, oh that's domestic terrorism.' They're not, not even by the way the FBI treated it."

When Friend pointed out to his supervisors that they were violating FBI procedures, they turned on him.

"They said that I was a simp for January 6," Friend recalls, "but I said, 'you have righteous cases here if somebody was engaging in violence, but as a matter of disclosure, you have to turn over Brady material [information favorable to the defendant] that you departed from your own rules. If the defense finds out about that, that's a bad black eye for us. What if the guy is a really bad dude and now you lost because you were so hellbent on hitting your numbers that you violated your own protocols and now he walks'? And they said to me, 'Well, Steve, we're not losing any of the cases.'"

And indeed, that was true. The DOJ has won convictions against nearly every January 6 defendant who has come before a Washington,

D.C. jury. And that is another reason why federal law enforcement made all its cases out of a jurisdiction that votes overwhelmingly Democrat. It is still unclear, however, when citizens on the left first resolved to punish fellow Americans for voting differently.

Between the Whitmer case and January 6, Friend's misgivings started to grow. When he was assigned to transport a January 6 suspect, he spoke out. "They were going to send a SWAT team, arrest him, and then my job was to take him from where we arrested him to court and drop him off. I said, 'This isn't fair, and this is dangerous. We're sending SWAT teams to guys' houses that said they'd cooperate. The guy said 18 months ago that he would cooperate, and you have no contact with him for a year and a half, and now you send a SWAT team to his house? He has no expectation that you're coming. There's lots of different ways you can bring him into custody. You guys are a hammer looking for a nail.'"

Friend's superiors couldn't understand why it mattered to him. "I said, 'You gave me training on identifying if I think that we're doing things the wrong way and I'm throwing the flag,' and they said, 'yeah, you have an oath of office, you have training, but your real duty is to the FBI, and you follow orders and do what you're told. What's your problem with it? And I just said we're supposed to be part of something bigger than that."

That was it for Friend. In 2022, he became an FBI whistleblower after making protected disclosures to Congress about the FBI's manipulative investigations of January 6 protestors. What had once been the world's premier law enforcement agency had become an arm of the ruling party, a homegrown version of a Soviet-style internal security service, an American Stasi serving not the people it was sworn to protect but the regime that funded and armed it. Thousands of Americans were swept up in the nationwide January 6 dragnet, detained for months, then years, their charges being bulked out with years-long sentencing enhancements. Many were broken by it, like Matthew Perna, a 37-year-old from Sharpsville, Pennsylvania.

"Matt decided to go to the Stop the Steal rally because he wanted to be part of what he thought was going to be a historic celebration," says his aunt Geri Perna. "He did not believe that the election results were going to be certified. And he felt that by joining this huge crowd, they would be heard, and something unprecedented would take place. And actually, something unprecedented did take place, and Matt got caught up in it."

Videotape shows that Perna walked into the Capitol through open doors past five Capitol Police officers. He held his cell phone aloft to record the events. He walked around for less than 15 minutes, then left through a different door.

"He went back to his hotel room and did a live Facebook feed where he talked about the day," says his aunt. "He was upset that Pence certified the vote and Biden was named President. He said it's not over yet. He meant that there will be investigations and that the truth will eventually come out."

Geri Perna tells me she was at home in Florida a week or so after and saw a Facebook post saying the FBI was looking for people who had attended the rally. "I clicked on the link and I was shocked to see my nephew's picture as one of the people that was wanted," she says. "And I let my family know. My brother visited Matt at 6:00 that morning and Matt already knew about it. He honestly didn't think he did anything wrong. He didn't hurt anybody, didn't steal anything, he didn't break anything."

He called the local FBI field office and explained who he was. The FBI made an appointment to visit him the following day. "Two officers showed up to question him about what happened," says Geri Perna. "He told them everything. Matt did not have an attorney because he thought this was just a mistake. And the FBI left that day giving Matt the impression that they had everything they needed."

When she heard about the meeting with the FBI, she got on a plane to Pennsylvania to see Matt. "We got an attorney," she says. "The FBI called, and they said they had a few more questions, and they showed up with five more officers and that's when they arrested Matt. They searched his home, confiscated his laptop and all his phones. They took him to the local office in New Castle, and they booked him then released him three hours later. They took the sweatshirt that he was wearing that day that said 'Make America Great Again' as evidence, and that was when the nightmare began."

Perna's attorney told him that he had nothing to worry about. He had no record, and all they would do was give him a slap on the wrist. "About ten days later," says Geri Perna, "they added the obstruction charge to over 200 of the defendants at the time, and Matt was one of them. And that's when everything got ugly. And this just began a series of postponements and delays. And Matt was constantly worried, what were they going to find? And every time there was a hearing, it got canceled and then postponed indefinitely. Matt's mental state began to deteriorate. He saw how many more people were being arrested and charged with very serious crimes and taken to the D.C. jail. Matt had guilty feelings because he was not in jail and other people were. Time was wearing on, the cases kept mounting, Christmas was approaching, and Matt had become a recluse in his home. He was always a healthy eater. He was now eating destructively. He just didn't care anymore."

Perna told his attorney that he wanted it to end as quickly as possible. The attorney told him that the quickest way to make it end would be to plead guilty.

"They weren't offering to drop any of the charges," says Geri Perna. "The lawyer told them that he was looking at a six- to twelve-month federal prison camp, with minimum security. Matt agreed to this. His late father suffered from Parkinson's disease, and they were going to use the fact that Matt was his caregiver to maybe get the sentence reduced to house arrest. That's what they were hoping."

On December 17, 2021, Perna pleaded guilty to obstruction of Congress, a felony, and three related misdemeanor charges.[15]

"His sentencing hearing was scheduled for March the third and a week before he called his attorney, and he said, 'I have a very bad feeling about my sentencing hearing being on March 3rd,'" she says. "That is the day his mother died. And honestly, I don't believe any of these dates are coincidental. They are playing with these people's minds. They are torturing them mentally, and Matt just did not want to have the hearing on that date."

His attorney told him that his hearing was postponed, but the prosecution was planning to ask the judge to add a sentencing enhancement, which could increase the sentence by many years.

"We later learned that Matt told his friend that he was looking at nine years. That just broke, Matt," says his aunt. "He called me sobbing on the phone. I could barely understand him. He could barely put a sentence together. He was stuttering. He was sobbing and he was apologizing over and over to me about how this impacted my friendships and how much guilt this poor kid felt for bringing our name into the newspapers. I kept telling him, 'don't worry, Matt. We're going to tackle this. And you have to have faith.' I think they had at this point convinced him that he deserved whatever they gave him. That Friday afternoon, early evening, my brother called me and told me to book a plane ticket because Matt had just hanged himself in his garage."

Matthew Perna's funeral was held March 2, 2022 in Hermitage, Pennsylvania. "We had an honor guard that requested to be there for the viewing the night before and then for the funeral," says his aunt. "They did a flag-folding ceremony and they handed my brother a flag, and my brother was confused and he said, 'I don't understand. Matt wasn't in the military. Aren't these funerals normally reserved for veterans?' And they told him, 'In our eyes, Matt was a bigger patriot than most of the veterans we've ever stood guard over.'"

The partisans in the FBI had driven a patriot, a good man, to despair. "We found out after he died about all of these amazing random acts of kindness that he did for people," she says. "People showed up at the funeral and told us about all the things he did. There was a family with a bunch of kids who'd been in a restaurant one day and Matt picked up the bill for them."

"I made a phone call when I was going through Matt's paperwork from his case. There was a phone number and a name in there for the prosecutor on Matt's case, the one that was going to try to push this sentencing enhancement. I called the number and got the prosecutor, and I said, 'I want to know why the sentencing enhancement'? And he says, 'let me start off by saying that if Matthew just could have waited another month, I don't think the sentencing enhancement would have stuck with the judge anyway.' And I said, 'Do you realize the threat of that enhancement and the jail time that went with it is the reason my nephew took his life'? And he says, 'well, there are many people in our department who felt very bad that Matt took his life.' And I said, 'You and the many people in your department are responsible for Matt taking his life.'"

Geri Perna advocates on behalf of January 6 defendants and speaks with the families constantly. "I don't know how many people have committed suicide over J6," she says. "You're never going to know. I've had three people reach out to me to tell me about friends or neighbors who killed themselves after they saw their picture on there. And you've never heard about them because they never got that far. But what it did to our family has changed us all. The direction this country has taken is unbelievable. And it doesn't seem to have a light at the end of the tunnel. We are a nation in distress."

9

INDESTRUCTIBLE TRUTH

"**D**onald Trump didn't need a new company and I didn't need a new job," says Devin Nunes. "We did this because we had no way to have a voice. We needed a voice, and millions of Americans and people around the world needed their voice back. I would have never left Congress to create Truth Social had they not done all the bad stuff that they did over the last ten years."

The former congressman has been Chief Executive Officer of Truth Social for more than two years when I visit him at the company's headquarters in Sarasota, Florida in spring 2024. He'd left the House of Representatives a year into his tenth term in January 2022. With Trump gone, and Republicans in the minority, there was no chance of advancing an America First agenda.

"People keep asking me why I left politics," says Nunes. "And I have to tell them, 'No, I'm at the pinnacle of it because we have nothing without basic communications. We have nothing. We will lose."

During and after the Trump presidency, Nunes watched with growing alarm as the suppression of conservatives by Big Tech accelerated from shadowbans and biased algorithms to outright expulsions from the platforms.

"I knew it was bad, and I wrote about that in my book, *Countdown to Socialism*," he says. "But I didn't know that they would go so crazy and start kicking people off all the social media platforms like that. Why not just shadowban them? It would have been easier. But they didn't care at that point. They just started banning people. There was a purge of center-right people who did nothing wrong. They just started outright kicking them off after the election."

"It was a dictator-type move," says Nunes. "How fast can we go and purge everybody and cut off their communications? It was old-school Chinese Communist Party, old-school Soviet Union, just flat-out Marxist-style step on their necks. Don't let them breathe. Wipe them out totally. They tried to wipe all these people out. They tried to disappear all these people, and they did. They even disappeared the president."

Nunes understood that the real battle had moved outside of Congress. Nothing he did on Capitol Hill would matter if he couldn't reach other Americans. And the country was lost if Americans couldn't speak freely with each other.

Nunes and I are driving through downtown Sarasota, the jewel of Florida's Gulf Coast. With new residential areas, upscale malls, and first-rate restaurants, the city has grown exponentially in the years since spring and summer 2020, when first Covid lockdowns and then the George Floyd riots drove disenfranchised blue city residents to the south. Nunes keeps an apartment here but still makes his home in the California Central Valley, where he was born and raised.

The first time I met him was in 2017 while he was investigating Russiagate. Then the chairman of the House Intelligence Committee, he was direct, certain of what he knew, determined to get answers to what he needed to know, and never flinched when he was taking fire from the security services and their media partners. He seems even surer now, more definitive in his conclusions and convictions. He has seen almost every stratagem the other side has in its arsenal. Having already proven his tactical skills and talent for improvising and innovating,

Nunes now has a comprehensive view of both the current battlefield and the larger war. He has the demeanor of a man who cannot afford to be surprised by anything, and he is not.

"We're in a very bad place as a country," he says. "There is a war of ideas, of ideologies taking place in the United States right now. I fought it in Congress and really I've fought it my whole life."

A "war of ideas" is always part of a larger kinetic conflict. Whether it was the Cold War or the Global War on Terror, one side, the majority of Americans, wants to lead normal lives and enjoy the blessings of peace and prosperity that generations dating back to the founders fought and died for. The minority is a committed revolutionary faction keen to replace the constitutional order with a new form of government, one that seeks to regulate the thought and behaviors of American citizens and strip us of our sovereignty on behalf of a ruling party, Obama's Shadow Network.

The ideologies they advance, socialism, globalism, etc., and policies they promote, from public health initiatives to race, gender, and climate activism, are a means of transferring middle-class American wealth to themselves and securing power against the majority of the American public. "It's about power," says Nunes. "They control the resources and create cults to control people."

Ordinary Americans are losing the war of ideas because our leadership cannot reach the masses of Americans who need that information in order to fight. "You can't have people's political beliefs censored so that when I tried to talk to my constituents back when I was an elected official, I couldn't reach them or other people around the country," says Nunes. "With Russiagate, I was lucky to get a message out, and we had to fight like hell every single day."

Russiagate was the testing ground. Nunes' investigation of the biggest political scandal in U.S. history should have awakened every American to the threat posed by a federal police force at liberty to target a presidential campaign. "In early 2018 I thought, 'okay, this is all done with,'" says Nunes. "'Here's our report. You guys are all in trouble. You broke the law. There's going to be a major investigation.' The biggest investigation in history should have started. People should have gone to jail—20, 30 people should have gone to jail. That would have ended it right there. And I thought that was going to happen in 2018."

He had not yet understood how profoundly the country's institutions—from law enforcement and the justice system to media and Big Tech—had been transformed. "I thought once this comes out, this is going to change the direction," says Nunes. "Did it change the direction? Yes. Did we expose the whole thing? Absolutely. Did anybody go to jail? No. And because nobody went to jail, they had nothing to fear, so they did even worse. They doubled down. So come 2020, they realized they could take people like me and others and limit or block them so it didn't matter how many tweets I put out or how many Instagram posts or how many times I said, 'hey, look at this report, everybody, these guys all lie and you should go look at it!'"

It was like shouting in a wind tunnel. "The fake news ignored it," Nunes says. "Nothing would ever go viral on Twitter or Facebook or YouTube or anywhere. So you really were down to just a few news programs. And so yes, we fought. We fought like hell and we got to like low forties, maybe forty-five percent of the American people who knew Russiagate was a fabricated hoax. But still, to this day, maybe we're close to fifty percent, but ninety percent should know what it was really about."

Social media is the central component in the left's propaganda campaign, its distribution center. "Social media is so important," he says, "and the left was brilliant and evil to go in and basically take everybody out with an invisible hand. We'd had some success with social media. Trump won in 2016 because of Facebook. Facebook didn't help him, he just used what was more or less a free and open system. He'd go out and do Facebook Live and get 50,000 people, 80,000 people. I watched it in '16 and I said, 'wow, this is real.'"

Nunes says he saw it himself with his own engagement. "I experienced it with Parler in 2020. I got 400,000 followers in four months. I'd never experienced anything like that before. I was reaching hundreds of thousands of people."

With January 6, the opposition's information ecosystem was rolled back to year zero. "Parler was finished. I was on Rumble and that was it. There were no alternatives. All of 2021 I'm in Congress, and I posted to Facebook where I have half a million followers but only get five people to view it. I put it up on Twitter and nobody could see it."

Nunes explains that experiencing that suppression directly, watching his ability to communicate with constituents and others shrink in real time shaped his understanding of the war of ideas. "Maybe you have to go through it to believe it and understand it," he says. "I watched it happen. It's real when you're seeing your real interaction with followers. It's real when your app stops working on your phone because Big Tech companies gang up to ban a platform like they did to Parler. And it's real when you get on Truth Social and you get real followers. So I think there aren't many people who lived it like I did and as President Trump did."

What January 6 showed him was he that couldn't take for granted even the forty-five to fifty percent of the American people he had reached to explain Russiagate. If the tech platforms wanted to shut down the right, while the FBI and DOJ rounded up the opposition for exercising its free speech rights, it could all be gone in a moment's notice—and never return. Protecting free speech was the first and necessary move to defend America from a regime of tyranny.

BUILDING A BEACHHEAD

"We had to build something that was indestructible," says Nunes. "We saw what had happened to Parler. So I knew one of the keys is to make sure you have reliable data centers with a reliable cloud because that's the backbone of the platform."

By "indestructible," Nunes means self-reliant. A platform like Parler that depends on the Big Tech leviathans—Amazon, Google, Apple, etc.—for its existence has to adhere to their ideological convictions or face extinction.

As one of Truth Social's technology officers explains to me in the company's downtown offices, "We are indestructible because our infrastructure is built so that Truth can be hosted on any server and not depend on specific technologies built by the big cloud companies."

As it turns out, it is cheaper to build it yourself. "Sure, the big cloud companies offer most of all those tools for free," says the tech officer. "But they charge for server use, by the hour. For Truth, we developed all the necessary tools in-house, which required time and engineers, but that's more cost-effective in the long run as we don't need to pay those high pricing models."

Many platforms work with the big cloud companies like Amazon Web Services mainly because they offer various tools that make launching a new platform easy. "But the problem with this approach," he says, "is that the platform becomes tightly coupled with the cloud company, and if the platform gets canceled, then they are in trouble. Also, it makes future moves to another company that might offer better pricing or some other incentive more challenging."

Truth Social touched down in Sarasota in summer 2022. Other potential headquarters were Texas and Tennessee but, in addition to its proximity to Mar-a-Lago, there was another reason that made Sarasota ideal. Rumble already had an office there, and the video platform had become a major partner of Trump's social media start-up, Trump Media & Technology Group. "I already had been working with Rumble as a user," says Nunes. "I was one of its first big creators. And now Rumble hosts Truth's servers."

The Rumble office is in a beautiful three-story villa overlooking the Sarasota Bay, with conference rooms named after some of its top creators like Dan Bongino, Dave Rubin—founder of Locals, which

Rumble bought in 2022—and Nunes.

Rumble's 41-year-old CEO Chris Pavlovski recounts to me the first time he and Nunes spoke. "I got a call in the summer of 2020 from the ranking member of the U.S. House Intelligence Committee," says Pavlovski. "And being a Canadian, I thought I was under some kind of investigation. But Devin asked me, 'Chris, if I bring my content to Rumble and I search for my name, am I going to find it'? 'Yes,' I said. 'Absolutely you're going to be able to find your content on Rumble.' He says, 'okay, we're going to bring it to Rumble.' So he brings all the content to Rumble and within two to three months, he has about 300,000 subscribers, compared to YouTube, which he'd been on for like four or five years and only had 10,000 subs."

Pavlovski believes that live streaming and video will come to dominate television. "YouTube is already at ten percent of all viewership of connected and traditional TVs in the U.S," he says. "And Rumble will grow up to be a dominant player in the TV space. It doesn't have the size and scale of YouTube, but we're seeing the same movement for long-form content, like podcasts and live streams. You can look at YouTube and Rumble and other platforms as similar to cable networks that you kind of see on cable television today, and these platforms will have a certain set of content, like some sports, exclusive content, and viewers will be flipping between different apps on their TVs rather than different channels."

"The younger generation doesn't want to subscribe to cable," he continues. "And they're obsessed with the internet, so they already know where to go and find things. And a lot of that viewership will move to companies like Rumble. They'll watch Dan Bongino on Rumble rather than watch the talent that's on cable."

Bongino joined the platform in September 2020 and brought with him more conservatives, talent, viewers, and eventually financers. By May 2021, Rumble began attracting outside investors, including Peter Thiel, 2024 presidential candidate Vivek Ramaswamy, and 2024 vice-presidential nominee Senator J. D. Vance.

"We went public in September of 2022 with a multi-billion-dollar market cap," says Pavlovski. "Rumble has a pretty good handle on the conservative space, with influencers and creators, and has expanded into sports and various other program categories."

Still, Pavlovski does not see the company, or its mission, as conservative.

"Rumble is neutral," he says. "Previously all the video platforms were pretty adamant about free speech and free expression and allowing people to speak their minds. Jack Dorsey talked about it, everyone in this space did. Everybody was in the center and all the platforms shared the same perspective, the internet is free and open. But then at some point in the last 5 to 10 years, they all picked a side and moved left, pro-censorship. Rumble just stayed where it was. We didn't move the goalposts. We're neutral, right in the center. We don't take sides and we don't pick sides. We welcome everyone. We just stayed consistent and fair, and we're all by ourselves in the middle."

Pavlovski acknowledges that Truth Social and Elon Musk's acquisition of Twitter has pulled the center of gravity slightly back to the center. "So the free-speech space has gotten a lot more crowded, which is a good thing," says Pavlovski. "There are more companies in that center with a neutral perspective."

He was instrumental in fortifying Truth from the beginning. As soon as Nunes took the Truth Social job December 2021, Rumble started building out the fledgling platform's infrastructure. "When we received investment, one of the priorities was to start building out our own infrastructure, especially after watching what happened to Parler and how Amazon tilted the scales in a way that was completely inappropriate, probably one of the worst decisions in the history of corporate America. It was imperative that we not rely on any of the incumbent Big Tech companies, so we started building out our own cloud immediately. Truth Social became the first company to start using our cloud."

With the server issue resolved, Nunes' next big task was to get into the app stores. Truth Social launched first on Apple. "It took us a little while to get in their app store," he says. "Then it took us an extra five, six months to get in the Google Play Store. And that was because Google was not approving us, even though we should have been approved. Luckily, I was able to use some of my old contacts with reasonable people within those companies, as well as members of Congress, to drag them along. And finally, in the fall of '22 we were approved in the Google Play Store."

Nunes says he is not really going by timelines. The Truth team builds and when the product is ready they deliver. "And we've got everything," says Nunes. "You can do anything that you can do on TikTok, Instagram, Twitter, Reddit even. You can do it all on Truth Social. It may not be as big right now, but it's vibrant. And it is bigger than all of these companies were when they were two years in. All that was built in a short amount of time with very little money."

Nunes explains how Truth recently introduced streaming videos. "That's our next big product," he says. "So that all this content that's out there, that's been hidden by streaming linear TV now gets to come out into the sun. There are center-right news sites like One America News, Newsmax, Real America's Voice that have been banned everywhere. You're lucky to find them. You may have Newsmax on—pick your service that you use, but they're channel 4383 or something ridiculous. I was trying to find Newsmax recently, I typed it in, and it doesn't come up. I knew Newsmax was on there, but it doesn't come up in the search."

Religious channels, says Nunes, are another crucial part of Truth's mission to rescue and restore the canceled. "So we're building all that out. We're building the infrastructure for these people to ride on. We're the beachhead. We have a really talented team that believes in the cause. Without us, everything else crumbles."

FACEBOOK PAPERS AND TWITTER FILES

In October 2021, in order to shore up its communications infrastructure, the Shadow Network made a move against its least reliable tech oligarch.

It was not enough that Mark Zuckerberg had spent more than $400 million on local 2020 elections to help boost Democratic turnout. That was just a fine he paid in hopes of forgiveness for his original sin—failing to keep Trump off Facebook in 2016. The following year, Obama insiders sent a fake whistleblower after Zuckerberg to testify before Congress that Facebook was bad for teenage girls.

The narrative unfolded like a Hollywood drama, its lead a courageous young woman trying to make the world a better place, only to get caught up in the machinations of a large corporation that threatened not only the health of young women but also American democracy itself.

The star was Frances Haugen, an attractive former Facebook executive in her late thirties who passed thousands of pages of internal documents to the Securities and Exchange Commission and the press. The previously unknown data engineer testified in an October 2021 Senate hearing, "Protecting Kids Online: Testimony from a Facebook Whistleblower," two days after her public debut on *60 Minutes.*

Why did she turn on Facebook? Ostensibly because she wanted her former employer to do better. "We can have social media that brings out the best in humanity," she posted on her personal website.

And yet Haugen's work at Facebook had nothing to do with improving the human condition or helping teenage girls through adolescence. Her job was to censor information damaging to the Shadow Network's political instrument, the Democratic Party. She joined the company in 2019 reportedly on the condition that she be assigned to its civic integrity unit, responsible for tracking "misinformation" related to the 2020 election. Famously, the unit censored pre-election reports of the Hunter Biden laptop.

That is, Haugen was not an independent whistleblower fighting to rein in the excesses of Big Tech. Rather, she was a political operative engaged in corporate espionage and information warfare. The purpose of the operation was the same as Obama's November 2016 chat with Zuckerberg about "disinformation"—to warn Facebook to stay on his side.

The anti-Facebook operation was built on the same model as those that had targeted Trump. The first impeachment also started with a "whistleblower," CIA analyst Eric Ciaramella, who filed a whistleblower complaint concerning Trump's phone call with the President of Ukraine. Similarly, the Steele dossier served as the model for "The Facebook Papers," a self-congratulatory exercise in propaganda masquerading as investigative reporting, sourced to the documents Haugen exfiltrated from her former employer.

"The Facebook Papers represents a unique collaboration between 17 American news organizations," according to promotional copy. "Journalists from a variety of newsrooms, large and small, worked together to gain access to thousands of pages of internal company documents obtained by Frances Haugen, the former Facebook product-manager-turned-whistleblower."

Of course, no one had to gain access to anything to participate in a "media event" that merely distributed pre-packaged "reports" to content providers who reprinted progressive talking points as news.

According to The Facebook Papers, the social media company knows from its own internal research that it has a negative effect on the self-image of teenage girls. Yet since a major engine of post-World War II American prosperity is the corporate effort to persuade females to buy things to improve their appearance, it hardly comes as news that Facebook knows that it, too, profits from mass consumer culture.

An even more absurd "revelation" to come out of Haugen's "truth-telling" was that Facebook feared the site is losing popularity with young people. Facebook has not been popular with anyone under 25 since the mid-2000s. It is for older people to keep up with their grand-children's birthday parties, music recitals, and little league games. It is how they stay in touch with friends and others who are semi or fully homebound. Facebook executives have known for years the product is a favored platform for elderly users, and it is the central fact of the company's financial model.

Because older voters tend to be more conservative, there is significant engagement with conservative news on Facebook. And that is why Obama's network regularly circles back to shake down Zuckerberg and remind him who is in charge.

The Facebook Whistleblower op was run by Bill Burton, former deputy press secretary in the Obama White House. Burton's wife Kelly Ward Burton was president of the National Democratic Redistricting Committee, a key piece of party machinery chaired by Obama's self-described wingman, former Attorney General Eric Holder. The operation's financial sponsor was eBay founder Pierre Omidyar. Along with George Soros, the French-born tech oligarch is also one of the major donors to the Sixteen Thirty Fund, a dark-money Democratic party group that spent $410 million during the 2020 election, more than the Democratic National Committee.[1]

Omidyar also bankrolled an operation to keep Elon Musk from buying Twitter.[2] In January 2022, Musk started buying Twitter stock and in April offered $44 billion for the company. After half a year of legal threats and haggling, the deal was finalized in October. Then the Omidyar-backed operation intensified its efforts. One cell sent a letter to Twitter's advertisers warning that Musk's acquisition would "toxify our information ecosystem and be a direct threat to public safety, especially among those already most vulnerable and marginalized." They told companies to "pull your advertising spending from Twitter" if Musk lifted the ban on Trump and other Republican officials.

Another Omidyar-funded organization sent a letter to the DOJ and other federal agencies demanding they investigate Musk's purchase of Twitter. According to the letter, "People in the United States and around the world are watching a single man radically alter this essential communications platform to favor his own personal interests and political views."[3]

Nonetheless, Musk hit the ground running. He reinstated Trump's account, fired half the staff, including the CEO and general counsel, and scored a win for transparency when he invited Matt Taibbi and several other journalists to post and comment on internal documents from the company's previous regime.

Some users, however, were disappointed that Musk had not chosen instead to download documents directly to his platform and let the public sort through them. After all, crowd-sourcing news and analysis is the fundamental genius of the platform, with popular and well-known accounts combining with smaller, sometimes anonymous users to piece together important stories the media is not covering. Nunes, in fact, has often credited the Russiagate corner of Twitter for aiding his investigation.

The rollout of the Twitter Files also produced awkward, and avoidable, errors. For instance, after Taibbi published the first installment of internal documents, he revealed that the company's deputy general counsel was vetting the documents before he received them—that was James Baker, the former FBI man at the center of Russiagate. "The news that Baker was reviewing the 'Twitter files' surprised everyone involved," admitted Taibbi.

That apparently included Musk, who suggested Baker may have deleted some of the files he was supposed to be reviewing. Although Musk eventually fired Baker, it seems Musk had forgotten that he had been warned about Baker months before, when journalist and filmmaker Mike Cernovich brought it to his attention on the website he was buying. "This is who is inside Twitter," Cernovich tweeted. "He facilitated fraud."[4] Musk replied: "Sounds pretty bad."[5]

Still, the Twitter Files exposed crucial details regarding the FBI's 2020 election interference operation, including the following:

- The FBI paid Twitter nearly $3.5 million, apparently for actions in connection with the 2020 election—nominally a payout for the platform's work censoring "dangerous" content that had been flagged as mis- or disinformation.
- In the week before the election, the FBI field office in charge of investigating Hunter Biden sent multiple censorship requests to Twitter.[6]
- Elvis Chan, from the FBI's San Francisco office, was the Bureau's chief liaison with Twitter and other tech companies, and helped "prime" the company to attribute reports of Hunter Biden's laptop to a Russian hack and leak operation.

The Twitter Files also provided indications of the success of Nunes' investigation—the spy agencies were forced to move much of their operations targeting Americans out of the federal government and into the private sector, which faced less legal restraints in surveilling and censoring Americans.

With the Twitter Files, Musk had done more in a matter of months to shed light on crimes committed by U.S. officials than Barr and Durham did during their three-year investigation. The internal documents showed that Twitter had become a crucial component of the national security apparatus. Stripping it from the Shadow Network is perhaps worth many times more than the $44 billion Musk paid for it.

"Elon has done a very good job," Trump tells me. "And he never would have bought Twitter if it weren't for me. Musk is indeed a passionate defender of free speech, but it was the success and excitement of the Truth Social launch that motivated him to throw his hat in the ring.

"I like Elon and I'm glad he did it because, overall, that's good," says Trump. "The other guys were bad people. They were sick people. It's not the way it used to be. I don't know how it's doing. But at least he got rid of that cancer there because those people are cancer. Those are the people we've been fighting for a long time."

OBAMA TAKES OWNERSHIP OF THE CENSORSHIP CAMPAIGN

In April 2022, when Musk first bid on Twitter, Barack Obama embarked on a "disinformation" tour. Visiting two of America's top universities to promote the un-American virtues of censorship, Obama once again waved his hand to announce that he was still in charge.

He first visited his hometown to speak at the University of Chicago conference, "Disinformation and the Erosion of Democracy." Other guests included Anne Applebaum, an early advocate of the Russian collusion hoax who pushed the FBI-contrived fiction in dozens of her *Washington Post* columns. Also in attendance was former CISA head Chris Krebs, famous for congressional testimony in which he contended the 2020 election was the most secure ever.

Obama sat for a live interview with *Atlantic Magazine* editor Jeffrey Goldberg in which the former president sketched out his program for combatting disinformation.

"I do think that the tech companies are going to be increasingly the dominant players," Obama intoned. "They are private companies, which means that they are already making a range of decisions about not just what is on or not on their platforms, but also what gets amplified and what does not. And I think it is reasonable for us as a society to have a debate and then to put in place a combination of regulatory measures and industry norms that leave intact the opportunity for these platforms to make money, but say to them that there's certain practices you engage in that we don't think are good for our society and we're going to discourage."[7]

In short, if tech companies want to stay in business and make money, they must silence those we tell them to censor.

Obama saved his keynote speech on disinformation for the second stop on his April tour, Big Tech's academic research and development arm, Stanford University.

The day-long seminar featured speakers from the Stanford Internet Observatory (SIO), part of the private-sector consortium that teamed up with CISA to censor the opposition's concerns about Covid and related voting procedures during the 2020 election cycle. SIO and the other components of the Election Integrity Partnership had all been rewarded with grant money by the Biden administration for greasing its path to the White House.[8] The SIO and the University of Washington's Center for an Informed Public received $3 million from the National Science Foundation "to study ways to apply collaborative, rapid-response research to mitigate online disinformation." Graphika, a private analytics firm, won nearly $5 million from the Pentagon after the 2020 election for "research on cross-platform detection to counter malign influence" and another $2 million in 2021. Since 2021, the Atlantic Council has received at least $4.7 million in federal grants.

Obama warmed up the audience with a ritual denunciation of Trump and the opposition: "Democratic backsliding is not restricted to distant lands," he said. "Right here, in the United States of America, we just saw a sitting president deny the clear results of an election and help incite a violent insurrection at the nation's Capitol."

Then the former president advanced lies about election integrity legislation written to address the irregularities of the 2020 vote: "A majority of his party, including many who occupy some of the highest offices in the land, continue to cast doubt on the legitimacy of the last election, and are using it to justify laws that restrict the vote, making it easier to overturn the will of the people in states where they hold power."[9]

He likened his American opponents to the nation's foreign adversaries. "People like Putin and Steve Bannon," said Obama, "understand it's not necessary for people to believe this information in order to weaken democratic institutions. You just have to flood a country's public square with enough raw sewage. You just have to raise enough questions, spread enough dirt, plant enough conspiracy theorizing that citizens no longer know what to believe."

Such a statement was especially remarkable for a man who had used the highest office in the land to weaponize Russiagate, the most destructive conspiracy theory in U.S. history.

Then he moved to the heart of the matter—laying the foundations for a whole-of-society campaign to strip fellow Americans of their right to free speech. "I'm pretty close to a First Amendment absolutist," he claimed. "That said, the First Amendment is a check on the power of the state. It doesn't apply to private companies like Facebook or Twitter, any more than it applies to editorial decisions made by *The New York Times* or Fox News. Never has. Social media companies already make choices about what is or is not allowed on their platforms and how that content appears, both explicitly through content moderation, and implicitly through algorithms."

According to Obama, social media companies were dishonest when they "called themselves neutral platforms with no editorial role in what their users saw. They insisted that the content people see on social media has no impact on their beliefs or behavior—even though their business models and their profits are based on telling advertisers the exact opposite."

It was time to hold them accountable. "A regulatory structure, a smart one, needs to be in place, designed in consultation with tech companies, and experts and communities that are affected, including communities of color and others that sometimes are not well represented here in Silicon Valley, that will allow these companies to operate effectively while also slowing the spread of harmful content. In some cases, industry standards may replace or substitute for regulation, but regulation has to be part of the answer."

In other words, he had gone to Silicon Valley to threaten his listeners that he would ruin their financial model by stripping away social media's liability exemptions. The option he gave them was to forget about "neutrality" altogether and work in coordination with the spy services to impose a scorched-earth policy against the Obama faction's opponents. And if they made the right choice, Obama showed, there was money in it for them.

"To the employees of these companies, and to the students here at Stanford who might well be future employees of these companies, you have the power to move things in the right direction. You can advocate for change; you can be part of this redesign," Obama declared. "And if not, you can vote with your feet and go work with companies that are trying to do the right thing."

It was a roll-out for the censorship industry, credentialed by the 44th President of the United States.

"In effect, Obama announced that the funding channels are open for people who want to do disinformation work," says Mike Benz, Executive Director of the Foundation for *Freedom* Online. "It's like what happened with climate change. If you were an academic who wanted federal funding for anything, you made sure you made reference to climate to get grants. Same now with disinformation. Obama was saying, 'here's where the puck is moving, so skate here if you want federal funding.'"

Obama was preaching to the converted. According to a Pew Research poll from the previous year, sixty-five percent of Democrats believed the government should take steps to restrict "false information," even if it means limiting freedom of information, and seventy-six percent believe that tech companies should do it. And it was Obama who converted them through the regime of censorship, surveillance, and election interference that he presides over.

"Once Obama won his second term he was willing to do all the things outside of the norm," says Nunes. "And the small group that he surrounded himself with made a point of going after intelligence. People say that the deep state's been around for a long time. And that's true, but it was never as organized as Obama was to go after the FBI, to go after the military, to go after the court system. They seeded in people at the top. At the end of the day, it's twenty, thirty people that are making the decisions. This is not like thousands and thousands of people that we're fighting. This is Team Obama."

The issue is not the Deep State with an army of faceless bureaucrats just waiting to take a shot at a president who threatens their jobs. Rather, there is a revolutionary program led by a select group of people determined to transform a country they despise.

Nunes maps out the Shadow Network—a circle of Obama operatives and donors that intersects with a circle of oligarchs from Big Tech and Wall Street. "If fifteen, twenty people had gone to jail for the Russia hoax, that would have solved a lot of problems. Even five, but probably twenty deserved it, including some of the Obama people. If the system works right then we're not in this position," says Nunes. Instead, he and his team were again at war.

Nunes says he was not looking for this mission. "I'd rather be with my family," he says. "I don't want to fight. I've been away from my wife and my kids for half their life or more. But these are sacrifices that are being made, because we're in very dark times. So it's not that I want to fight, but I'm not going to sit and take it. I'm one of the only ones who will actually fight. It's not that I enjoy it. I don't enjoy it. I do it because no one else will."

10

THE BUILDERS AND THE DESTROYERS

"Trump is a construction guy first," says Devin Nunes. "It's his passion. He loves to build things, and he loves people that know how to do it. And those people have to work and get dirty. They have to use their head. They have to use their hands, they have to use their muscles, they have to use everything. And this is what the elites in this country don't know—he realizes that a guy with a hammer and some tools is a super valuable person. The people who know how to operate big, heavy machinery, those people have a lot of really important skills. Without them a lot of this stuff doesn't get built in this country. And Trump built so many great things in New York City. You can go see them. He's built them, remodeled them. Look what he did with Mar-a-Lago."

The twenty-acre Palm Beach estate in the Spanish Revival style is bordered by the Atlantic Ocean on one side with Florida's Intracoastal Waterway on the other. It was completed in 1927 at a cost of $7 million, the equivalent today of $120 million, at the time the most expensive non-royal residence in the world. Its owner Marjorie Merriweather Post, the cereal heiress and at the time the richest woman in America, bequeathed it to the National Park Service at her death in 1973 to be used as a winter White House. The government found the upkeep costly and in 1981 returned it to the Post foundation, which put it up for sale.[1]

Trump initially offered a reported $28 million. The bid was rejected, but he persisted and after a financial downturn sealed the deal for $5 million. He turned it into a private club, and unlike many others in the area, he admitted Jews and blacks, and was the first in Palm Beach to accept gay couples.[2] He built a 20,000 square foot ballroom, where as president he hosted world leaders like President of the People's Republic of China Xi Jinping, former Brazilian President Jair Bolsonaro, and Shinzo Abe, the late Prime Minister of Japan.

On August 8, 2022, Mar-a-Lago was raided by the FBI, the regime's praetorian guard. It was the first time the home of an American president had ever been raided. With another norm shattered, among other institutions and traditions, customs and mores desecrated and defiled, the Shadow Network walked the country another step closer to the abyss. And for what? Like every other unprecedented action taken against the opposition and its leader, from Russiagate to January 6 prosecutions, the raid was an instrument to cover up their own crimes.

In March 2021, Biden aides began to sort through documents left in his office at the Penn Biden Center, the Washington, D.C. think-tank bearing his name.[3] Among his belongings was a cache of classified documents from his years as vice president and senator. It was a crime to mishandle classified documents, a crime that Hillary Clinton should have been charged with in 2016. By 2022, framing Trump to protect Democratic presidential candidates had become a well-established pattern: as the Trump-Russia collusion narrative was purposed, initially, to deflect attention from Clinton's use of a private email server, and as the first impeachment of Trump deflected attention from evidence of Biden's corrupt dealings in Ukraine, Biden's mishandling of classified documents was turned inside out to ensnare the opposition leader and imprison him.

For this latest sequence in the anti-Trump plot, another institution was enlisted alongside federal law enforcement agencies and the media—the National Archives and Records Administration, or NARA.

One of NARA's most generous patrons is David Rubenstein, co-founder of the Washington, D.C.-based private equity firm the Carlyle Group. In 2013, the David M. Rubenstein Gallery at the National Archives was completed at a cost of $13.5 million. He was also a top Biden ally who regularly hosted the Biden family at his Nantucket estate for Thanksgiving.

NARA is supposed to be above the political fray. "Its mission is the preservation of historical American documents and Executive Branch recorded information," says records management executive Don Lueders.

But Rubenstein's philanthropic mission involves capturing U.S. institutions to make them serve the Shadow Network's desecration and defilement of American history. For instance, he donated $20 million to refurbish parts of Thomas Jefferson's Monticello home in a makeover that recasts the founding father's legacy as an object lesson in systemic racism.[4] Ibram X. Kendi's titles are available for purchase at Monticello's David M. Rubenstein Visitor Center. Likewise, the permanent David M. Rubenstein exhibit at the National Archives, "Records of Rights," focuses on America's disenfranchisement and mistreatment of minorities.

"It's not up to NARA to interpret documents," says Lueders. "That's what Museums are for." Lueders has worked in electronic records managements at the highest levels of the federal government for more than two decades. He tells me that "NARA's responsibility is to preserve this information in a manner in which it cannot be changed or destroyed. And this has kept NARA from becoming politically partisan." That began to change in the Obama years thanks to Rubenstein.

The Carlyle Group founder appears to exercise considerable influence over the staffing of senior NARA personnel. Its chief archivist

Colleen Shogan previously served as the Director of the David M. Rubenstein Center at the White House Historical Center.[5] Her predecessor at NARA, David Ferreiro, was Duke University librarian from 1996 to 2004 while Rubenstein was chairman of the Duke Board of Trustees. "As Archivist of the United States," says Lueders, "Ferreiro prioritized uncovering records that were believed to be biased against certain identity groups, while significantly diminishing the agency's mission to permanently preserve American history and government records in a secure, immutable manner."

With his tenure as archivist winding down in 2021, Ferreiro struck his final blow for the resistance when he referred Trump to the Department of Justice for a criminal investigation that led to the FBI raid. The archivist told media that he remembered watching coverage of inauguration day and seeing someone carrying a white bankers box as Trump left the White House. The NARA official said that he wondered, "What the hell's in that box?" That observation, said Ferriero, "began a whole process of trying to determine whether any records had not been turned over to the Archives."[6]

But NARA already had possession of Trump's presidential records. "Virtually all presidential records today are born digitally and by NARA's own rules must be preserved in an electronic format," says Lueders. The Mar-a-Lago op all hung on an obvious fact obscured by the media: government records in the digital age, with rare exceptions, like handwritten notes and personal letters, originate not on paper but rather on electronic devices.

"The preservation of digital presidential records is the responsibility of the White House Office of Records Management (WHORM)," says Lueders. "When the President leaves the White House, WHORM gathers up all the president's digital records and accessions them to NARA, where they are permanently preserved in compliance with the Presidential Record Act. If the original, digital records were not already preserved on National Archives servers, NARA should have questioned WHORM leadership, not raided the former president's home."

Whatever was in that box Ferreiro said he saw leaving with Trump was not government records. "According to the definition of a presidential record these analog printouts are non-record documents produced only for convenience of reference," says Lueders. "Final disposition of this non-record material is at the discretion of the president."

Since the president is the ultimate declassification authority, there was never any ground for a case against Trump. Nonetheless, Ferreiro had set the stage for another paper coup.

By May 2021, NARA chief counsel Gary Stern was already consulting with the White House about the Trump documents.[7] Then he began to pressure Trump, writing Trump's lawyers that "two dozen boxes of original presidential records" had not been transferred to NARA.[8] It appears that the only items not already in NARA's possession that Ferreiro had identified were correspondence with North Korean leader Kim Jong Un and a letter Obama left for him in the White House at the beginning of Trump's presidency.[9]

Both documents are arguably personal rather than presidential records, but NARA and the DOJ used them as a pretext to get access to the rest of the documents Trump had taken from the White House. This operation, too, was modeled after Russiagate. Just as the FBI had obtained the spy warrant to search the 2016 Trump team's electronic communications for any dirt that might crash his campaign, NARA used the Kim and Obama letters to jimmy its way into Mar-a-Lago to see what they could find to frame him for a crime.

In January, after months of back-and-forth between the Archives and Trump's lawyers, NARA retrieved fifteen boxes of paper records from Mar-a-Lago.[10] "NARA had no right to claim that material should be returned to the Archives, because they were already in possession of the originals, by law," says Lueders. "This should have ended the investigation because any evidence found after this point should be considered 'fruit of the poison tree.'"

On February 9, 2022, NARA alerted federal law enforcement that the fifteen boxes contained classified information. It was now time to raise the pressure on Trump by taking the plot public. So, the same day, Congresswoman Carolyn Maloney wrote a letter to NARA asking if the fifteen boxes included classified information. NARA officials responded that they did, and that they were in communication with the Justice Department.[11]

The White House told the Archives that Biden would not honor Trump's claim to presidential privilege, and that was the signal for NARA to make a criminal referral to the DOJ against the opposition leader. The investigation launched in April, and a federal grand jury was impaneled to deliberate whether Trump had violated the Presidential Records Act or had unlawfully possessed national security information. The grand jury concluded that "there had been a violation of the law."[12]

The DOJ got a grand jury subpoena to search Mar-a-Lago, and on June 3 a DOJ lawyer and three FBI agents went to Trump's house. He hailed them cheerfully. "Look," he said to the law enforcement officials, "whatever you need let us know."[13] The agents asked to see the storage locker where he kept mementos from his term in office, and on June 22, the DOJ subpoenaed surveillance video footage of it. Now it was up to Attorney General Merrick Garland to pull the trigger.[14]

He stalled for weeks, even though Biden had made clear he wanted his top law enforcement official to bust Trump.[15] Maybe Garland was wondering whether it was a good idea to raid the home of a former president. Or perhaps he was just giving the White House time to move pieces into place for when news of Biden's crime went public. Regardless, Garland greenlighted the warrant application on August 5, and the FBI sent a team down from Washington to conduct the search.

After the raid, the anti-Trump hysteria reached near Russia-hoax levels, with the media accusing the president of selling nuclear secrets to Saudi Arabia, a crime for which, suggested presidential historian Michael Beschloss and former CIA chief Michael Hayden, he should be executed.[16]

And yet inside the FBI, agents from field offices across the country began to flood the ombudsman's office with complaints.

"I've lost just about all faith in our leadership," wrote one unidentified agent. "Obviously they forgot Crossfire Hurricane. If he took documents, give him a call and ask for them back. Like…Seriously? My own agency…A bunch of democrat political hacks up top."[17]

The complaint continued: "While you are at it, please ask them why we break out all the tools to enforce a federal misdemeanor of someone walking through the Capitol on January 6th…but people can violate [the law] every day and harass Supreme Court Justices in broad day light on the news and NOTHING is done about it."

Another wrote: "Absolute embarrassment of the recently formed Banana Republic Bu[reau]," wrote another. "People are threatening us more than usual due to the actions of the few…The 7th floor needs to lead and provide faith back in our organization if it's even possible."

Details of the raid caused more concern in other law enforcement circles. "They sent the Hostage Rescue Team to Mar-a-Lago, which is a tier-one asset," says former FBI agent Steve Friend, referring to federal law enforcement's version of Delta Force and the SEALS teams. "So two conclusions: the process was part of the punishment, and regular agents couldn't be trusted to do the search."

In any case, says Friend, "the Bureau's decision to utilize an overwhelming show of force for a situation which clearly necessitated a consent search demonstrates how the FBI is no longer nonpartisan or dedicated to a fair process. Law enforcement is supposed to investigate criminal violations, collect evidence, and present the case in court. Retribution is not within its mandate. But the raid on Mar-a-Lago reveals the FBI is wholly committed to abuse its processes as a punishment for its perceived political enemies."

At the same time, the government was running Biden's cover up. At the end of June 2022, White House counsel Dana Remus went to the Penn Biden Center to take possession of the material in Biden's office.[18] She must have known how damaging it was because she left the administration within weeks to serve as Biden's outside counsel.

Remus was a longtime Obama ally. She had served in the Obama White House and was later general counsel for the Obama Foundation. Obama officiated her 2018 wedding. In October she joined Covington and Burling, home to Obama's first attorney general Eric Holder, and within a month the White House lawyer who assisted in the cover up was handling the classified documents case.[19]

With everything in place, the White House notified NARA on November 2, more than eighteen months after Biden aides began sorting through boxes containing classified documents. Two days later NARA reported the news to the DOJ, which handed it off to the U.S. Attorney for Chicago, the capital of ObamaWorld, for further review—and to ensure news of Biden's crime would not leak before the mid-term elections. It was not until the second week of January the story was finally leaked to friendly reporters, and Garland appointed a special counsel to investigate Biden's case to make the Trump investigation look even-handed.

But according to the media, what Trump had done was much worse. The difference between the two cases, they explained, was that Biden had cooperated with investigators whereas Trump had repeatedly delayed. But that was a lie. The difference was this: during his term as president, Trump was able to declassify any documents in his possession, an authority that Biden, as a senator and vice president, did not have. Trump was investigated under a false pretext and framed, while Biden used federal government agencies to cover up his crime.

NARA's involvement in the anti-Trump plot is a sign of future trouble for the country's information ecosystem, even more daunting and comprehensive than the censorship in which social media platforms regularly engage. It signals that the Shadow Network is able not only to suppress political opposition but also to rewrite the historical record to suit its destructively transformational program.

"The politicization of NARA will shape future accounts of American history," says Lueders. "Federal records that do not fit a specific narrative, as determined by NARA bureaucrats, can be legally destroyed at any time based on an Archivist-approved retention schedule. At the same time, information that supports the current narrative can be marked for long-term preservation—or even designated as a historical record and preserved permanently at the National Archives."

Even worse is the use of artificial intelligence in managing federal agency records. "The AI solutions are essentially trained to align with their creators' worldview," says Lueders. "If these AI technologies find government records contradictory to that worldview, they are free to mark it for destruction immediately. This would alter the public's understanding of American history forever without us ever knowing why."

TOMBSTONE FOR THE JUSTICE SYSTEM

After the stage was set for Trump's prosecution, John Durham, having been appointed special counsel to investigate the FBI's Trump-Russia probe, made it clear there would be no accountability for Shadow Network participants' previous crimes and malfeasance.

On May 15, 2023, the Justice Department finally released his long-awaited report.

"Based on the evidence gathered in the multiple exhaustive and costly investigations of these matters," Durham wrote, "neither U.S. law enforcement nor the Intelligence Community appears to have possessed any actual evidence of collusion in their holdings at the commencement of the Crossfire Hurricane investigation."[20]

In other words, it was all a lie. The FBI never had anything tying Trump to Russia, nor did the CIA. No one did. The NSA had no signals intelligence on collusion. Adam Schiff lied when he said he had seen more than circumstantial evidence that Trump colluded with Russia. When John Brennan testified before the House Intelligence Committee that he had given the FBI all the evidence he had on the Trump team's ties to Russia, he was lying. Leaks to the press, most likely from Brennan, that European services passed on intelligence to their U.S.

partners were also lies. Brennan's Intelligence Community Assessment that claimed Trump's ascent to the White House was aided by Moscow was a lie. And most consequential of all, Barack Obama used the executive authority vested in him by the American people to credential a lie.

But there would be no further prosecutions. That was okay with William Barr. "I've said all along that's dangerous to get into the business of saying that the standard is how many people you prosecute," Barr said of Durham's work, "because the object here was to find out what happened and to tell the story, to get to the bottom of it."[21] That was nonsense: books are written to tell stories, the goal of launching a criminal investigation of corrupt government officials is to hold them accountable and to deter future crimes.

The report uncovered at least one significant fact previously unknown—FBI Director James Comey had himself run Crossfire Hurricane. The anti-Trump plot had not been cooked up by a rogue band of middle-management bureaucrats like FBI agents Peter Strzok and Lisa Page. No, it was Obama's domestic spy chief who ran point on the Shadow Network's 2016 election interference operation.

According to the report, the Trump investigation was opened at the "direction of Deputy Director Andrew McCabe," and he was acting on behalf of the director. Comey, according to the report, "was getting daily briefings" and "was intimately involved with the team that was working the case." It was "a top priority for Director Comey." According to the report, "the FISA was something McCabe definitely knew Comey wanted." With delays in securing the warrant to spy on the Trump campaign, Comey pressed McCabe repeatedly, asking, "Where is the FISA, where is the FISA? What's the status with the … FISA?"

How did Durham know about Comey's role, since neither Comey nor McCabe spoke with him, and he did not compel them to cooperate? The information came from interviews DOJ Inspector General Michael Horowitz had conducted with McCabe for his December 2019 report on the FISA warrant on Trump associate Carter Page. Horowitz kept

Comey's role out of the report because, like Durham's report, it was part of a cover up, what President Richard M. Nixon's aides called a "limited hangout." That's the standard spy service gambit they employed as the Watergate scandal started to unfold—when it's no longer possible to sustain a phony cover story, dangle some partial truths in public and acknowledge some small, albeit honest, miscues in order to keep the most damning parts of the truth under wraps.

No one was going to jail, no one was going to be held accountable.

Durham had earlier charged Perkins Coie attorney Michael Sussmann and Steele dossier source Igor Danchenko, but even before his final report was issued both men walked out of Washington, D.C. courtrooms without even a blot on their resumes. Durham had also charged Kevin Clinesmith when he found that the FBI lawyer had falsified a government record to obtain the FISA warrant to spy on the Trump campaign. But by the time of the Durham report, Clinesmith had already been readmitted to the D.C. Bar as a member in good standing.[22]

Durham's investigation was worse than a failure. As Devin Nunes told Fox News' Maria Bartiromo, the report "reads like the tombstone for the justice system." And the epitaph: "Here lies the justice system," said Nunes, "we knew there was criminality, and we couldn't do anything about it."[23]

Nunes and his team had made numerous criminal referrals in 2019, and four years later Durham had nothing to show for it. "It's a really sad day for America," Nunes told Bartiromo. The report was evidence that the justice system had collapsed, not just the FBI and DOJ but also the judicial branch. Nunes enumerated only the most egregious examples of corruption in the court system: first, there was the FISA court judge who signed off on the warrant to spy on Trump and his circle. Second was Judge Emmitt Sullivan, who violated the separation of powers when he took it upon himself to prosecute Michael Flynn after the DOJ dropped its fraudulent case against Trump's first national security advisor. And finally, said Nunes, there was the Florida magistrate who had signed the warrant to raid Mar-a-Lago.

It was part of the massive lawfare campaign against Trump that included:

- The May 30, 2024, conviction of Trump in a Manhattan court for matters related to business records.
- The August 14, 2023, indictment of Trump and eighteen others in Fulton County, Georgia, for election interference.
- The efforts by numerous states, led by Colorado, to throw Trump off their ballots for allegedly participating in an insurrection against the United States. In March 2024, the Supreme Court unanimously decided that the GOP nominee could not be removed from the ballot.
- The 2022 lawsuit won by sex-advice columnist E. Jean Carroll, who claimed that Trump had sexually assaulted her in the mid-1990s. She could not remember exactly when, nor could the witnesses she called, but the New York City court system was determined to add its dagger to the bloody bouquet of knives out for Trump.

Crucially, there was also Jack Smith, the special prosecutor named by Merrick Garland in November 2022 to spearhead the Biden administration's lawfare campaign. He brought two cases against Trump: the first, in Miami, Florida on June 8, 2023, related to documents the president kept from his term in office, which was thrown out on July 24, 2024 after Justice Clarence Thomas showed that Smith's appointment was unconstitutional. Smith filed his second case, concerning January 6 and election interference, in Washington, D.C., on August 1, 2023.

As for the special counsel tapped to investigate Biden's case, Robert Hur, he declined to indict Biden because a jury was supposedly unlikely to convict someone they would perceive as a "well-meaning, elderly man with a poor memory."[24]

The America First movement often remarks that the country now has a two-tier system of justice—jail for January 6 defendants, for instance, and get-out-of-jail-free cards for BLM and Antifa rioters. But that assessment is not accurate. In the current system, law is an instrument the regime uses to punish political opponents, while everything is licit for the ruling party. That is, the current system is lawless.

The failure to hold anyone accountable for Russiagate incentivized lawlessness. Without indictments ready before the summer of 2020, Durham and Barr guaranteed that the same institutions, industries, and individuals that interfered in the 2016 vote would be free to try again in the 2020 election. And they did.

The plain fact is that the Shadow Network rewards lawlessness. George Soros pays district attorneys to turn felons loose against American families. Washington, D.C. federal court judges routinely violate the constitutional rights of January 6 defendants by detaining them unlawfully and delaying their trials. When they finally get their day in court, their Sixth Amendment right to an impartial jury is trashed by a justice system drawing from a pool that voted overwhelmingly Democratic and was brainwashed by the press to cheer on the defendants' impoverishment, imprisonment, and in the case of some like Matthew Perna, their death.

By opening our borders to criminals and terrorists from around the world, the Obama faction has effectively erased the Constitution and brought Americans back to the frontier. The founding fathers gave us the law, but without the men of hard resolve who enforced the constitutional order, there was only frontier justice or no justice at all. By collapsing that order, those elected to keep Americans safe have put our lives and property at risk through the purposeful destruction of the justice system and the erosion of our national and individual sovereignty. They have brought the wilderness to our front doors.

Restoring order and fighting off the dark forces unleashed against us will demand the same sort of resilience and courage that built it, the spirit of the frontier.

The Durham report closes only the first chapter of Russiagate. We have known most of the important facts for some time now, thanks to Nunes' investigation. It started March 22, 2017, when as chairman of the House Intelligence Committee he convened a press conference to say he had seen evidence of spying on Trump's presidential transition team. But it's far from over.

Russiagate is the basic template on which all the subsequent campaigns targeting Trump and the opposition are based—from Charlottesville and the first impeachment to the second one and January 6, and from the Mar-a-Lago raid to the attempt on the opposition leader's life. Russiagate, Nunes has said, "changed the course of human history."[25]

It is important to know that history in order to recognize the inevitable campaigns against our security and sanity in the future. Also, we need to know it well enough to retell it or that history will be forgotten. No one else will tell it, and certainly not the media, which willingly served as the essential platform for Russiagate. Without the media, the intelligence services' efforts would have been futile, for how else could they have launched such an operation?

And the education system will not relay this history honestly, either. For the foreseeable future, blue city schools will brainwash American kids into believing that the 45th President of the United States was a Russian asset. And if current trends continue, the official institution tasked with preserving American history, the National Archives, is likely to record as fact the lie perpetrated by John Brennan at Obama's behest—that Trump owed his presidency to a foreign power. There will be little in the standard account revealing how Obama interfered with the 2016 election, desecrated the transfer of executive authority, and delegitimized his successor's authority in order to initiate what amounts to a cold civil war.

"WE LEARNED HOW TO CODE"

Because Truth Social is one of the cornerstones of the opposition's communications infrastructure, it is hardly surprising the Shadow Network fought Nunes from the start. When he became CEO of the newly created Trump Media & Technology Group (TMTG) in January 2022, the company had already signed an agreement to combine with a special purpose acquisition company, or SPAC—a shell company whose purpose is to take another company public by merging with it. The SPAC that would merge with TMTG was called Digital World Acquisition Corp (DWAC).

A few weeks before Nunes joined TMTG, DWAC reported that it was under federal investigation. Several people associated with DWAC were eventually prosecuted for insider trading or fraud. Although none of the charges applied to TMTG or any of its employees, the Securities and Exchange Commission (SEC) used the investigation as a pretext to delay the merger.

"The SEC is supposed to, one, protect small companies like our startup and make sure that we can get access to the capital markets," says Nunes. "And then in the SPAC, they're supposed to protect retail shareholders first and foremost. But the SEC didn't care about either. They should have made sure the deal got done quickly and then go deal with any bad apples. Instead, they punished us and they punished the retail shareholders. They wanted the president and me to walk away."

Gary Gensler was appointed by Biden to head the SEC. He had been Chief Financial Officer of the Hillary Clinton presidential campaign, which paid Fusion GPS to produce the Steele dossier with funds laundered through the law firm Perkins Coie. Gensler later testified before Congress that despite being its CFO, he had not been aware of the Clinton Campaign's payment for the dossier.[26] His testimony contradicted that of former Clinton Campaign President John Podesta, who told Nunes' committee that Gensler "established the financial controls" at the campaign. When asked who would have managed invoices from Perkins Coie, Podesta replied, "Well, at the top was Gary."[27]

"At the SEC, Gensler is at the top," says Nunes. "He's the leader. He's the one who should have stepped in. Plenty of people in Congress asked him to step in and stop this madness. And credit goes to people on the Financial Services Committee like Dan Musa from Pennsylvania, Greg Steube from Florida, and some of the others from the Florida congressional delegation. They just started saying, 'hey, what the hell's going on here?' If there's ever a criminal investigation into these activities, you're going to find exactly what we found in the Russia hoax. You're going to see the same people doing things that they shouldn't have been doing. Except this time, they were manipulating billions of dollars."

Melissa Hodgman was acting director of the SEC's Enforcement Division.[28] She was the wife of disgraced FBI agent Peter Strzok, whose misdeeds and damning text messages were also highlighted by Nunes' investigation, including the fact that Strzok was cheating on Hodgman with Strzok's colleague at the Department of Justice, Lisa Page.

"We knew Hodgman was at the highest level of the SEC," says Nunes. "We know what her husband did before. We know what Gensler had done before. That said, we fought them because we wanted to protect the retail shareholders. And we needed access to the capital markets so that we can go build this company."

The Shadow Network wanted to block the deal. Trump and the opposition stood to gain access to a prominent, censorship-free social media platform. Furthermore, Trump was poised to profit handsomely if the company were successful—just as the left was trying to bankrupt him through a lawfare campaign that forced him to spend millions on his legal defense.

Investors had already poured hundreds of millions of dollars into DWAC as a means to invest in TMTG before it went public. But TMTG could neither access those funds nor issue its own stock until the SEC approved the merger. So months ticked by, and the months turned to years, but the SEC continued withholding approval, dragging TMTG through one of the longest SPAC merger processes in history.

Despite the merger being held in limbo, TMTG launched the Truth Social platform on February 21, 2022. Quickly gaining millions of users, the platform provided a refuge for many conservatives banned from other platforms or simply exhausted by the constant suppression of their points of view. Among them was Donald Trump himself, who announced his return to social media with a Truth Social post declaring, "I'm back! #Covfefe," with a photo of the former president on his phone outside his home at Mar-a-Lago.

In March 2024, two-and-a-half years after DWAC and TMTG announced their intent to merge, the SEC finally agreed to a settlement with DWAC and approved the deal. As Nunes noted, the sudden approval was announced after Republican Members of Congress began addressing questions to Gensler and the SEC about the drawn-out approval process.

The corporate media was shocked to realize that a merger they had long written off as doomed would now move forward. With TMTG having refused to rely on Big Tech for operating Truth Social, instead choosing Rumble Cloud service as its infrastructure backbone, the former president now had an uncancellable platform where he could re-connect with his base.

The press responded with non-stop attacks on every element of Truth Social. They hurled accusations of corruption, influence peddling, self-dealing, fraud, and every other imaginable offense, leading TMTG to file multiple defamation lawsuits.

"About a week before the merger happened, the media suddenly realized we weren't going to get beaten down and defeated by the SEC," says Jack Langer, who led Nunes' communications efforts in Congress and now works at Truth Social. "The ensuing onslaught was amazing. It wasn't so much a series of attacks as it was just one, continuous attack cycle. For a few months it was as intense as during the peaks of the

Russia collusion hoax. There is something about Truth Social that the media really, really doesn't like."

The corporate media's hive mentality was especially evident in one story that is now the subject of defamation litigation. A November 13, 2023, *Hollywood Reporter* story claimed TMTG had lost $73 million since its launch. But the number was wrong. As the publication later admitted, its report was based on misreading a line item from TMTG's financial results, misinterpreting a $50 million profit for 2022 as a $50 million loss.[29]

Still, dozens of media outlets re-reported the false figure. Even with full access to TMTG's public filing, the reporters parroted the initial negative spin without even checking if the figure they were reporting was accurate.

Despite the media, the SEC, and attacks on the company's stock by short sellers—including numerous examples of what appears to be illegal naked short selling—Truth Social is now sitting on nearly $350 million in cash on its balance sheet with which to expand the platform.

As Nunes often notes, based on the fate of Parler, Truth Social built its own infrastructure in a deliberate move to avoid relying on Big Tech. It took the same approach with the August 2024 rollout of its streaming service, building a network of data centers, servers, and routers, as well as software, to keep their independence from tech oligarchs.

"They told us to learn how to code, so we learned how to code," says Nunes. "They told us to build our own, so we built our own. And now Donald Trump is a tech start-up billionaire."

Truth Social is a cornerstone of the new patriot economy, or what Dan Bongino calls the parallel economy—an alternative commerce network whose creators and customers reject Big Tech, woke corporations, as well as government interference in commerce and in the free exchange of goods and ideas. With the opposition deplatformed, debanked, and denied legal representation, and opposition-run enterprises boycotted and, in the case of Parler, destroyed, many Americans are simply opting out, to the greatest degree possible, of left-leaning corporate America. Instead, they are building their own economic infrastructure from the ground up to create a network of businesses and services immune to prevailing political biases.

"We have a beautiful product," says Nunes. "We have a great partnership with Rumble. We have an indestructible platform built all internally, operating globally, and one of the fastest-growing social media sites in history. Nobody grew as fast as we did. I don't think there's any other example even close to us out there, especially with as little money as we spent. Don't forget that. We built this for a fraction of what these other companies were built for. Twitter has been operating for fifteen, twenty years and has never been profitable. Facebook went for years without being profitable. We built by taking the best of all those companies' features, and put them into one platform without political censorship. We have millions of users. We have a vibrant community. We get better every day."

CHURCH OF AMERICA

"I want to thank, in particular, Devin," says Donald Trump. "Devin's done an incredible job. He's very special."

Several hundred guests have gathered at Mar-a-Lago on a beautiful spring evening to celebrate Truth Social. The company had finally gotten free of the SEC, finished the merger with DWAC, debuted on the Nasdaq exchange, and now the platform's owner has a tech start-up worth billions. He has been on the road since 6:00 a.m. campaigning, returning late to Palm Beach. Guests hoped the candidate would stick his head in for a few minutes, say thanks, and congratulate Truth Social staff before turning in to prepare for another day on the campaign trail. But that is not Trump's style. He draws energy from the crowd, and at 10:30 p.m. he is still regaling his guests.

"I gave him the Presidential Medal of Freedom because when I came into office, I heard there's a strange man down in the basement of the White House," Trump says of Nunes. "And he was with an even far stranger man named Kash Patel." Standing on the raised patio behind Trump, Nunes and Patel share a laugh.

"And these two guys were in the basement of the White House for a long period of time, going through documents and going through papers because they felt that the Russia, Russia, Russia Hoax was indeed a hoax. They felt it," says Trump. "And they spent four months in the basement of the White House going through documents. Who would do this? I mean, you have to be a certain type of person to do this. And every day I'd come in they'd say, 'yes, they're here again.' And I thought it was amazing, but I had no idea it was going to end up being so important."

Nunes and Patel get a warm round of applause and thank the president. "Truth has become so important. It's strong, it's dedicated," says Trump. "They will do everything they can to hurt it," he says of the cadres that have been hunting him for nearly a decade. "And what they'd like to do is hurt my voice. But the big thing is that it's such a powerful voice."

Trump praises the builders who launched Truth. "I love our engineers. I think the platform works better than any other platform, and I know them all very well. And I want to thank the engineers because they're brilliant and they're patriotic. So thank you to everybody here. We're going to make this thing so successful. I think it's got the possibility of really being legendary."

Everyone who's been to a Trump rally or speaking event knows the rhythm. He talks about policy and political issues and hits the important points, but what listeners really come for is the camaraderie of being together with Trump and other supporters.

It is a bad time for the country. The people running America, Obama's Shadow Network, are powerful and dangerous and they are waging a campaign of fear against the American people. To Trump supporters, it is self-evident that they are confronted by an evil force.

But no one comes to a Trump talk demoralized. They come for community, the other Americans that Trump has stirred with his message of national greatness, and the greatness of Americans, all of us.

Trump loves being with friends. He turns to singer Lee Greenwood, whose "Proud to be an American" is the president's theme song. Trump thanks him. "That voice is still great. You're amazing."

Jon Voigt is here, too. "This guy did the greatest movies, every single one" says Trump, and goes on to list *The Champ*, *Midnight Cowboy*, and *Deliverance* as his favorites. "Jon Voight is a fantastic man, a wonderful person, and he does things on me, he puts them out on his feed that are so beautiful that sometimes I break down in tears. I break down and start crying," says Trump. "But I'm only kidding. My public doesn't want to see me cry," Trump pauses. "He puts out things saying how important it is that we take back our country."

He sees Sebastian Gorka in the crowd and calls out. "Hello, Seb. This guy is so loyal," Trump tells the crowd and then speaks to his former aide as if it was just the two of them meeting in a hallway: "Everything good?" Trump asks him. "You're doing good?"

"President Trump is unlike any politician in Washington D.C., because he isn't a politician," Gorka tells me later. "And amazingly, despite having been elected to the highest office in the land, and becoming the most powerful man in the world, he very much remains the outsider and not a politician because the establishment still hates him and wants him imprisoned. Or worse. His efficacy as a speaker is a function of that authenticity. When I first met him, it was in the summer of 2015, and I was asked to advise him on national security issues for the primary debate. Within the first few minutes I realized two things about the man: he completely loves America and wants to save it from those who hate it and want to destroy it. And whether you're a steelworker from Ohio, or a former counterterrorism expert born in the UK, you recognized that in him and you want to support him and help him save the republic."

"We have enemies outside and inside," Trump tells his guests. "The enemy on the outside, that's Russia and China, and all the rest. If you have a smart president, they're no problem." But the enemy from within, says Trump, "these people are communists. What we have is an old-style Soviet Union where they go after their political opponents with law enforcement. They raided this house. This house was raided. This house was not meant to be raided."

It's the first time I saw it this way. The issue isn't just that it was the first time the home of a former president, and leader of the opposition, was raided by the government he once led. It was also an invasion of the home of an American man who is proud of his house and his ability to care for his family. He is also proud of taking care of his country and encourages his guests to do the same. "Make sure that on election day, there's no cheating," says Trump. "They have no shame. They'll do anything they can. They are really horrible people who I believe hate our country."

Evidence that more election fraud was planned for 2024 would soon begin to surface. For instance, in August, Pennsylvania's Department of State posted on Twitter: "Pennsylvanians won't always know the final results of all races on election night. Any changes in results that occur as counties continue to count ballots are not evidence that an election is 'rigged.'"[30]

In fact, delaying the announcement of election results is typically seen the world over as evidence of fraud. U.S. officials once saw it that way, too, at least up until the 2020 election when questioning election results became grounds for indicting the opposition leader and his top aides.

For instance, delays in announcing results of the first round of Peru's 2000 election—three days for the presidential race, more than a month for congressional contests, and a "mysterious" lapse in the transport of ballot boxes to vote count centers—got the Clinton administration's attention.[31] A State Department spokesman warned the Peruvian government "to take every possible measure to ensure that the next round of voting fully meets democratic standards of openness, transparency and fairness."[32]

The Peruvian campaign was marked by other irregularities, too, as watchdog groups found evidence that incumbent Alberto Fujimori's operatives had manipulated the media, forged voter registration signatures, and transported pre-marked ballots.

Those sound like the irregularities identified in the 2020 U.S. elections because the distinguishing characteristics of election fraud are always the same. There are not that many ways to rig an election, and it does not take a professional election monitor to recognize fraud.

Delayed election results are correlated not only with fraud but also violence. According to a study of African elections from 1997 to 2022, "The length of time between elections and the announcement of the official results acts as a signal of possible voter fraud, thereby increasing incentives for post-election violence."[33]

Likewise, paused ballot-counts and lengthy delays in announcing results in Honduras' 2017 presidential elections led to widespread violence including seventeen deaths. Here again, the U.S. State Department noticed—the irregularities, said U.S. diplomats, indicated that "much-needed electoral reforms should be undertaken."[34]

So, are Democratic Party officials preparing the way for violence after the 2024 elections? They are certainly talking about it.

Asked by a reporter if he was confident that there would be a peaceful transfer of power after the 2024 election, Joe Biden answered "If Trump wins, no I'm not confident at all." Then, seemingly correcting himself, the president said, "I mean if Trump loses, I'm not confident at all. He means what he says, we don't take him seriously. He means it, all the stuff about if we lose there will be a bloodbath."[35]

Biden was referring to a comment Trump made in March about Chinese efforts to build auto manufacturing plants in Mexico. The export of those cars to America, Trump said, would result in a bloodbath for the U.S. auto industry. Naturally, the Biden campaign used the figure of speech to accuse Trump of inciting "political violence."[36]

In mid-summer, a video circulated on social media featuring Democrat Congressman Jamie Raskin explaining how Congress will remove Trump by invoking Section 3 of the Fourteenth Amendment prohibiting anyone "engaged in insurrection or rebellion" from holding office. "It's going to be up to us on January 6, 2025, to tell the rampaging Trump mobs that he's disqualified," said Raskin. "And then we need bodyguards for everybody in civil war conditions."[37]

That is one violent scenario. But there is another scripted by Rosa Brooks, the former Obama Pentagon official whose 2020 wargaming with the Transition Integrity Project is credited by the press for its "accuracy." Brooks, according to the *Guardian*, "imagined the then far-fetched idea that Trump might refuse to concede defeat, and, by claiming widespread fraud in mail-in ballots, unleash dark forces culminating in violence. Every implausible detail of the simulations came to pass in the lead-up to the US Capitol attack on 6 January 2021." The fact is, Brooks' work is widely acknowledged as the Shadow Network's communications center for post-election contingency planning.

For 2024 she teamed up with Barton Gellman to run a series of wargames in May and June under the auspices of the Democracy Futures Project (DFP), part of the Brennan Center for Justice at New York University. Two opposing teams were staffed by former government officials with large professional networks to read into the post-election operation. Mid-level operatives got their directions on July 30 with the simultaneous publication of several articles describing wargame scenarios conducted months before.

It was a rollout, like the proliferation of articles published about the TIP in the summer and fall of 2020. But with articles published on the same day, the 2024 campaign feels like the July 2016 rollout of the Trump-Russia information operation when the *New Yorker*, *Atlantic Magazine*, the *Weekly Standard*, Slate, and others ran articles sourced to Fusion GPS, the Clinton campaign contractors who produced the Steele dossier. This time the big names are the *New Republic*, the *Guardian*, the *Washington Post*, which ran a piece by Gellman, and Brooks herself writing for the *Bulwark*.[38]

Curiously, the scenarios, at least those disclosed, assume a Trump victory. The narrative is driven by self-congratulatory mirror-imaging and projection where the defenders of democracy face down the steady growth of authoritarianism in a second Trump term. According to DFP's information warfare operation, it is not Biden and Harris who use the power of the federal government against their opponents. No, it's Trump. It is a Trump administration that forces out top military officials. Why? For "objecting to Trump's cozy relationship with Russia." And it is Trump's CIA and DOJ that are getting rid of national security officials for "raising concerns about the politicization of intelligence and the pressure to launch ideologically motivated investigations." It is Trump who will use the IRS to go after nonprofits. And it is on Trump's instructions that leftwing journalists are targeted and Democrat-aligned media outlets are under investigation while the FCC revokes broadcast licenses.

The scenario reads like a paranoid fantasy, but it is really a carefully scripted inversion of reality to rewrite history and obscure the crimes of the left that have laid waste to the republic. Thus, taking purposeful misdirection to its logical conclusion, Brooks writes that "while Team Trump had a clear leader, the opposition was dispirited and rudderless." In other words, no one, not even Barack Obama, the man who has claimed responsibility for transforming America since he first took office in 2009, is responsible for what has been done and will be done to transform America by driving its people against each other.

One Brooks scenario involves political and military officials "resisting efforts to federalize their national guard units and send them to quell anti-Trump protests in major U.S. cities." That is, the post-election playbook calls for widespread violence so intense that the president invokes the Insurrection Act. One iteration of the scenario posits a split in the senior ranks of the U.S. military after Trump replaces the chiefs of staff with officers who comply with his order and deploy forces to put down the riots.

This is where the political violence cultivated by the left is leading. After the attempt on Trump's life, Democratic Party officials and the media denied any connection between the shooting and their inflammatory rhetoric labeling him a fascist, would-be dictator, traitor, spy, Putin stooge, etc.

In fact, some blamed Trump himself. After *pro forma* denunciations of the attempted public execution of the opposition leader, the Shadow Network's media courtiers said that Trump and his aspiring assassin were cut from the same cloth: "The gunman and Trump, at their opposite ends of a bullet's trajectory, are nonetheless joined together as common enemies of law and democracy," wrote George W. Bush speechwriter David Frum.

In other words, Trump has polarized the country so profoundly that he is ultimately responsible for the attempt on his own life. But that account is another inversion of reality, tailored to suit the bloodlust of a dark regime. It is the logic of terror: *it is only the violence of our victims that drove us to slaughter them.* This self-serving logic not only gets the left off the hook for past depredations, but also serves as the pretext for future terror against Trump, his aides, and supporters. *It's okay to target them because they brought it upon themselves.*

But it was not Trump who split the country. Rather, political violence is the poisonous fruit that Obama cultivated with the January 5 coup and the CIA assessment designed to undermine his successor's presidency and hobble his administration with phony investigations sourced to the perverted fantasies of an FBI informant once employed by British intelligence. Lending the U.S. government's executive authority to an information operation contending that half of the country supported a foreign agent to govern the country was weaponized to destabilize America and make its people fearful and angry.

216

These are the products of an elite campaign to demoralize and desecrate a republic: among others, the widespread prosecution of political opponents that was normalized in the wake of January 6; censoring Americans for objecting to the Covid-inspired voting procedures; mandating vaccines and impoverishing those who resisted experimental medical treatments; recasting Trump supporters as domestic terrorists; opening borders to usher foreign criminals into working-class and middle-class communities; convicting elderly women for praying in front of abortion clinics; and dispatching the FBI to raid the home of the opposition leader, unlawfully deputizing an officer to prosecute him, all culminating in an attempt on his life.

Back at the Truth Social party at Mar-a-Lago, Trump is closing out his remarks. "I'm a messenger," he says. He has been campaigning all day and speaking to his guests for nearly an hour. "That's all I'm doing. I'm not a bad messenger, but I'm a messenger, and I'm representing millions and millions of people. I think I'm representing 200 million people in this country. MAGA is the greatest movement in the history of our country."

The Shadow Network is determined, ruthless, and has unlimited access to money and other resources. Still, its victory is anything but inevitable. The America First movement comprises millions of tough fighters, fierce patriots, and brave dissidents. Trump re-awakened something strong and beautiful in Americans—a force that grows naturally from the shared purpose of those who will walk together through fire.

ACKNOWLEDGMENTS

Thanks to all who shared their insight with me for this book. Also, thanks to my editors and colleagues at *Tablet Magazine*, where some of this work appeared previously in different form. Thanks to Devin Nunes and his team at Truth Social. Thanks to friends and neighbors, in particular the Ackerman, Badran, and Richards families, Gail Holdcraft and Glenn Hughes. And greatest thanks of all to my wife Catherine and son Augie.

NOTES

CHAPTER ONE: THE SILENCING

1 Bobby Allen, Tamara Keith, "Twitter Permanently Suspends Trump, Citing 'Risk Of Further Incitement Of Violence,'" NPR, January 8, 2021, https://www.npr.org/2021/01/08/954760928/twitter-bans-president-trump-citing-risk-of-further-incitement-of-violence.

2 Devin Nunes, Countdown to Socialism (New York, NY: Encounter Books, 2020), 59-60.

3 Molly Ball, "The Secret History of the Shadow Campaign That Saved the 2020 Election," Time, February 4, 2021, https://time.com/5936036/secret-2020-election-campaign/.

4 Barack Obama, "Our Remarks at the 2024 Democratic National Convention," Medium blogpost, August 21, 2024, https://barackobama.medium.com/our-remarks-at-the-2024-democratic-national-convention-4b1f8a9dce8c.

5 Kamala Harris, Speech for 2024 Democratic National Committee Convention, https://www.nytimes.com/2024/08/23/us/politics/kamala-harris-speech-transcript.html.

6 Collin Rugg (@CollinRugg), "NEW: Kamala Harris says the U.S. needs to "close the page" on the last decade, prompting Dana Bash to point out that a third of that time was with her in office. Kamala: 'I believe the American people deserve a new way forward and turn the page on the last decade...' Bash: 'The last three-and-a-half years has been part of your administration?,'" X, August 29, 2024, 9:43 p.m., https://x.com/CollinRugg/status/1829334152338174319.

7 Albert R. Hunt, "The 'Female Obama' Tries to Be Just Familiar Enough," Bloomberg, October 9, 2018, https://www.bloomberg.com/view/articles/2018-10-09/midterm-elections-kamala-harris-channels-obama-for-democrats.

8 Donie O'Sullivan, "Kamala Harris calls on Twitter CEO to suspend Donald Trump," CNN, October 2, 2019, https://www.cnn.com/2019/10/02/politics/kamala-harris-donald-trump-twitter/index.html.

CHAPTER TWO: THE JANUARY 5 CONSPIRACY

1 Jim Rutenberg, "Media's Next Challenge: Overcoming the Threat of Fake News," New York Times, November 6, 2016, https://www.nytimes.com/2016/11/07/business/media/medias-next-challenge-overcoming-the-threat-of-fake-news.html.

2 Max Read, "Donald Trump Won Because of Facebook," New York Magazine, November 9, 2016, https://nymag.com/intelligencer/2016/11/donald-trump-won-because-of-facebook.html.

3 Jasper Jackson, "Mark Zuckerberg vows more action to tackle fake news on Facebook," Guardian (US), November 13, 2016, https://www.theguardian.com/technology/2016/nov/13/mark-zuckerberg-vows-more-action-to-tackle-fake-news-on-facebook.

4 Gardiner Harris and Melissa Eddy, "Obama, With Angela Merkel in Berlin, Assails Spread of Fake News," New York Times, November 17, 2018, https://www.nytimes.com/2016/11/18/world/europe/obama-angela-merkel-donald-trump.html.

5 Issie Lapowsky, "Here's How Facebook Actually Won Trump the Presidency," WIRED, November 15, 2016, https://www.wired.com/2016/11/facebook-won-trump-election-not-just-fake-news/.

6 Darren Samuelsohn, "Trump raises $9 million off debate night Facebook Live events," Politico, October 20, 2016, https://www.politico.com/story/2016/10/trump-raises-9-million-off-debate-night-facebook-live-events-230126.

7 Kelsey Sutton, "Trump campaign advisers to host nightly Facebook live show through Election Day," Politico, October 24, 2016, https://www.politico.com/blogs/on-media/2016/10/trump-campaign-advisers-to-host-nightly-facebook-live-show-through-election-day-230265.

8 Philip Bump, "'60 Minutes' profiles the genius who won Trump's campaign: Facebook," Washington Post, October 9, 2017, https://www.washingtonpost.com/news/politics/wp/2017/10/09/60-minutes-profiles-the-genius-who-won-trumps-campaign-facebook/.

9 Adam Entous, Elizabeth Dwoskin and Craig Timberg, "Obama tried to give Zuckerberg a wake-up call over fake news on Facebook," Washington Post, September 24, 2017, https://www.washingtonpost.com/business/economy/obama-tried-to-give-zuckerberg-a-wake-up-call-over-fake-news-on-facebook/2017/09/24/15d19b12-ddac-4ad5-ac6e-ef909e1c1284_story.html#.

10 Glenn Greenwald, Ewen MacAskill, "NSA Prism program taps in to user data of Apple, Google and others," Guardian (US), June 7, 2013, https://www.theguardian.com/world/2013/jun/06/us-tech-giants-nsa-data.

11 Robert Litt, "The New Intelligence Sharing Procedures Are Not About Law Enforcement," Just Security, March 30, 2016, https://www.justsecurity.org/30327/intelligence-sharing-procedures-not-law-enforcement/.

12 Charlie Savage, "N.S.A. Gets More Latitude to Share Intercepted Communications," New York Times, January 12, 2017, https://www.nytimes.com/2017/01/12/us/politics/nsa-gets-more-latitude-to-share-intercepted-communications.html.

13 Andy Greenberg, "Just in Time for Trump, the NSA Loosens Its Privacy Rules," WIRED, January 12, 2017, https://www.wired.com/2017/01/just-time-trump-nsa-loosens-privacy-rules/.

14 FBI, "Statement by FBI Director James B. Comey on the Investigation of Secretary Hillary Clinton's Use of a Personal E-Mail System," press

release, July 5, 2016, https://www.fbi.gov/news/press-releases/statement-by-fbi-director-james-b-comey-on-the-investigation-of-secretary-hillary-clinton2019s-use-of-a-personal-e-mail-system.

15 "Grassley, Graham Uncover 'Unusual Email' Sent By Susan Rice To Herself On President Trump's Inauguration Day," News Releases, Chuck Grassley Senate, released February 12, 2018, https://www.grassley.senate.gov/news/news-releases/grassley-graham-uncover-unusual-email-sent-susan-rice-herself-president-trump-s#:~:text=In%20particular%2C%20Ambassador%20Rice%20wrote,communities%20'by%20the%20book'.

16 Adam Entous, Ellen Nakashima and Greg Miller, "Secret CIA assessment says Russia was trying to help Trump win White House," Washington Post, December 9, 2016, https://www.washingtonpost.com/world/national-security/obama-orders-review-of-russian-hacking-during-presidential-campaign/2016/12/09/31d6b300-be2a-11e6-94ac-3d324840106c_story.html.

17 David E. Sanger and Scott Shane, "Russian Hackers Acted to Aid Trump in Election, U.S. Says," New York Times, December 9, 2016, https://www.nytimes.com/2016/12/09/us/obama-russia-election-hack.html.

18 William M. Arkin, Ken Dilanian and Cynthia McFadden, "U.S. Officials: Putin Personally Involved in U.S. Election Hack," NBC News, December 14, 2016, https://www.nbcnews.com/news/us-news/u-s-officials-putin-personally-involved-u-s-election-hack-n696146.

19 Office of the Director of National Intelligence, "Background to 'Assessing Russian Activities and Intentions in Recent US Elections': The Analytic Process and Cyber Incident Attribution," January 6, 2017, https://www.dni.gov/files/documents/ICA_2017_01.pdf.

20 Aaron Mate, "Hidden Over 2 Years: Dem Cyber-Firm's Sworn Testimony It Had No Proof of Russian Hack of DNC," RealClear Investigations, May 13, 2020, https://www.realclearinvestigations.com/articles/2020/05/13/hidden_over_2_years_dem_cyber-firms_sworn_testimony_it_had_no_proof_of_russian_hack_of_dnc_123596.html.

21 David Choi, "Former Homeland Security head issues fiery statement on the Trump-Russia investigation," Business Insider, June 20, 2017, https://www.businessinsider.com/jeh-johnson-intelligence-committee-hearing-statement-russia-election-hack-2017-6; Department of Homeland Security, "Statement by Secretary Jeh Johnson on the Designation of Election Infrastructure as a Critical Infrastructure Subsector," January 6, 2017, https://www.dhs.gov/news/2017/01/06/statement-secretary-johnson-designation-election-infrastructure-critical.

22 Tim Starks, "DHS labels elections as 'critical infrastructure,'" Politico, January 6, 2017, https://www.politico.com/story/2017/01/elections-critical-infrastructure-homeland-security-233304.

23 Eric Geller, "Elections security: Federal help or power grab?," Politico, August 28, 2016, https://www.politico.com/story/2016/08/election-cyber-security-georgia-227475.

24 https://www.washingtonpost.com/world/national-security/russian-government-hackers-do-not-appear-to-have-targeted-

DISAPPEARING THE PRESIDENT

vermont-utility-say-people-close-to-investigation/2017/01/02/70c25956-d12c-11e6-945a-76f69a399dd5_story.html

25 Erica Hendry, "Read Jeh Johnson's prepared testimony on Russia," PBS News, June 20, 2017, https://www.pbs.org/newshour/politics/read-jeh-johnsons-prepared-testimony-russia.

CHAPTER THREE: THE COUNTERINSURGENTS

1 Dwight D. Eisenhower Memorial Commission, "Dwight D. Eisenhower and Science & Technology," November, 2008, https://web.archive.org/web/20101027163454/http://eisenhowermemorial.org/onepage/IKE%20%26%20Science.Oct08.EN.FINAL%20%28v2%29.pdf.

2 Sean Gallagher, "50 years ago today, the Internet was born. Sort of," Ars Technica, October 29, 2019, https://arstechnica.com/information-technology/2019/10/50-years-ago-today-the-internet-was-born-sort-of/.

3 https://www.youtube.com/watch?v=yVWgnBQBJx8

4 https://www.feinstein.senate.gov/public/index.cfm/2018/1/schiff-feinstein-request-twitter-and-facebook-conduct-investigation-of-russian-bot-activity-in-releasethememo-campaign

5 https://democrats-intelligence.house.gov/uploadedfiles/final_feinstein_schiff_1.23.18.pdf

6 https://www.nato.int/cps/en/natohq/opinions_166392.htm

7 Andrew Weisburd, Clint Watts, and Jim Berger, "Trolling for Trump: How Russia Is Trying to Destroy Our Democracy," War on the Rocks, November 6, 2016, https://warontherocks.com/2016/11/trolling-for-trump-how-russia-is-trying-to-destroy-our-democracy/.

8 https://avalon.law.yale.edu/18th_century/fed68.asp

9 Josh Rogin, "National Security Figures Launch Project to Counter Russian Mischief," Washington Post, July 11, 2017, https://www.washingtonpost.com/news/josh-rogin/wp/2017/07/11/national-security-figures-launch-project-to-counter-russian-mischief/.

10 https://www.nbcnews.com/politics/congress/right-wing-demand-releasethememo-endorsed-russian-bots-trolls-n839141

11 Spencer Ackerman, "Source: Twitter Pins #ReleaseTheMemo on Republicans, Not Russia," Daily Beast, January 23, 2018, https://www.thedailybeast.com/source-twitter-pins-releasethememo-on-republicans-not-russia#:~:text=The%20online%20groundswell%20urging%20the,widely%20since%20late%20last%20week.

12 Matt Taibbi (@mtaibbi), "1.THREAD: Twitter Files #15 MOVE OVER, JAYSON BLAIR: TWITTER FILES EXPOSE NEXT GREAT MEDIA FRAUD," X, January 27, 2023, 12:49 p.m., https://x.com/mtaibbi/status/1619029772977455105.

13 Vijaya Gadde, Twitter General Counsel letter to The Honorable Dianne Feinstein and The Honorable Adam Schiff, January 26, 2018, https://democrats-intelligence.house.gov/uploadedfiles/twitter_response_jan_26.pdf.

14 https://www.feinstein.senate.gov/public/_cache/files/6/4/64bd3267-fdc9-
46fb-b265-589dc5d08eff/8DBC13B7F818DA79F0E8C614A8F8159D.
facebook-response-to-feinstein-schiff-1.26.18.pdf
15 "Feinstein, Schiff Send Follow Up Letter to Twitter and Facebook on
#ReleaseTheMemo Campaign," U.S. Senate Committee on The Judiciary,
January 31, 2018, https://www.judiciary.senate.gov/press/dem/releases/
feinstein-schiff-send-follow-up-letter-to-twitter-and-facebook-on-
releasethememo-campaign.
16 Twitter, "Retrospective Review: Twitter, Inc. and the 2018 Midterm Elections
in the United States," January 31, 2019 (updated February 4, 2019), https://
cdn.cms-twdigitalassets.com/content/dam/blog-twitter/official/en_us/
company/2019/2018-retrospective-review.pdf.

CHAPTER FOUR: COERCED AND CAJOLED: BIG TECH JOINS THE FRAY

1 "What We Investigate: Combating Foreign Influence," FBI.gov, August 30,
2018, https://www.fbi.gov/investigate/counterintelligence/foreign-influence.
2 Masood Farivar, "FBI Task Force Sharing Information About Online Trolls,"
VOA, August 6, 2018, https://www.voanews.com/a/fbi-task-force-sharing-
information-about-online-trolls/4516728.html.
3 Connor O'Brien, "FBI director: Russia 'continues to engage in malign
influence operations' against U.S.," Politico, July 18, 2018, https://
www.politico.com/story/2018/07/18/fbi-wray-russia-meddling-
732337#:~:text=My%20view%20has%20not%20changed,at%20sowing%20
discord%20and%20divisiveness.".
4 Matt Taibbi (@mtaibbi), "7. The FBI's social media-focused task force, known
as FTIF, created in the wake of the 2016 election, swelled to 80 agents and
corresponded with Twitter to identify alleged foreign influence and election
tampering of all kinds," X, December 16, 2022, 4:00 p.m., https://twitter.com/
mtaibbi/status/1603857548645318656.
5 Seth Fiegerman, "Obama's staff is taking over Silicon Valley," CNNMoney,
August 11, 2016, https://money.cnn.com/2016/08/11/technology/obama-
staff-silicon-valley/.
6 Lindsay Holst, "President Obama Asks Todd Park to Continue
Administration Service in New Role after Returning to Silicon Valley,"
Obama White House, August 28, 2014, https://obamawhitehouse.
archives.gov/blog/2014/08/28/president-obama-asks-todd-park-continue-
administration-service-new-role-after-return.
7 Cecilia Kang and Juliet Eilperin, "Why Silicon Valley is the new revolving
door for Obama staffers," Washington Post, February 28, 2015, https://www.
washingtonpost.com/business/economy/as-obama-nears-close-of-his-
tenure-commitment-to-silicon-valley-is-clear/2015/02/27/3bee8088-bc8e-
11e4-bdfa-b8e8f594e6ee_story.html.
8 Ibid.
9 Brian Stelter, "The Facebooker Who Friended Obama," New York Times, July
7, 2008, https://www.nytimes.com/2008/07/07/technology/07hughes.html.

10 Ibid.

11 Chance Miller, "New data shows Google has met with White House officials over 400 times since 2009," 9to5Google, April 26, 2016, https://9to5google.com/2016/04/26/google-close-ties-with-the-white-house/.

12 Ina Fried, "Google's Schmidt: Society not ready for technology," CNET, August 4, 2010, http://archive.today/2012.07.14-193124/http://news.cnet.com/8301-13860_3-20012704-56.html.

13 Claire Miller, "New Book on Google Shows Gaffes in China," New York Times, March 31, 2011, https://www.nytimes.com/2011/04/01/business/01author.html.

14 Tech Transparency Project, "Eric Schmidt: Obama's Chief Corporate Ally," April 26, 2016, https://www.techtransparencyproject.org/articles/eric-schmidt-obamas-chief-corporate-ally.

15 Tom Hamburger, Matea Gold, "Google, once disdainful of lobbying, now a master of Washington influence," Washington Post, April 12, 2014, https://www.washingtonpost.com/politics/how-google-is-transforming-power-and-politicsgoogle-once-disdainful-of-lobbying-now-a-master-of-washington-influence/2014/04/12/51648b92-b4d3-11e3-8cb6-284052554d74_story.html.

16 David Dayen, "The Android Administration: Google's Remarkably Close Relationship With the Obama White House, in Two Charts," The Intercept, April 22, 2016, https://theintercept.com/2016/04/22/googles-remarkably-close-relationship-with-the-obama-white-house-in-two-charts/.

17 Steve Henn, "Almost All Tech Execs At White House Supported Obama Campaign," NPR, December 17, 2013, https://www.npr.org/sections/alltechconsidered/2013/12/16/251787365/um-chaddickerson-how-did-you-get-an-invite-to-the-white-house.

18 Jackie Calmes, Nick Wingfield, "Tech Leaders and Obama Find Shared Problem: Fading Public Trust," New York Times, December 17, 2013, https://www.nytimes.com/2013/12/18/us/politics/as-tech-industry-leaders-meet-with-obama-nsa-ruling-looms-large.html.

19 Shirin Ghaffary, "Edward Snowden says Facebook is just as untrustworthy as the NSA," Vox, October 31, 2019, https://www.vox.com/recode/2019/10/31/20940532/edward-snowden-facebook-nsa-whistleblower.

20 Communications Decency Act of 1996, US Code 47 (2024), § 230, https://www.law.cornell.edu/uscode/text/47/230.

21 James Baker, Letter to Twitter, September 9, 2014, https://www.washingtonpost.com/r/2010-2019/WashingtonPost/2014/10/07/National-Security/Graphics/Exhibit%205%20-%2020140909%20FBI%20Letter%20to%20Twitter.pdf?tid=a_inl_manual.

22 Andrew Mallin, "Former FBI lawyer hits back at critics of Russia investigation origins," ABC News, May 10, 2019, https://abcnews.go.com/Politics/fbi-lawyer-hits-back-critics-russia-investigation-origins/story?id=62964016.

23 Rob Copeland, "Inside James Comey's Bizarre $7M Job as a Top Hedge Fund's In-House Inquisitor," Vanity Fair, November 5, 2023, https://www.vanityfair.com/news/2023/11/james-comey-dalio-bridgewater-the-fund.

24 Ellen Nakashima, Devlin Barrett, and Adam Entous, "FBI obtained FISA warrant to monitor former Trump adviser Carter Page," Washington Post, April 11, 2017, https://www.washingtonpost.com/world/national-security/fbi-obtained-fisa-warrant-to-monitor-former-trump-adviser-carter-page/2017/04/11/620192ea-1e0e-11e7-ad74-3a742a6e93a7_story.html.

25 Paul Sperry, "The Checkered Past of the FBI Cyber Contractor Who 'Spied' on Trump," RealClear Investigations, February 17, 2022, https://www.realclearinvestigations.com/articles/2022/02/17/the_checkered_past_of_the_fbi_computer_contractor_who_spied_on_trump_816761.html.

26 Zach Whittacker, "Meet the shadowy tech brokers that deliver your data to the NSA," ZDNET, September 5, 2014, https://www.zdnet.com/article/meet-the-shadowy-tech-brokers-that-deliver-your-data-to-the-nsa/.

27 United States of America v. Michael A. Sussmann, Indictment (United States District Court for the District of Colombia September 16, 2021), https://www.justice.gov/sco/press-release/file/1433511/download.

28 Charlie Savage and Adam Goldman, "Trump-Era Special Counsel Secures Indictment of Lawyer for Firm With Democratic Ties," New York Times, September 16, 2021, https://www.nytimes.com/2021/09/16/us/politics/michael-sussmann-indictment-durham-investigation.html.

29 Aaron Mate, "Hidden Over 2 Years: Dem Cyber-Firm's Sworn Testimony It Had No Proof of Russian Hack of DNC," RealClear Investigations, May 13, 2020, https://www.realclearinvestigations.com/articles/2020/05/13/hidden_over_2_years_dem_cyber-firms_sworn_testimony_it_had_no_proof_of_russian_hack_of_dnc_123596.html.

30 UndeadFOIA, "Confirmation: Alfa Bank Researchers Worked on DNC Hack," Sleuth News, September 11, 2023, https://undeadfoia.substack.com/p/confirmation-alfa-bank-researchers.

31 David E. Sanger, "Obama Strikes Back at Russia for Election Hacking," New York Times, December 29, 2016, https://www.nytimes.com/2016/12/29/us/politics/russia-election-hacking-sanctions.html.

32 Matt Taibbi and UndeadFOIA, "Forget Collusion. Was "Interference" Also Fake News?," Racket News, September 26, 2023, https://www.racket.news/p/forget-collusion-was-interference?utm_source=post-email-title&publication_id=1042&post_id=137179945&utm_campaign=email-post-title&isFreemail=false&r=byeq&utm_medium=email.

33 "$1.3 Million in Grants from Omidyar Network, Open Society Foundations Will Expand Poynter's International Fact-Checking Network," PR Newswire, June 29, 2017, https://www.prnewswire.com/news-releases/13-million-in-grants-from-omidyar-network-open-society-foundations-will-expand-poynters-international-fact-checking-network-300481553.html.

34 Alexios Mantzarlis, "Facebook's fake news problem won't fix itself," Poynter, October 28, 2016, https://www.poynter.org/fact-checking/2016/facebooks-fake-news-problem-wont-fix-itself/.

35 Richard Stengel, "Why America needs a hate speech law," Washington Post, October 29, 2019, https://www.washingtonpost.com/opinions/2019/10/29/why-america-needs-a-hate-speech-law/.

36 Name Redacted (@NameRedacted247), "Why has Meta hired more than 160 individuals from the US Intelligence Community since 2018?...," X, August 4, 2023, 7:01 a.m., http://archive.today/2023.08.05-135433/https://twitter.com/NameRedacted247/status/1687358111235932161.

37 Ibid., "Dawn Burton (She/Her)- Current Google Director/Chief of Staff Privacy & Safety. Former Twitter Senior Director Trust & Safety 3 years. Former FBI Deputy Chief of Staff to Former Director James Comey- 4 years. Former DOJ 6 years...," X, December 27, 2022, 12:52 a.m., http://archive.today/2022.12.28-044239/https://twitter.com/NameRedacted247/status/1607539912659849217.

38 Emma James, "Revealed: Twitter's Top Ranks Were Filled with over a Dozen Ex-FBI Agents and Executives Which Stitched Social Media Giant Even Closer to the Bureau - as 'twitter Files' Uncover Cooperation over Account Details," Daily Mail Online, December 17, 2022, https://www.dailymail.co.uk/news/article-11549091/FBI-agent-blasts-Twitters-gross-subservience-intelligence-agency-meddling-revealed.html.

39 Michael Shellenberger (@shellenberger), "29. As of 2020, there were so many former FBI employees — "Bu alumni" — working at Twitter that they had created their own private Slack channel and a crib sheet to onboard new FBI arrivals," X, December 19, 2022, 12:44 p.m., https://twitter.com/shellenberger/status/1604895371360374784/photo/1.

40 Name Redacted (@NameRedacted247), "Dawn Burton (She/Her)- Current Google Director/Chief of Staff Privacy & Safety. Former Twitter Senior Director Trust & Safety 3 years. Former FBI Deputy Chief of Staff to Former Director James Comey- 4 years. Former DOJ 6 years...," X, December 27, 2022, 12:52 a.m., http://archive.today/2022.12.28-044239/https://twitter.com/NameRedacted247/status/1607539912659849217.

41 Rachael Bade and Rebecca Morin, "Ex-FBI general counsel faced criminal leak probe," Politico, January 15, 2019, https://www.politico.com/story/2019/01/15/fbi-general-counsel-criminal-investigation-1101774.

42 Joseph A. Wulfsohn, "Jim Baker, ousted Twitter lawyer and ex-FBI official involved in Russiagate, was a CNN analyst in between jobs," Fox News, December 8, 2022, https://www.foxnews.com/media/jim-baker-ousted-twitter-lawyer-ex-fbi-official-involved-russiagate-cnn-analyst-between-jobs.

43 Diana Glebova, "EXCLUSIVE: DOJ Probed Tara Reade's Twitter After She Issued Allegations About Joe Biden's Sexual Harassment, Docs Show," Daily Caller, December 2, 2022, https://dailycaller.com/2022/12/02/doj-tara-reade-twitter-joe-biden-sexual-assault-allegations/.

44 Robert Kelner, email to Jeff Jordan, https://www.fec.gov/files/legal/murs/7827/7827_08.pdf.

45 Michael Shellenberger (@Shellenberger), "20. Time and again, FBI asks Twitter for evidence of foreign influence & Twitter responds that they aren't finding anything worth reporting. "[W]e haven't yet identified activity that we'd typically refer to you (or even flag as interesting in the foreign influence context)."" X, December 19, 2022, 12:21 p.m., https://twitter.com/shellenberger/status/1604879477732831235.

46 Michael Shellenberger (@Shellenberger), "12. And yet, during all of 2020, the FBI and other law enforcement agencies repeatedly primed Yoel Roth to dismiss reports of Hunter Biden's laptop as a Russian "hack and leak" operation. This is from a sworn declaration by Roth given in December 2020.," X, December 19, 2022, 12:21 p.m., https://twitter.com/shellenberger/status/1604889734378967041.

47 Joseph Clark, "'Twitter Files' show FBI offered executives top secret info to guide 2020 election censorship," Washinton Times, December 19, 2022, https://www.washingtontimes.com/news/2022/dec/19/twitter-files-show-fbi-offered-executives-top-secr/.

48 "Rudy Giuliani: This is how the FBI spied on me," Newsmax post on YouTube, December 14, 2022, https://www.youtube.com/watch?v=8_B-X1oiPME.

49 Steven Nelson and Samuel Chamberlain, "Ex-Twitter executives now say they forget key details of censoring Post's Hunter Biden laptop scoop," New York Post, February 8, 2023, https://nypost.com/2023/02/08/house-panel-seeks-out-collusion-between-fbi-twitter-execs-who-censored-hunter-biden-laptop-story/.

CHAPTER FIVE: HOW TO COUP

1 George F. Kennan, "The Inauguration of Organized Political Warfare," April 30, 1948, Wilson Center Digital Archive, https://digitalarchive.wilsoncenter.org/document/george-f-kennan-inauguration-organized-political-warfare.

2 John M. Broder, "Political Meddling by Outsiders: Not New for U.S.," New York Times, March 31, 1997, https://www.nytimes.com/1997/03/31/us/political-meddling-by-outsiders-not-new-for-us.html.

3 The Select Committee to Study Governmental Operations with Respect to Intelligence Activities, "Covert Action in Chile: 1963-1973," 94th Cong., 1st sess., 1975, https://web.archive.org/web/20100504030947/http://www.fas.org/irp/ops/policy/church-chile.htm.

4 Peter Theroux, "Remembering a CIA Coup in Iran That Never Was," Tablet Magazine, March 5, 2023, https://www.tabletmag.com/sections/israel-middle-east/articles/cia-coup-in-iran-that-never-was-mossadegh.

5 Robert Parry, "CIA's Hidden Hand in 'Democracy' Groups," Consortium News, January 8, 2015, https://consortiumnews.com/2015/01/08/cias-hidden-hand-in-democracy-groups/.

6 William J. Casey, Letter to the Honorable Edwin Meese, undated, https://consortiumnews.com/wp-content/uploads/2016/10/casey-meese.pdf.

7 David Ignatius, "Innocence Abroad: The New World of Spyless Coups," Washington Post, September 21, 1991, https://www.washingtonpost.com/archive/opinions/1991/09/22/innocence-abroad-the-new-world-of-spyless-coups/92bb989a-de6e-4bb8-99b9-462c76b59a16/.

8 Scott Shane and Ron Nixon, "Charges Against U.S.-Aided Groups Come With History of Distrust in Egypt," New York Times, February 6, 2012, https://www.nytimes.com/2012/02/07/world/middleeast/in-egypt-a-history-of-distrust-of-us-aided-groups.html.

9 Ron Nixon, "U.S. Groups Helped Nurture Arab Uprisings," New York Times, April 14, 2011, https://www.nytimes.com/2011/04/15/world/15aid.html.

10 Darien Cavanaugh, "Arab Spring Activists Relied on Social Media — And America Taught Them How to Use It," War is Boring, October 3, 2016, https://medium.com/war-is-boring/arab-spring-activists-relied-on-social-media-and-america-taught-them-how-to-use-it-3eb5a1bda2d8.

11 Agence France-Presse, "US trains activists to evade security forces," RawStory, April 8, 2011, https://www.rawstory.com/2011/04/us-trains-activists-to-evade-security-forces/.

12 Kate Bolduan, "Chief of firm involved in breach is Obama adviser," CNN, March 22, 2008, https://www.cnn.com/2008/POLITICS/03/22/passport.files/index.html?iref=newssearch.

13 David Rohde, "The politics of espionage in the Obama-Brennan era," Reuters, November 2, 2016, https://www.reuters.com/article/world/the-politics-of-espionage-in-the-obama-brennan-era-idUSKBN12X1L6/.

14 Carl Gershman, "Former Soviet states stand up to Russia. Will the U.S.?," Washington Post, September 26, 2013, https://www.washingtonpost.com/opinions/former-soviet-states-stand-up-to-russia-will-the-us/2013/09/26/b5ad2be4-246a-11e3-b75d-5b7f66349852_story.html

15 Paul Blumenthal, "U.S. Obscures Foreign Aid To Ukraine, But Here's Where Some Goes," Huffington Post, March 7, 2014, https://www.huffpost.com/entry/us-foreign-aid-ukraine_n_4914682.

16 "About the CCL," Center for Civil Liberties, accessed August 29, 2024, https://ccl.org.ua/en/about-the-ccl/.

17 Katrina Elledge, "Ukraine: Dissident Capabilities in the Cyber Age," in Beyond Propaganda, ed. Legatum Institute Transitions Forum, November 2015, https://lif.blob.core.windows.net/lif/docs/default-source/publications/cyber-propaganda-2015-final-pdf.pdf?sfvrsn=2.

18 Omidyar Network, "Omidyar Network Supports 15 Transparency and Accountability Organizations with Grants Totaling $9.7m," PR Newswire, December 11, 2014, https://www.prnewswire.com/news-releases/omidyar-network-supports-15-transparency-and-accountability-organizations-with-grants-totaling-97m-300008325.html.

19 Federal Bureau of Investigation (FBI), CHS Reporting Document, June 30, 2020, https://www.grassley.senate.gov/imo/media/doc/fd_1023_obtained_by_senator_grassley_-_biden.pdf.

20 Michael J. Morrell, "I Ran the C.I.A. Now I'm Endorsing Hillary Clinton.," New York Times, August 5, 2016, https://www.nytimes.com/2016/08/05/opinion/campaign-stops/i-ran-the-cia-now-im-endorsing-hillary-clinton.html.

21 Natasha Bertrand, "Hunter Biden story is Russian disinfo, dozens of former intel officials say," Politico, October 19, 2020, https://www.politico.com/news/2020/10/19/hunter-biden-story-russian-disinfo-430276.

22 "Presidential Debate at Belmont University in Nashville, Tennessee," The Commission on Presidential Debates, transcript, https://www.debates.org/voter-education/debate-transcripts/october-22-2020-debate-transcript/.

23 Houston Keene, "CIA approved former top spy signing Hunter Biden laptop letter," Fox News, May 8, 2023, https://www.foxnews.com/politics/cia-approved-former-top-spy-signing-hunter-biden-laptop-letter.

CHAPTER SIX: CENSORSHIP KILLS

1 Chandelis Duster, "Obama urges Americans to continue social distancing despite Trump's wishes to reopen economy," CNN, March 25, 2020, https://www.cnn.com/2020/03/25/politics/barack-obama-social-distancing/index.html.

2 Barack Obama (@BarackObama), "These are the burdens our medical heroes already face in NYC. It's only going to get harder across the country. Another reason to maintain social distancing policies at least until we have comprehensive testing in place. Not just for our sake—for theirs.," X, March 25, 2020, 10:11 a.m., https://twitter.com/BarackObama/status/124281647157 2545536?s=20.

3 Chandelis Duster, "Obama urges Americans to continue social distancing despite Trump's wishes to reopen economy," CNN, March 25, 2020, https://www.cnn.com/2020/03/25/politics/barack-obama-social-distancing/index.html.

4 Robert Kuznia, Curt Devine and Drew Griffin, "Severe shortages of swabs and other supplies hamper coronavirus testing," CNN, March 18, 2020, https://www.cnn.com/2020/03/18/us/coronovirus-testing-supply-shortages-invs/index.html.

5 Eleni Patrozou and Leonard A. Mermel, "Does Influenza Transmission Occur from Asymptomatic Infection or Prior to Symptom Onset?," Public Health Reports 124, no. 2, (March-April 2009): 193–196, https://www.ncbi.nlm.nih.gov/pmc/articles/PMC2646474/#:~:text=Asymptomatic%20individuals%20may%20shed%20influenza%20virus%2C%20but%20studies%20have%20not,such%20people%20effectively%20transmit%20influenza.

6 Daniel Horowitz, "Horowitz: A severely symptomatic lie about asymptomatic spread," Blaze Media, November 23, 2020, https://www.theblaze.com/column/opinion/ready-horowitz-a-severely-symptomatic-lie-about-asymptomatic-spread; Pure@heart (@Pureomheart), "Dr. Fauci: 'In all the history of respiratory viruses of any type, asymptomatic transmission has never been the driver of outbreaks,'" X, August 29, 2020, https://x.com/Pureomheart/status/1299665701054095361.

7 Andrew Romano, "Fauci once dismissed concerns about 'silent carriers' of coronavirus. Not anymore," Yahoo News, updated April 7, 2020, https://news.yahoo.com/fauci-once-dismissed-concerns-about-silent-carriers-of-coronavirus-not-anymore-161718057.html.

8 FBI, "Amerithrax or Anthrax Investigation," FBI.gov, https://www.fbi.gov/history/famous-cases/amerithrax-or-anthrax-investigation.

9 "U.S. Government Gain-of-Function Deliberative Process and Research Funding Pause on Selected Gain-of-Function Research Involving Influenza, MERS, and SARS Viruses," Office of the Assistant Secretary for Preparedness and Response, U.S. Department of Health and Human Services, accessed

August 31, 2024, https://www.phe.gov/s3/dualuse/Documents/gain-of-function.pdf.

10 Rowan Jacobsen, "Inside the risky bat-virus engineering that links America to Wuhan," MIT Technology Review, June 29, 2021, https://www.congress.gov/117/meeting/house/114658/documents/HHRG-117-IF14-20220427-SD003.pdf.

11 Zack Quaintance, "Coronavirus: Obama Speaks at Zoom Meeting of U.S. Mayors," Government Technology, April 9, 2020, https://www.govtech.com/health/coronavirus-obama-speaks-at-zoom-meeting-of-us-mayors.html.

12 Dan Merica and Caroline Kelly, "Obama to mayors on coronavirus: The biggest mistake leaders 'can make in these situations is to misinform,'" CNN, April 10, 2020, https://www.cnn.com/2020/04/09/politics/obama-mayors-coronavirus/index.html.

13 Barack Obama (@BarackObama), "Social distancing bends the curve and relieves some pressure on our heroic medical professionals. But in order to shift off current policies, the key will be a robust system of testing and monitoring – something we have yet to put in place nationwide.," X, April 8, 2020, https://twitter.com/BarackObama/status/1247890918440448003?s=20.

14 Donald J. Trump (@realDonaldTrump), "Once we OPEN UP OUR GREAT COUNTRY, and it will be sooner rather than later, the horror of the Invisible Enemy, except for those that sadly lost a family member or friend, must be quickly forgotten. Our Economy will BOOM, perhaps like never before!!!," X, April 8, 2020, https://twitter.com/realDonaldTrump/status/1247900240155295745?s=20.

15 Will Feuer and Noah Higgins-Dunn, "Asymptomatic spread of coronavirus is 'very rare,' WHO says," CNBC, June 8, 2020, https://www.cnbc.com/2020/06/08/asymptomatic-coronavirus-patients-arent-spreading-new-infections-who-says.html.

16 Berkeley Lovelace Jr., "Dr. Anthony Fauci says WHO's remark on asymptomatic coronavirus spread 'was not correct,'" CNBC, June 10, 2020, https://www.cnbc.com/2020/06/10/dr-anthony-fauci-says-whos-remark-on-asymptomatic-coronavirus-spread-was-not-correct.html.

17 Berkeley Lovelace Jr., Jasmine Kim, and Will Feuer, "WHO walks back comments on asymptomatic coronavirus spread, says much is still unknown," CNBC, June 9, 2020, https://www.cnbc.com/2020/06/09/who-scrambles-to-clarify-comments-on-asymptomatic-coronavirus-spread-much-is-still-unknown.html.

18 Edward Peter Stringham, "How a Free Society Deals with Pandemics, According to Legendary Epidemiologist and Smallpox Eradicator Donald Henderson," American Institute for Economic Research, May 21, 2020, https://www.aier.org/article/how-a-free-society-deals-with-pandemics-according-to-legendary-epidemiologist-and-smallpox-eradicator-donald-henderson/.

19 Deepa Seetharaman, "Facebook, Twitter Take Down Video of Trump Saying Children 'Almost Immune' From Covid-19," Wall Street Journal, August 5,

2020, https://www.wsj.com/articles/facebook-twitter-take-down-video-of-trump-saying-children-almost-immune-from-covid-19-11596674533.

20 Kaitlan Collins, "Trump adds coronavirus adviser who echoes his unscientific claims," CNN, August 12, 2020, https://www.cnn.com/2020/08/12/politics/scott-atlas-donald-trump-coronavirus/index.html.

21 Ninety-nine Stanford Medicine Faculty, Open letter from Stanford Doctors on Scott Atlas, September 9, 2020, https://int.nyt.com/data/documenttools/read-the-open-letter-from-stanford-doctors-on-scott-atlas/813b50f72b6543b4/full.pdf.

22 Audrey Bloom, "From Stanford to the rabbinate: Phil Pizzo moving on," Stanford Daily, April 10, 2022, https://stanforddaily.com/2022/04/10/from-stanford-to-the-rabbinate-phil-pizzo-moving-on/.

23 "Great Barrington Declaration," Great Barrington Declaration, accessed August 31, 2024, https://gbdeclaration.org.

24 "Focused Protection," Great Barrington Declaration, November 25, 2020. https://gbdeclaration.org/focused-protection/.

25 "How Fauci and Collins Shut Down Covid Debate," Wall Street Journal, editorial, December 21, 2021, https://www.wsj.com/articles/fauci-collins-emails-great-barrington-declaration-covid-pandemic-lockdown-11640129116.

26 Marcia Frellick, "Critics Blast Controversial Declaration in Favor of Herd Immunity," Medscape, October 14, 2020, https://www.medscape.com/viewarticle/939147#vp_2.

27 Anthony Fauci, "Today's Doctor meeting and Task Force," email to Francis Collins, October 18, 2020, https://www.aier.org/wp-content/uploads/2021/12/FauciBirx.pdf.

28 Jeremy Diamond and Paul LeBlanc, "Twitter removes tweet from Trump coronavirus adviser that undermined importance of masks," CNN, October 18, 2020, https://www.cnn.com/2020/10/17/politics/scott-atlas-face-masks-coronavirus/index.html;

29 Betsy Klein, "Birx tells friends she was relieved after Trump adviser Scott Atlas' inaccurate mask tweet was removed," CNN, October 19, 2020, https://www.cnn.com/2020/10/19/politics/scott-atlas-deborah-birx-task-force/index.html.

30 Rachel Scully, "Birx: Fauci, other colleagues on Trump team had resignation pact," The Hill, April 26, 2022, https://thehill.com/blogs/blog-briefing-room/3463388-birx-fauci-other-colleagues-on-trump-team-had-resignation-pact/.

31 Yael Halon, "Trump adviser Dr. Scott Atlas clarifies 'rise up' tweet after backlash from Biden, Michigan governor," Fox News, November 16, 2020, https://www.foxnews.com/politics/dr-scott-atlas-tweet-rise-up-michigan-governor-whitmer-joe-biden.

32 Stanford University, "Faculty Senate condemns COVID-19 actions of Hoover's Scott Atlas," Stanford Report, November 20th, 2020, https://news.stanford.edu/2020/11/20/faculty-senate-condemns-actions-hoover-fellow-scott-atlas/.

33 James Bovard, "Private-federal censorship machine targeted TRUE 'misinformation,'" New York Post, March 17, 2023, https://nypost. com/2023/03/17/private-federal-censorship-machine-targeted-true-misinformation/.

34 Christopher St. Aubin and Jacob Liedke, "Most Americans favor restrictions on false information, violent content online," Pew Research Center, July 30, 2023, https://www.pewresearch.org/short-reads/2023/07/20/most-americans-favor-restrictions-on-false-information-violent-content-online/.

35 Aaron Kheriaty and Gerard V. Bradley, "University Vaccine Mandates Violate Medical Ethics," Wall Street Journal, June 14, 2021, https://www.wsj.com/ articles/university-vaccine-mandates-violate-medical-ethics-11623689220.

CHAPTER SEVEN: THE FIXERS

1 @RNDog12, "Donald Barr served in the Army as an Italian interpreter in a POW camp and as a member of the OSS "Target team" in Germany," June 30, 2024, 3:01 p.m., https://x.com/RNDog12/status/1807489708022239506/ photo/1.

2 "Headmaster and Dean to Debate for CWCC," Scarsdale Inquirer, October 7, 1971, https://news.hrvh.org/veridian/?a=d&d=scarsdaleinquire19711007.2.6 9&e=-------en-20--1--txt-txIN-------.

3 JPat Brown, "While at the CIA, William Barr drafted letters calling for an end to the Agency's moratorium on destroying records," MuckRock, April 16, 2019, https://www.muckrock.com/news/archives/2019/apr/16/cia-barr-crest/.

4 Brad Heath, "U.S. secretly tracked billions of calls for decades," USA Today, April 7, 2015, https://www.usatoday.com/story/news/2015/04/07/dea-bulk-telephone-surveillance-operation/70808616/.

5 Brad Heath, "Justice under AG Barr began vast surveillance program without legal review – in 1992, inspector general finds," USA Today, March 28, 2019, https://www.usatoday.com/story/news/politics/2019/03/28/review-finds-phone-data-dragnet-dea-doj-began-without-legal-review/3299438002/.

6 Office of the Inspector General, "A Review of the Drug Enforcement Administration's Use of Administrative Subpoenas to Collect or Exploit Bulk Data," U.S. Department of Justice, March 2019, https://oig.justice.gov/ reports/2019/o1901.pdf.

7 James Bamford, "The NSA Is Building the Country's Biggest Spy Center (Watch What You Say)," WIRED, March 15, 2012, https://www.wired. com/2012/03/ff-nsadatacenter/.

8 Glenn Greenwald, "NSA collecting phone records of millions of Verizon customers daily," Guardian, June 6, 2013, https://www.theguardian.com/ world/2013/jun/06/nsa-phone-records-verizon-court-order.

9 Luke O'Brien, "FBI Confirms Contracts with AT&T, Verizon and MCI," WIRED, March 28, 2007, https://www.wired.com/2007/03/fbi-confirms-co/; Victor Nava, "FBI paid Twitter $3.4M for doing its dirty work on users, damning email shows," New York Post, December 2019, https://nypost.

com/2022/12/19/fbi-reimbursed-twitter-for-doing-its-dirty-work-on-users/.

10 Ryan Singel, "FBI Patriot Act Abuse Documents: What Special Project Lives in FBI HQ Room 4944?," WIRED, July 10, 2007, https://www.wired.com/2007/07/fbi-patriot-act/; John Solomon and Carrie Johnson, "FBI broke law for years in phone record searches," Washington Post, January 19, 2010, https://www.washingtonpost.com/wp-dyn/content/article/2010/01/18/AR2010011803982_pf.html.

11 Mark Hosenball, "Terror Watch: A Secret Lobbying Campaign," Newsweek, September 19, 2007, https://www.newsweek.com/terror-watch-secret-lobbying-campaign-99841.

12 William Barr, "Former attorney general: Trump was right to fire Sally Yates," Washington Post, February 1, 2017, https://www.washingtonpost.com/opinions/former-attorney-general-trump-was-right-to-fire-sally-yates/2017/02/01/5981d890-e809-11e6-80c2-30e57e57e05d_story.html.

13 William Barr, "Former attorney general: Trump made the right call on Comey," Washington Post, May 12, 2017, https://www.washingtonpost.com/opinions/former-attorney-general-trump-made-the-right-call-on-comey/2017/05/12/0e858436-372d-11e7-b4ee-434b6d506b37_story.html.

14 Peter Baker, "'Lock Her Up' Becomes More Than a Slogan," New York Times, November 14, 2017, https://www.nytimes.com/2017/11/14/us/politics/trump-pressure-clinton-investigation.html.

15 Matt Zapotosky, "As Mueller builds his Russia special-counsel team, every hire is under scrutiny," Washington Post, July 5, 2017, https://www.washingtonpost.com/news/post-politics/wp/2017/07/05/as-mueller-grows-his-russia-special-counsel-team-every-hire-is-under-scrutiny/.

16 "Attorney General William P. Barr Delivers Remarks on the Release of the Report on the Investigation into Russian Interference in the 2016 Presidential Election," Office of Public Affairs, U.S. Department of Justice, April 18, 2019, https://www.justice.gov/opa/speech/attorney-general-william-p-barr-delivers-remarks-release-report-investigation-russian.

17 Kevin Johnson, "Attorney general says he will review government 'spying' on Trump campaign; 'I am concerned,'" USA Today, April 10, 2019, https://www.usatoday.com/story/news/politics/2019/04/10/ag-barr-says-spying-did-occur-trump-campaign-reviewing-legality/3421411002/.

18 "Department of Justice Statement on the Investigation into the Destruction of Videotapes by CIA Personnel," Office of Public Affairs, U.S. Department of Justice, November 9, 2010, https://www.justice.gov/opa/pr/department-justice-statement-investigation-destruction-videotapes-cia-personnel.

19 Aaron Kliegman, "Emergency rule emergency? How authorities are invoking crises to exercise unprecedented power," Just the News, September 28, 2022, https://justthenews.com/government/courts-law/emergency-rule-how-authorities-are-using-crises-exercise-unprecedented-power.

20 "Building Confidence in U.S. Elections," Report on the Commission of Federal Election Reform, September 2005.

21 Barack Obama (@BarackObama), "Let's not use the tragedy of a pandemic to compromise our democracy. Check the facts of vote by

mail.," X, April 10, 2020, 5:08 p.m., https://twitter.com/BarackObama/status/1248719432563732482.

22 Barack Obama (@BarackObama), "Everyone should have the right to vote safely, and we have the power to make that happen. This shouldn't be a partisan issue.," X, April 10, 2020, 5:08 p.m., https://twitter.com/BarackObama/status/1248719429904429056

23 Sean Davis, "Obama's Campaign Paid $972,000 To Law Firm That Secretly Paid Fusion GPS In 2016," The Federalist, October 29, 2017, https://thefederalist.com/2017/10/29/obamas-campaign-gave-972000-law-firm-funneled-money-fusion-gps/

24 "15 Days to Slow the Spread," Trump White House, March 16, 2020, https://trumpwhitehouse.archives.gov/articles/15-days-slow-spread/; Marc Elias, "The virus means we'll be voting by mail. But that won't be easy," Washington Post, March 16, 2020, https://www.washingtonpost.com/opinions/2020/03/16/virus-means-well-be-voting-by-mail-that-wont-be-easy/.

25 Committee on the Judiciary and the Select Subcommittee on the Weaponization of the Federal Government, "The Weaponization of CISA: How a 'Cybersecurity' Agency Colluded with Big Tech and 'Disinformation' Partners to Censor Americans,", June 26, 2023, https://judiciary.house.gov/sites/evo-subsites/republicans-judiciary.house.gov/files/evo-media-document/cisa-staff-report6-26-23.pdf.

26 Natalie Schachar, "Barbara Ehrenreich, Explorer of Prosperity's Dark Side, Dies at 81," New York Times, September 2, 2022, https://www.nytimes.com/2022/09/02/books/barbara-ehrenreich-dead.html.

27 Rosa Brooks, "What's the worst that could happen?," Washington Post, September 3, 2020, https://www.washingtonpost.com/outlook/2020/09/03/trump-stay-in-office/.

28 bid.

29 Transition Integrity Project, "Preventing a Disrupted Presidential Election and Transition," August 3, 2020, https://s3.documentcloud.org/documents/7013152/Preventing-a-Disrupted-Presidential-Election-and.pdf, p. 1

30 Ibid., p. 1

31 Ibid., p. 1

32 Ibid., p. 2

33 Ibid., p. 2

34 Ibid., p. 19

35 Ibid., p. 10

36 Melissa Quinn, "Barr doesn't expect investigations of Obama, Biden stemming from Russia review," CBS News, May 18, 2020, https://www.cbsnews.com/news/william-barr-barack-obama-fbi-probe-trump-campaign-russia-no-investigations/.

37 Brooke Singman, "DNI declassifies Brennan notes, CIA memo on Hillary Clinton 'stirring up' scandal between Trump, Russia," Fox News, October

6, 2020, https://www.foxnews.com/politics/dni-brennan-notes-cia-memo-clinton.

38 Ronn Blitzer, "Barr hints at 'developments' in Durham probe this summer, says racism not 'systemic' problem in law enforcement," Fox News, June 21, 2020, https://www.foxnews.com/politics/barr-durham-probe-should-have-some-developments-this-summer.

39 "FBI Attorney Admits Altering Email Used for FISA Application During 'Crossfire Hurricane' Investigation," United States Attorney's Office, District of Connecticut, August 19, 2020, https://www.justice.gov/usao-ct/pr/fbi-attorney-admits-altering-email-used-fisa-application-during-crossfire-hurricane#:~:text=Clinesmith%20pleaded%20guilty%20to%20one,fine%20of%20up%20to%20%24250%2C000.

40 Alayna Treene, "Barr tells Republicans Durham report won't be ready by election," Axios, October 9, 2020, https://www.axios.com/2020/10/09/barr-durham-report-election.

41 Jerry Dunleavy, "Hunter Biden evidence wrongly labeled disinformation by FBI: Whistleblower," Washington Examiner, July 25, 2022, https://www.washingtonexaminer.com/news/justice/whistleblowers-hunter-biden-wrongly-labeled-disinformation-fbi.

42 Margot Cleveland, "Bill Barr Confirms Rep. Jamie Raskin Lied About Biden Family Corruption Investigation," The Federalist, June 7, 2023, https://thefederalist.com/2023/06/07/exclusive-bill-barr-confirms-rep-jamie-raskin-lied-about-biden-family-corruption-investigation/.

43 Naveen Athrappully, "'Dirty Trick': Barr Blasts Letter Framing Hunter Biden Laptop as Russian Disinformation," The Epoch Times, April 28, 2023, https://www.theepochtimes.com/us/dirty-trick-barr-blasts-letter-framing-hunter-biden-laptop-as-russian-disinformation-5226194.

44 Shane Harris, Ellen Nakashima, Greg Miller and Josh Dawsey, "White House was warned Giuliani was target of Russian intelligence operation to feed misinformation to Trump," Washington Post, October 15, 2020, https://www.washingtonpost.com/national-security/giuliani-biden-ukraine-russian-disinformation/2020/10/15/43158900-0ef5-11eb-b1e8-16b59b92b36d_story.html.

45 Evan Perez, "FBI says it has 'nothing to add' to Ratcliffe's claim on Russian disinformation," CNN, October 21, 2020, https://www.cnn.com/2020/10/21/politics/fbi-russia-disinformation/index.html.

46 Julie Kelly, "The FBI-Tainted Whitmer 'Kidnap Plot' You've Heard Next to Nothing About," RealClearInvestigations, January 3, 2024, https://www.realclearinvestigations.com/articles/2024/01/03/the_fbi-tainted_whitmer_kidnap_plot_youve_heard_next_to_nothing_about_1001971.html.

47 Jessica Garrison and Ken Bensinger, "An FBI Agent In The Michigan Kidnapping Case Has Pleaded No Contest To Assaulting His Wife," Buzzfeed News, December 20, 2021, https://www.buzzfeednews.com/article/jessicagarrison/fbi-michigan-kidnapping-case-plea-assault.

48 Kevin Bensinger, "The Side Hustle Of An FBI Agent In The Michigan Kidnapping Case Is Relevant, Defense Lawyers Argued," Buzzfeed News,

December 31, 2021, https://www.buzzfeednews.com/article/kenbensinger/michigan-kidnapping-plot-fbi-agent-business.

CHAPTER EIGHT: DISAPPEARING THE OPPOSITION

1 Pew Research Center, "The voting experience in 2020," November 20, 2020, https://www.pewresearch.org/politics/2020/11/20/the-voting-experience-in-2020/.

2 The Heritage Foundation, "The TRUTH About Election Fraud | Texas AG Ken Paxton at #Heritage50," April 27, 2023, https://www.youtube.com/watch?v=4eTG32YC_Uw.

3 Mark Hosenball, "U.S. ethics groups say Barr uses DOJ as political tool, call for his impeachment," Reuters, October 12, 2020, https://www.reuters.com/article/world/u-s-ethics-groups-say-barr-uses-doj-as-political-tool-call-for-his-impeachment-idUSL1N2H31D9/.

4 Citizens for Responsibility and Ethics in Washington, "Abuse of power: The case for Attorney General Bill Barr's impeachment," report, July 28, 2020, https://www.citizensforethics.org/reports-investigations/crew-reports/abuse-of-power-the-case-for-attorney-general-bill-barrs-impeachment/; Joe Schoffstall, "Soros Gave $1.35M to 'Nonpartisan' Watchdog Inundating Trump with Lawsuits," Washington Free Beacon, December 20, 2018, https://freebeacon.com/politics/soros-gave-1-35m-to-nonpartisan-watchdog-inundating-trump-with-lawsuits/.

5 Michael Balsamo, "Disputing Trump, Barr says no widespread election fraud," Associated Press, June 28, 2022, https://apnews.com/article/barr-no-widespread-election-fraud-b1f1488796c9a98c4b1a9061a6c7f49d.

6 Sophia Cai, "Barr tells Jan. 6 panel: Trump "detached from reality" on voter fraud," Axios, June 13, 2022, https://www.axios.com/2022/06/13/bill-barr-trump-detached-reality-election-fraud.

7 William Barr, "When I Confronted Trump About Election Fraud" Wall Street Journal, March 3, 2022, https://www.wsj.com/articles/william-barr-when-i-confronted-trump-about-election-fraud-11646323237.

8 "Barr says Justice Department has no evidence of widespread fraud in election," CBS News, December 1, 2020, https://www.cbsnews.com/news/barr-no-election-fraud-evidence-doj/.

9 Nikolas Lanum, "Bill Barr says Joe Biden lied to Americans about Hunter Biden laptop: 'I was very disturbed,'" Fox News, March 21, 2022, https://www.foxnews.com/media/bill-barr-joe-biden-lied-hunter-biden-laptop.

10 Melissa Goldin, "Misinfo about 'suitcases' of ballots and a burst pipe in 2020 return after Trump's Georgia indictment," Associated Press, August 17, 2023, https://apnews.com/article/fact-check-trump-indictment-fulton-suitcases-pipe-654281257169.

11 "Permanent suspension of @realDonaldTrump," Twitter (now X), January 8, 2021, https://blog.x.com/en_us/topics/company/2020/suspension.

12 Emma Colton, "Conservatives fed up with 'censorship' on Twitter jump to Parler," Washington Examiner, June 24, 2020, https://www.

washingtonexaminer.com/news/1460270/conservatives-fed-up-with-censorship-on-twitter-jump-to-parler/.

13 Vidhi Choudhary, "Apple CEO Tim Cook Says Parler Suspension and Free Speech Unrelated," TheStreet, January 15, 2021, https://www.thestreet.com/investing/apple-chief-tim-cook-says-parler-suspension-and-free-speech-unrelated.

14 "Statement of Christopher Wray," Department of Justice, March 2, 2021, https://www.judiciary.senate.gov/imo/media/doc/SJC%20Oversight%20Hearing%20-%20FBI%20Director%20Wray%20SFR%20-%203.2.2021.pdf.

15 "Pennsylvania Man Pleads Guilty to Felony Charge For Obstructing Congress During Jan. 6 Capitol Breach," United States Attorney's Office, District of Columbia, December 17, 2021, https://www.justice.gov/usao-dc/pr/pennsylvania-man-pleads-guilty-felony-charge-obstructing-congress-during-jan-6-capitol#:~:text=Perna%20pleaded%20guilty%20in%20the,2021%2C%20and%20indicted%20on%20Feb.

CHAPTER NINE: INDESTRUCTIBLE TRUTH

1 Kenneth P. Vogel and Shane Goldmacher, "Democrats Decried Dark Money. Then They Won With It in 2020.," New York Times, August 21, 2022, https://www.nytimes.com/2022/01/29/us/politics/democrats-dark-money-donors.html.

2 Alana Goodman, "Mystery Solved: Left-Wing Billionaire Pierre Omidyar Bankrolls Shadowy Anti-Musk Group," Washington Free Beacon, February 21, 2023, https://freebeacon.com/latest-news/mystery-solved-left-wing-billionaire-pierre-omidyar-bankrolls-shadowy-anti-musk-group/.

3 Open Markets Institute, letter to federal agencies regarding Musk's Twitter takeover, November 16, 2022, https://static1.squarespace.com/static/5e449c8c3ef68d752f3e70dc/t/63754d1ba9540f651d2ef646/1668631835775/OMI+-+Musk-Twitter+-+FINAL.pdf.

4 Mike Cernovich (@Cernovich), "Twitter lawyer Jim Baker, when general counsel of the FBI, personally arranged a meeting between the FBI and Michael Sussmann. In this meeting, Sussmann presented fabricated evidence in the Alfa bank matter," X, April 26, 2022, 10:43 p.m., https://twitter.com/cernovich/status/1519145293287092225.

5 Brad Maloney (@br4dm4l0n3y), "He at least knew one day after Twitter accepted his purchase offer (25 April).," X, December 6, 2022, 9:25 p.m., https://twitter.com/br4dm4l0n3y/status/1600315522624651265.

6 Margot Cleveland, "FBI Office Investigating Hunter Biden Sent Twitter Numerous Censorship Requests Right Before 2020 Election," The Federalist, December 27, 2022, https://thefederalist.com/2022/12/27/fbi-office-investigating-hunter-biden-sent-twitter-numerous-censorship-requests-right-before-2020-election/.

7 Jacob Stern, "Obama: I Underestimated the Threat of Disinformation," Atlantic, April 7, 2022, https://www.theatlantic.com/ideas/archive/2022/04/barack-obama-interview-disinformation-ukraine/629496/.

8   Greg Piper and John Solomon, "Outsourced censorship: Feds used private entity to target millions of social posts in 2020," Just the News, September 29, 2022, https://justthenews.com/government/federal-agencies/biden-administration-rewarded-private-entities-got-2020-election.

9   Justin Hendrix, "Transcript: Barack Obama Speech on Technology and Democracy," Tech Policy Press, April 21, 2022, https://www.techpolicy.press/transcript-barack-obama-speech-on-technology-and-democracy/.

CHAPTER TEN: THE BUILDERS AND THE DESTROYERS

1   Sam Dangremond and Leena Kim, "A History of Mar-a-Lago, Donald Trump's Palm Beach Home," Town&Country, June 13, 2023, https://www.townandcountrymag.com/style/home-decor/a7144/mar-a-lago-history/.

2   Maggie Haberman, "Mar-a-Lago, the Future Winter White House and Home of the Calmer Trump," New York Times, January 1, 2017, https://www.nytimes.com/2017/01/01/us/trump-mar-a-lago-future-winter-white-house.html.

3   James Comer, letter to Edward Siskel, October 11, 2023, https://oversight.house.gov/wp-content/uploads/2023/10/WH-Classified-Documents-10.11.23_Final.pdf.

4   Monticello, "Monticello's Historic Mountaintop Project to Receive Second $10 Million Gift," press release, May 2, 2015, https://www.monticello.org/press/news-releases/news-releases-2015-2017/monticello-s-historic-mountaintop-project-to-receive-second-10-million-gift/; Mary Kay Linge and Jon Levine, "Monticello is going woke — and trashing Thomas Jefferson's legacy in the process," New York Post, July 9, 2022, https://nypost.com/2022/07/09/monticello-draws-criticism-after-trashing-thomas-jefferson/.

5   White House Historical Association, "Colleen Shogan - White House Historical Association," accessed September 6, 2024, https://www.whitehousehistory.org/presidential-sites-summit/presidential-sites-summit-speakers-2023/colleen-shogan;

6   Margot Cleveland, "Records Suggest A Backbench Bureaucrat's Partisan Grievance Spurred The FBI's Nakedly Political Raid On Trump," The Federalist, August 15, 2022, https://thefederalist.com/2022/08/15/from-bureaucrat-hack-to-grand-jury-witch-hunt-the-dojs-trump-raid-smells-like-spygate/.

7   John Solomon and Steven Richards, "Unsealed docs expose early collaboration between Archives, Biden White House in Trump prosecution," Just the News, April 23, 2024, https://justthenews.com/accountability/political-ethics/new-court-docs-show-archives-biden-wh-coordinated-trump-probe.

8   Josh Dawsey and Jacqueline Alemany, "Archives asked for records in 2021 after Trump lawyer agreed they should be returned, email says," Washington Post, August 24, 2022, https://www.washingtonpost.com/national-security/2022/08/24/trump-records-archives-2021/.

9 Email conversation between Gary Stern and David Ferriero, starting May 5, 2021, 9:48 a.m., https://justthenews.com/sites/default/files/2024-04/Case%20 9.23-cr-80101-AMC%20Document%20469-1.pdf.

10 Jacqueline Alemany, Josh Dawsey, Tom Hamburger and Ashley Parker, "National Archives had to retrieve Trump White House records from Mar-a-Lago," Washington Post, February 7, 2022, https://www.washingtonpost.com/ politics/2022/02/07/trump-records-mar-a-lago/.

11 David Ferriero, letter to the Honorable Carolyn B. Maloney, February 18, 2022, https://www.archives.gov/files/foia/ferriero-response-to-02.09.2022-maloney-letter.02.18.2022.pdf.

12 Margot Cleveland, "Records Suggest A Backbench Bureaucrat's Partisan Grievance Spurred The FBI's Nakedly Political Raid On Trump," Federalist, August 15, 2022, https://thefederalist.com/2022/08/15/from-bureaucrat-hack-to-grand-jury-witch-hunt-the-dojs-trump-raid-smells-like-spygate/.

13 John Solomon, "Questions grow about Trump raid after revelation of grand jury subpoena, extensive cooperation," Just the News, August 10, 2022, https://justthenews.com/politics-policy/all-things-trump/trump-got-grand-jury-subpoena-spring-voluntarily-cooperated-home.

14 Sadie Gurman, "Merrick Garland Weighed Search of Trump's Mar-a-Lago for Weeks," Wall Street Journal, August 15, 2022, https://www.wsj.com/ articles/merrick-garland-weighed-search-of-trumps-mar-a-lago-for-weeks-11660601292.

15 Katie Benner, Katie Rogers and Michael S. Schmidt, "Garland Faces Growing Pressure as Jan. 6 Investigation Widens," New York Times, April 2, 2022 https://www.nytimes.com/2022/04/02/us/politics/merrick-garland-biden-trump.html.

16 Politicus Media, "Morning Joe Asks If Trump Was Selling Secrets To Saudi Arabia," August 24, 2022, https://www.youtube.com/ watch?v=NB0tdfBpVAA; Gabriel Hays, "MSNBC's Beschloss, former CIA director Hayden 'suggest' Trump be executed for having nuclear documents," Fox News, August 12, 2022, https://www.foxnews.com/media/msnbcs-beschloss-former-cia-director-hayden-suggest-trump-executed-having-nuclear-documents.

17 Julie Kelly (@julie_kelly2), "Notice of Trump's intent to file a lawsuit against DOJ for MAL raid in August 2022 contains internal FBI emails expressing shock at the unprecedented event: Chauncenette Morey was the FBI acting ombudsman at the time. Morey also noted the double standard in prosecuting J6ers vs other political demonstrators," August 12, 2024, 1:42 p.m., https://x.com/julie_kelly2/status/1823052418625454082?s=43&t=kGvu 1R4Po5SmjGa0Dwb6zw.

18 House Committee on Oversight and Accountability, Letter to White House Counsel Edward Siskel, October 11, 2023, https://oversight.house.gov/ wp-content/uploads/2023/10/WH-Classified-Documents-10.11.23_Final. pdf.

19 "Former White House Counsel Joins Covington," Covington & Burling,

press release, October 4, 2022, https://www.cov.com/en/news-and-insights/news/2022/10/former-white-house-counsel-joins-covington.

20 John H. Durham, "Report on Matters Related to Intelligence Activities and Investigations Arising Out of the 2016 Presidential Campaigns," May 12, 2023, https://justthenews.com/sites/default/files/2023-05/durhamreport.pdf.

21 Kathryn Watson, "Bill Barr says Trump's classified documents case is his biggest legal risk: 'I don't think that argument's gonna fly,'" CBS News, May 19, 2023, https://www.cbsnews.com/news/bill-barr-interview-trump-classified-documents-special-counsel-decision/.

22 Paul Sperry, "DC Bar Restores Convicted FBI Russiagate Forger to 'Good Standing' Amid Irregularities and Leniency," RealClearInvestigations, December 16, 2021, https://www.realclearinvestigations.com/articles/2021/12/16/dc_bar_lets_convicted_fbi_russiagate_lawyer_back_in_good_standing_as_court_cuts_him_more_slack_807964.html.

23 "Durham report release revealed a failed 'stunt' by the Hillary Clinton campaign: Devin Nunes," Fox News, May 21, 2023, https://www.foxnews.com/video/6327971325112.

24 Arden Farhi, "What Biden told then-special counsel Robert Hur in their 5-hour interview, according to the transcript," CBS News, updated March 12, 2024, https://www.cbsnews.com/news/biden-special-counsel-robert-hur-transcript-reviewed/.

25 Michael Katz, "Devin Nunes to Newsmax: Durham Report Should 'Scare Living Hell Out of Everyone,'" Newsmax, May 15, 2023, https://www.newsmax.com/newsmax-tv/devin-nunes-durham-report-fbi/2023/05/15/id/1119899/.

26 Timothy H. J. Nerozzi, "Donalds grills Biden SEC commissioner on Steele dossier payment," Fox News, April 19, 2023, https://www.foxnews.com/politics/donalds-grills-biden-sec-commissioner-steele-dossier-payment.

27 John Podesta Testimony to the House Permanent Select Committee on Intelligence, December 4, 2017, https://intelligence.house.gov/uploadedfiles/john_podesta_testimony_dec_4_2017.pdf.

28 U.S. Securities and Exchange Commission, "Melissa Hodgman Named Acting Director of Division of Enforcement," press release, January 22, 2021, https://www.sec.gov/newsroom/press-releases/2021-15.

29 Alex Weprin, "Trump's Truth Social Lost Tens of Millions Since Launch, New Filing Shows," The Hollywood Reporter, November 13, 2023.

30 PA Department of State (@PAStateDept), "Pennsylvanians won't always know the final results of all races on election night. Any changes in results that occur as counties continue to count ballots are not evidence that an election is "rigged." See the full explanation at http://vote.pa.gov/FactCheck.," August 8, 2024, https://twitter.com/PAStateDept/status/1821589896773128621.

31 "Alberto Fujimori Wins Re-Election in Peru, Amid Wide Complaints of Fraud," NotiSur, June 9, 2000, https://digitalrepository.unm.edu/cgi/viewcontent.cgi?article=13787&context=notisur.

32 Sebastian Rotella, "A Delay in Vote Count Raises Tensions in Peru," Los Angeles Times, April 11, 2000, https://www.latimes.com/archives/la-xpm-2000-apr-11-mn-18381-story.html.

33 Ghadafi Saibu, "On the Edge: Delays in Election Results and Electoral Violence in Sub-Sahara Africa," German Institute of Development and Sustainability, 2023, https://www.idos-research.de/fileadmin/migratedNewsAssets/Files/DP_19.2023.pdf.

34 Sarah Kinosian, "US recognizes re-election of Honduras president despite fraud allegations," Guardian, December 22, 2017, https://www.theguardian.com/world/2017/dec/22/us-recognizes-re-election-of-honduras-president-despite-calls-for-a-new-vote.

35 "Biden warns about transfer of power if Trump loses 2024 race," Washington Post, video, August 11, 2024, https://www.washingtonpost.com/video/politics/biden-warns-about-transfer-of-power-if-trump-loses-2024-race/2024/08/11/91f7f909-2a24-4fbf-a7f0-597def9101c1_video.html.

36 Robert Farley, "Trump's 'Bloodbath' Comment," FactCheck.org, March 18, 2024, https://www.factcheck.org/2024/03/trumps-bloodbath-comment/.

37 M. D. Kittle, "Firebrand Leftist Jamie Raskin Said Congress Must 'Disqualify' Trump, Predicted 'Civil War Conditions,'" The Federalist, August 6, 2024, https://thefederalist.com/2024/08/06/firebrand-leftist-jamie-raskin-said-congress-must-disqualify-trump-predicted-civil-war-conditions/.

38 David Rothkopf, "Here's How President Trump Would Run Roughshod Over Our Democracy," New Republic, July 30, 2024, https://newrepublic.com/article/184344/heres-president-trump-run-roughshod-democracy; Ed Pilkington and Kira Lerner, "Washington insiders simulated a second Trump presidency. Can a role-play save democracy?," Guardian, July 30, 2024, https://www.theguardian.com/us-news/article/2024/jul/30/washington-dc-role-play-second-trump-term?CMP=share_btn_url; Barton Gellman, "How to harden our defenses against an authoritarian president," Washington Post, July 30, 2024, https://www.washingtonpost.com/opinions/2024/07/30/trump-authoritarian-president-government-defend/; Rosa Brooks, "Democracy Will Suffer a Relatively Quiet Death. We Simulated It.," Bulwark, July 30, 2024, https://www.thebulwark.com/p/democracy-suffer-quiet-death-simulated-trump.